EDUCATION AND CULTURE IN EUROPEAN COMMUNITY LAW

European Community Law Series
Series Editor: Rosa Greaves, Professor of Law, Durham University
Founding Editor: Professor D. Lasok, QC, University of Exeter

European Community Law is having an important impact upon the law of the United Kingdom and other countries concerned with EC legislation. This new series provides authoritative and up-to-date accounts of specific topics and areas. The volumes are addressed to legal practitioners, in-house lawyers, businessmen and to all those who need to communicate with lawyers in this field.

Already published volumes include:
1 Peter Stone, *Copyright Law in the UK and the European Community*

2 Frank Wooldridge, *Company Law in the UK and the European Community*

3 Rosa Greaves, *Transport Law of the European Community*

4 Friedl Weiss, *Public Procurement in European Community Law*

5 A. J. Easson, *Taxation in the European Community*

6 Frans van Kray, *Tourism and the Hotel and Catering Industries in the EC*

7 Timothy Portwood, *Mergers under EEC Competition Law*

Future volumes will include:
Philippe Bourin, *The European Investment Bank: Its Structure and Functions in Financing Community and Non-Community Projects*

David Freestone, *Environment Protection in European Community Law*

Syamal Chatterjee, *Legal Aspects of Drug Control and Treatment of Drug-dependent Persons within the European Community*

Timothy Portwood, *Joint Ventures under EEC Competition Law*

European Community Law Series

8

EDUCATION AND CULTURE in European Community Law

Joseph A. McMahon

THE ATHLONE PRESS
London & Atlantic Highlands, NJ

First published 1995 by The Athlone Press Ltd
1 Park Drive, London NW11 7SG and
165 First Avenue, Atlantic Highlands, NJ 07716

British Library Cataloguing in Publication Data
A catalogue record for this book is available from the British Library
ISBN 0-485-70013-1

Library of Congress Cataloging in Publication Data
McMahon, Joseph A., 1960–
Education and culture in European Community law / Joseph A. McMahon.
p. cm. – (European Community law series; 8)
Includes bibliographical references and index.
ISBN 0-485-70013-1
1. Educational law and legislation – European Economic Community countries. 2. European Economic Community countries – Cultural policy. I. Title. II. Series.
KJE6266.M37 1995
344.4'07 – dc20
[344.047] *94-21692*
CIP

Typeset by Datix International Limited, Bungay, Suffolk
Printed and bound in Great Britain by
WBC Book Manufacturers Limited, Bridgend

Contents

Series Preface vii
Volume Preface ix

PART 1 EDUCATION

Chapter 1: The Development of Community Competence 3

Taking the First Steps 3
A Community Education Action Programme 8
A People's Europe 14

Chapter 2: Specific Programmes 21

Erasmus 21
Comett 30
Lingua 36
Tempus 39
A Right of Residence for Students 43
Conclusion 47

Chapter 3: The Extension of Community Competence 51

The Educational Rights of Migrants and their Children 51
Article 12 of Regulation 1612/68 52
Article 7 of Regulation 1612/68 59
The Concept of Vocational Training 66
Towards a Definition 67
A Definition 70
Refining the Definition 74
Education as a Service 79
The Mutual Recognition of Qualifications 81

Specific Directives 82
General Principles 84
The General Directive 87
Other Issues 91
Conclusion 94

Chapter 4: From Maastricht to the Future 97

A Review: 1976–93 97
The Maastricht Provisions 105
A Conclusion 117

PART 2 CULTURE

Chapter 5: The Emergence and Development of Community Competence 121

Taking the First Steps 122
Towards Stronger Action 129
'A Fresh Boost' 137
The Audio-visual Sector 140
The Book Sector 144
Training in the Cultural Sector 148
Business Sponsorship 151
Other Areas 152
Conclusions 156

Chapter 6: From Maastricht to the Future 161

A Review: 1977–93 161
The Maastricht Provisions 164
A Conclusion 172

Notes 177
Table of European Communities Legislation 203
Table of Cases from the European Court of Justice 207
Bibliography 211
Index 217

Series Preface

West European integration has become an irreversible and ever-expanding process affecting directly not only the Member States of the European Community but also business interests and individuals in all walks of life. The prediction that, in time, 80 per cent of the national legislation will eventually emanate from Brussels may not be accurate. But the volume of regulations and directives so far produced in the Community has already assumed formidable dimensions. Consequently textbooks, commentaries and source publications have grown in size to the point of being too voluminous to be handled by anyone interested in a particular area. Moreover, in view of the abundance of material, large publications cannot always do justice to every topic which merits treatment in depth.

In response to this challenge, The Athlone European Community Law Series is addressed mainly to legal practice and the business world and also to students of law. The Series consists of concise and relatively short monographs designed to break new ground and fill the gaps in the existing literature. In monographs unencumbered with general information but still within the context of the integrative process, the Series offers guidance to the practitioner, businessman and others concerned with Community Legislation.

Volumes in the Series take more or less self-contained subjects, and the Series will eventually compose a specialist library.

Rosa Greaves, Series Editor
D. Lasok, Founding Editor

Volume Preface

The intention of this Series is to break new ground by filling in the gaps in existing knowledge in European Community Law. It may seem odd, therefore, to have one of the books on education and culture, as these areas are not traditionally associated with European Community Law. The original Treaty of Rome contains very few references to education; indeed most of the references to education relate to vocational training rather than education generally. This is not surprising given the predominantly economic emphasis of the Treaty of Rome. Education policy thus emerges from a limited Treaty base. In contrast, the Community's policy on culture emerges from an even narrower basis. However, the move towards greater integration, typified by the Single European Act and, more recently, by the Treaty on European Union, has involved an extension of the competencies of the Community into many areas not envisaged by the Treaty of Rome. In one sense the belated recognition of the Community's competence in these areas has benefited the Community and the Member States. Through the development of policies in the areas of education and culture in a period when Community competence was not fully established the broad parameters of such action have been accepted by all the Member States: intitial reluctance to accept Community competence in these areas has been steadily overcome. A major contribution to this acceptance, especially in education, has been the integrationist (or interventionist) approach of the European Court of Justice. The attitude of the Court to the issue of culture has not been so supportive.

The initial impression is therefore false. Education and culture are areas where the Community has striven to construct a legal framework which guarantees the rights of the citizens of the Community. It is also possible to view these areas as an example of how the Community will develop in the future given the increasing emphasis on doctrines such as subsidiarity and intergovernmentalism. Indeed, it is possible to view both areas as prime examples of the principle of subsidiarity at work. I hope that through the elaboration of the development and extension of Community competence in both these areas, from the Treaty of Rome to the Treaty on European Union, a greater understanding and appreciation will emerge.

Part 1 of the book concentrates on education. The first two chapters trace the development of the competence of the Community in this area from the Treaty of Rome up to the recent case overturning the legal basis of the directive on the right of residence of students. Chapter 3 is devoted to the case law of the European Court of Justice on education. Three particular areas are chosen for examination: the rights of migrant workers and their children under Regulation 1612/68; the concept of vocational training; and the mutual recognition of qualifications. The final chapter of Part 1 examines the provisions of the Treaty on European Union (The Maastricht Treaty) dealing with education. An assessment is made of these provisions and some indication of the likely future development of the competence of the Community in education is attempted. Part 2 concentrates on culture. Given the more recent emergence of Community action in the cultural area this part is shorter than Part 1; this is due to some extent to the unsupportive role played by the European Court. The emergence and development of Community competence in this area are combined into a single chapter. Part 2 ends with an assessment of the provisions of the Treaty on European Union as they relate to culture. Whereas the development and extension of Community competence in these two areas are roughly comparable, the provisions of the Treaty on European Union will mark a watershed; education will continue to develop as an area of Community competence but culture will remain an area where action is largely symbolic.

I would like to thank the many people who have helped in the work on this book. I would like to thank Professor Lasok for affording me the opportunity to write in such an interesting area. The staff in the Official Publications Section of the Library here at Queen's deserve a special mention for all their assistance. I would also like to thank all those at The Athlone Press who have helped in the production of this book. Special thanks must also go to the Faculty and School of Law for allowing me the time to write this book. As ever, the patience of my wife and son in enduring my absences, both physical and mental, is greatly appreciated. I would like to dedicate this book to them.

Joseph A. McMahon

Part 1
Education

Notes

1

The Development of Community Competence

The original Treaty of Rome includes few references to education. Article 41 states that in order to promote the objectives of the Common Agricultural Policy, provision could be made within that policy for 'an effective coordination of efforts in the spheres of vocational training'. In the context of the right of establishment, Article 57(1) refers to 'the mutual recognition of diplomas, certificates and other evidence of formal qualifications'. In the context of social policy, Article 118 gives the Commission the task of promoting 'close co-operation between the Member States in the social field'. Basic and advanced vocational training is one of the areas particularly referred to and this is further developed in Article 128 which states:

> The Council shall, acting on a proposal from the Commission and after consulting the Economic and Social Committee, lay down general principles for implementing a common vocational training policy capable of contributing to the harmonious development both of the national economies and of the common market.

From these meagre beginnings the Community would develop an education policy which has moved beyond the economic perspective of these articles towards a genuine social policy. The purpose of this chapter is to trace the development of that policy from the Treaty provisions outlined above.

TAKING THE FIRST STEPS

Education is of course a sensitive area; national traditions are particularly strong; education systems differ widely in their organization, content and outlook; national governments are

> reluctant to sacrifice the individuality of their particular systems. This impedes progress towards an education policy of the Community, however modest; again and again objections to education measures have been raised by member governments on grounds of national sovereignty.[1]

The initial reluctance of the Community to take action in the area of education reflected the concerns identified above. Indeed the concern with national sovereignty prevented action for the first fourteen years of the Community's existence. However, action was taken in 1971. One of the reasons for this was final Communique of the Conference of Heads of State or Government held at The Hague in December 1969. Point four of the Communique reaffirmed that the Community was more than an economic association of states; social goals were, therefore, considered equally important.[2] Meeting within the Council for the first time in November 1971 the Ministers of Education of the Member States referred specifically to The Hague Communique. The resolution continues: 'Considering that the Treaty of Rome has already provided for and organized activities concerning *inter alia* the right of establishment and vocational training, but that they should be supplemented by greater cooperation in the field of education as such'.[3] The significance of this recital cannot be overestimated, for it established that general education and not just vocational training was an area which did fall within the competence of the European Community. The resolution went on to establish a working party which would have responsibility for devising ways of establishing active co-operation in the field of education.

Before the conclusion of the working party's deliberations the Commission enlisted the help of Professor Henri Janne, a former Belgian Minister of Education, to formulate the first principles of an education policy at Community level. The Commission assumed that education was an area where it had the responsibility of developing Community policies.[4] The subsequent report, known as the Janne Report, established a framework within which the first steps could be taken for a Community Education Action Programme. Janne enlisted a number of persons from the Member States and beyond to discuss the basic elements of a Community education policy.[5] The discussions were on the basis of two documents. The first of these documents, a Background Note, defined the major data on the European context of the problems of education.[6] According to the Background Note, a Community education policy would bring about a change in direction/dimension in the Community as it would be an expression of a 'desire for unity and the choice of a common destiny'. The second document was a Memo of Talks, which listed a number of points which a European education policy would have to deal with.[7] The results of the consultations and discussions were synthesized by Janne in the conclusion of the report which seeks to establish the scope of an education policy for the Community.

The report concludes that although there are within the Treaty certain provisions dealing with education, these provisions allow only for a 'bit-by-bit' approach to education.[8] Such an approach was considered to be inadequate and an overall concept of education is recommended. This concept seeks to place education within the economic, scientific and cultural policies which are already contained, or will emerge in the case of cultural policy, from both the Treaties of Rome.[9] Progress towards economic goals would be assisted if there were an educational policy. All aspects of education would therefore be covered by the Community's education policy but the report noted:[10] 'It is advisable scrupulously to respect national structures and traditions where education is concerned, but to promote a necessary harmonization by means of permanent concerted action at all levels and through more and more educational exchanges'.[10] An Educational and Cultural Council/Committee would be established.[11] This would allow the Member States to determine the extent to which they were pursuing common objectives and an appropriate European dimension in their educational policies. The end result would be a European Charter of Education providing a framework for educational thought in the Community.[12] The specific subject-matter of the education policy would include all subjects covered by the Treaty, as anything short of this would be fragmentary and destined to fail.[13] The policy, as a consequence of respecting national structures and traditions in education, would be complementary to national policies. The overall goal would be the gradual harmonization of the educational policies of the Member States.[14]

As for the specific content of the Community's education policy several areas were highlighted for inclusion. The policy would include the promotion of foreign languages.[15] A system for student and staff exchanges covering both schools and universities would be established.[16] Co-operation between universities would be encouraged through the creation of university consortia.[17] Interestingly, the report considered the equivalence of degrees and diplomas and concluded that harmonization was not an acceptable option. Final degrees and diplomas would be accepted by the Member States as equivalent provided that they were mentioned on a Community list. Where the duration of studies differed, traineeship systems in the country where the profession is to be exercised would be instituted.[18] Finally, the report concluded that permanent education was one of the priority areas for Community action. Permanent education was defined by the Report as referring to adult and continuous education throughout an individual's working life.[19]

The Janne Report noted that not all measures could be launched at the same time and a study group was recommended to establish priorities. The report concluded:

> At the beginning an educational policy should have sensitive antennae directed towards the whole socio-cultural environment. With a view to contacts, surveys and necessary investigations, a Study Group, because of its unofficial nature, would therefore be preferable to the immediate setting up of an Educational and Cultural Council; this will, however, be necessary in the second phase on the basis of experience already acquired.[20]

After welcoming the report the Commission promised that it would take up its suggestions. A response to the report emerged in the 1974 Commission communication to the Council on Education in the European Community. The Report confirms the point made by the Janne Report that educational co-operation within the Community was of equal importance with existing co-operation in other areas. Education was viewed 'an integral part of the overall development of the Community.'[21]

The common European policy advocated by the Commission would not be as extensive as that envisaged by the Janne Report: indeed the policy would be confined to three broad areas. The first area related to the need to improve and extend opportunities for educational exchanges for academic staff, researchers and students. Before action could be taken in this area, it was considered necessary to establish the existing scope of educational exchanges within the Community. One area of problems for student exchanges related to limits on admission, especially in higher education. As a further part of this field it was recognized that the problems of the equivalence of qualifications had to be solved. Yet the exchange of students was not to be limited to university students and staff but would also extend to teaching and research staff at the primary and secondary level. Opportunities for exchange were also to be extended to educational and youth administrators. In all areas pilot projects were envisaged as an appropriate mechanism by which to gather further information which would form the basis of future co-operative efforts.[22]

The second area concerned the education of the children of migrant workers. The need for action in this area was dictated by Article 48 of the Treaty and especially Article 12 of Regulation 1612/68, which provides for the admission of the children of migrant workers to the host state's educational system.[23] Special measures were considered necessary to promote the initial integration of the children, especially in relation to the language of the host state. These measures would be implemented after a series of studies on the issues had been undertaken and a period of consultation with the Member States.[24] The third and final area was the encouragement of a European dimension in education. This was considered necessary to enhance public understanding of and stimulation of interest in the Community.[25] It is in this area that the impact of the recommendations of the Janne Report are most obvious.

Four particular areas were highlighted as part of this European dimension. It was considered necessary to promote the learning of foreign languages. All students were to have the opportunity to study at least one language, and preferably two, in the course of their education. The anticipated role for the Commission was one of collecting and collating information on the teaching of foreign languages. Pilot studies and special fellowships were considered potential means of acquiring further information on which to base future co-operation.[26] The second area was the study of Europe.[27] This involved providing information on the Community and encouraging teaching and research about the Community. Once again, pilot studies and special fellowships were envisaged. The final areas of the European dimension to education involved co-operation between institutions of higher education and the establishment of European schools.[28]

To promote policy-making the Commission proposed a draft Resolution of the Council and the Ministers of Education meeting within the Council on co-operation in the field of education.[29] The content of the resolution reflects the three areas of co-operation: mobility of students; the education of the children of migrant workers; and a European dimension to education. In each area further information would be needed and/or pilot studies would be launched. To co-ordinate this information-gathering role, the draft resolution was accompanied by a draft decision on the establishment of a European Committee for Educational Cooperation.[30] This committee would have the task of pooling information and discussing educational questions of interest to the Community. On its own initiative or at the request of the Commission, the committee could prepare opinions or make reports. This advice would form the basis for the elaboration and development of the Community's educational policy.

The first steps had been taken. In 1971 the Council had launched the idea that education should be an area of Community concern. The Janne Report considered that the future educational policy of the Community should have an extremely wide scope, but the Commission envisaged a substantially more restricted educational policy. The elaboration and development of a more extensive policy would be the responsibility of a European Committee for Educational Co-operation, which would be chaired by a Commission representative. The next step would have to be taken by the Council in the light of the Commission's communication.

A COMMUNITY EDUCATION ACTION PROGRAMME

Meeting within the Council in June 1974 the Ministers of Education of the Member States considered the Commission communication and as a result passed a resolution on co-operation in the field of education.[31] The Preamble to the resolution recalls point 4 of the final Communique of The Hague Conference in 1969. It also confirms that co-peration in the field of education would be instituted, but not on the principles advocated by either the Janne Report or the Commission communication. Co-operation would be based on the following principles:

(i) the programme of cooperation initiated in the field of education, whilst reflecting the progressive harmonization of the economic and social policies in the Community, must be adapted to the specific objectives and requirements of this field,

(ii) on no account must education be regarded merely as a component of economic life,

(iii) educational cooperation must make allowance for the traditions of each country and the diversity of their respective educational policies and systems (Paragraph 1).

The goal of the Community action in the area of education was to be co-operation rather than the harmonization of existing policies and systems.

It is important to note the scope of the principles of co-operation in education. First, it ties the development of co-operation in education to the harmonization of economic and social policies within the Community. A clear link is thereby established between progress in both of these areas. Educational co-operation is not, however, to be pursued solely as part of the contribution which it can make to greater economic and social harmonization; educational co-operation was important for its own sake. This latter point is recognized in the second principle of co-operation. Secondly, by recognizing the diversity of educational systems and policies, the principles confirm that these systems and policies are not to be harmonized. The resolution, therefore, respects the sovereignty of the Member States in these areas. A means had thus been found of negating the most important factor which had impeded Community progress in this area for such a long period.

To further their co-operation in education the following seven priority spheres of action were identified:

(i) better facilities for the education and training of nationals and the children of nationals of other Member States of the Communities and non member countries;
(ii) the promotion of closer relations between educational systems in Europe;
(iii) the compilation of up-to-date documentation and statistics on education;
(iv) increased cooperation between institutes of higher education,
(v) improved possibilities for academic recognition of diplomas and periods of study,
(vi) the encouragement of freedom of movement and mobility of teachers, students and research workers in particular by the removal of administrative and social obstacles to the free movement of such persons and by the improved teaching of foreign languages,
(vii) the achievement of equal opportunity for free access to all forms of education.[32]

An Education Committee was established to foster co-operation in these seven areas. The Committee was composed of representatives of each of the Member States and of the Commission. The

Committee was to report to the Council on each of these areas before 30 June 1975.

Having agreed the principles of co-operation in the field of education and highlighted various priority areas for such co-operation, the next step was to establish an Action Programme in the field of education. This was duly established in February 1976.[33] The Preamble to the resolution establishing the programme makes specific reference to the 1974 resolution on co-operation in education (for example, it reaffirms the desire to achieve European co-operation in education). However, this resolution is much more comprehensive than its predecessor. Whereas the 1974 resolution merely listed seven priority areas, the 1976 resolution goes into much greater detail in all of these areas; this is not surprising given the role assigned to the Education Committee under the 1974 resolution. Taking as an example the area of Achievement of Equal Opportunity for Free Access to All Forms of Education, the Action Programme states: 'The achievement of equal opportunity for free access to all forms of education is an essential aim of the education policies of all the Member States and its importance must be stressed in conjunction with other economic and social policies, in order to achieve equality of opportunity in society'.

The Action Programme goes on to state the activities which will be organized at Community level in order to identify specific areas where joint Community/Member State action may be undertaken. These are largely to be facilitated by an exchange of views and experience between the Member States organized by the Community. In addition to this task, the following are identified as priority areas for action at Community level:

(i) the measures to be taken in the field of education to prepare young people for work, to facilitate their transition from study to working life and to increase their chances of finding employment, thereby reducing the risks of unemployment;
(ii) the provision, in the context of continuous education and training, of further education to young workers and young unemployed persons to improve their chances of finding employment. (Paragraph 2.2).

To co-ordinate and monitor the implementation of the Action Programme an Education Committee, having similar membership to the Education Committee set up under the 1974 resolution, was established. Its role would, however, be permanent as it was given the task of preparing papers on the future development of the

Community policy in education. The Action Programme envisaged further meetings of the Council to establish the future guidelines of the Community's education policy.

The 1976 resolution is significant for a number of reasons. First, it marks the arrival of education as an area of policy interest for the Community. The relative silence of the Treaty on education had thus been bypassed and the reservations of the Member States had been overcome. Secondly, education is to be an area of joint responsibility. This emerges from the content of the resolution which divides the actions to be undertaken by the Community from those to be undertaken by the Member States. Further evidence of this can be found in the title of the resolution: whereas the 1974 resolution was a resolution of the Ministers of Education meeting within the Council, the 1976 resolution was a resolution of the Council and of the Ministers of Education meeting within the Council. Finally, and partly as a continuation of the last point, the Education Committee occupies an anomalous position. Compared with other institutions assigned responsibility for the overseeing of a particular Community policy, the Education Committee functions more as a Committee of the Council rather than one of the Commission. It differs significantly from the European Committee for Educational Co-operation advocated in the 1974 Commission communication. For instance, it is not chaired by the Commission but by the Minister of Education from the Member State which holds the Presidency of the Council at the time of its meeting. Essentially, the Education Committee underlines the fact that responsibility for education is not entirely in the hands of the Community. Depending on the viewpoint adopted, it represents a good example of subsidiarity at work or an example of how the Community can work well at an intergovernmental level.

In implementing the Action Programme further guidance was provided for the Member States and the Community by another 1976 resolution of the Council and the Ministers of Education meeting within the Council.[34] The Member States were urged to take into account the conclusions and measures suggested by the Education Committee in the development of their national policies on education and vocational training. Various actions were also set out in the Resolution to be implemented by the Community.[35] In particular areas there would be pilot projects and studies to assist in the evaluation and development of national educational and vocational training policies. In addition the Community would organize study visits for specialists in the areas of vocational education and guidance. The financing of these measures was to be decided in accordance with the Community budgetary rules and procedures. These initiatives would run until 31 December 1980, however, before this date the Council and the Ministers of Education meeting within the Council had already extended the period for the programme of pilot projects to 31 December 1981.[36] Equally, that Council had also had the opportunity to discuss the general report of the Education Committee on the priority areas identified by the 1976 Action Programme.

The 1980 assessment of the Action Programme was agreed to in substance by the Council and the Ministers of Education meeting within the Council at their meeting on 27 June 1980.[37] The nature of the report is to examine each of the seven priority areas identified by the Action Programme and the measures undertaken at both the Member State and Community levels to implement the programme. Returning to the example chosen from the 1976 Action Programme of achievement of equal opportunity for free access to all forms of education, the report noted the range of activities undertaken both by the Member States and the Community.[38] Reports had been prepared on the organization of pre-primary education and the special education of handicapped children. The majority of the report in these areas concentrated on the preparation of girls for working life and equality of opportunity for girls and boys in society.[39] The Education Committee proposed a series of objectives reflecting not only the question of equal opportunity but also the larger issue of the unemployment problems facing young people arising from the recession. To reinforce the measures which the Education Committee considered should be taken to implement these objectives, further measures were proposed to be taken at Community level, consisting of the promotion of studies, research and the exchange of experience and information in selected areas.[40]

The difficult employment situation faced by young people which had been referred to in the Education Committee report was also raised in the context of a Joint Council of Ministers for Economic Affairs, Finance and Social Affairs which was held on 11 June 1981. On 22 June 1981 the Council and the Ministers of Education meeting within the Council discussed the conclusions of the Joint Council and concluded that education and training could make a contribution to the promotion of economic and social development within the Community, thus alleviating the problems caused by unemployment.[41] To ensure that this was successful, the Council emphasized the need to remove internal rigidities in the education system so that an integrated approach could be adopted to education, training and employment policies. The Commission and the Education Committee were given the responsibility to pursue this integrated approach through the exchange of information between the relevant authorities in the Member States. Both bodies were to make appropriate recommendations.

The emergence of an integrated approach was not surprising given the reorganization of the Commission in 1981.[42] Since January 1973 responsibility for education was placed under the ambit of Directorate General XII together with research and science policy. Vocational training, on the other hand, was within the ambit of Directorate General V, which dealt with social affairs. In 1981 education and vocational training policy were finally brought together under the ambit of Directorate General V – Social Policy. Education would thus assume a more significant role in the years to come. Greater emphasis was given to measures to improve the preparation of young people for work and measures which would facilitate their transition from education to working life. In a sense, the 1982 resolution of the Council and Ministers of Education meeting within the Council on this matter marks a new phase in the development of Community education policy.[43] Increasingly, educational policy was seen as making an important contribution to the alleviation of unemployment within the Community, especially youth unemployment.

This is not to suggest that other elements of educational co-operation were neglected but rather that co-operation in these other areas was refocused so that it could contribute to the new employment-related goals of educational policy. For example, the 1983 Council resolution on vocational training measures relating to new information technologies in its general guidelines makes reference to the need to implement special measures to improve the employment prospects of the unemployed by including studies relating to new technologies in their training programmes.[44] A similar guideline emerges from another resolution in 1983 on measures relating to the introduction of new information technologies in education.[45] As part of an 'adequate preparation' for working life, it was considered essential that young people in education should be taught how to use information technology. The emphasis in both resolutions was on the transition of young people from education to adult and working life.

A joint meeting of the Labour and Social Affairs Council and the Council and Ministers of Education meeting within the Council in June 1983 issued further guidance on this subject.[46] The conclusions of this joint session note that although eradicating unemployment necessitated the interplay of economic, financial and employment policies, education and vocational training policies could complement this interplay. Two main functions were assigned to education and vocational training policies in facilitating the transition of young people to adult and working life, namely:

(i) equipping all young people, in school as well as in supplementary out-of-school measures, with the knowledge, abilities and skills which are a prerequisite for successful access to further vocational training and entry into working life, also helping them to develop the personal and social attributes needed to face with self-confidence and initiative the increasing difficulties of transition and to find their place as young adults;

(ii) providing all young school-leavers either the opportunity to obtain a supplementary vocational qualification or systematic work experience.[47]

Co-operation would thus continue to have wider or more specific goals than those laid down in the 1976 Action Programme. That Programme had merely noted the contribution which co-operation in education could make to the development of the Community, now this co-operation was to complement the economic, financial and employment objectives of the Community. This emerges very clearly from the 1983 resolution of the Council on vocational training policies in the Community in the 1980s.[48] It appeared that after developing an education policy with limited objectives, the Community was gradually changing that policy towards the type of policy advocated by the Janne Report. Further changes to the scope of co-operation in education would emerge from the desire to create a People's Europe.

A PEOPLE'S EUROPE

Further guidelines for education in the period after 1985 emerged first from the Reports of the *ad hoc* Committee on a People's Europe, the Adonnino Report.[49] The Committee, which was established by the European Council meeting at Fontainbleau in June 1984, was given the mandate of pinpointing action which would enable the Community to respond to 'the expectations of the peoples of Europe by adopting measures to strengthen and promote its identity and its image both for its citizens and for the rest of the world'. The *ad hoc* Committee submitted its first report to the European Council meeting at Brussels in March 1985. This report pinpointed measures which would enable individuals to enjoy freedom of movement throughout the Community. It included sections on the recognition of professional qualifications[50] and a general right of residence.[51] A further report was requested for the next European Council meeting and was designed to add a new political, cultural and social dimension to the Community. The second report contained parts on both education and culture. The section of the report on education and vocational training begins by noting that, 'It is essential to involve and interest young people in the further development of Europe.'[52] What followed was a list of proposals aimed at the young people of Europe and constituting an extension of existing Community efforts. The six areas for action identified by the Adonnino Report were language training; exchanges between schools; voluntary work camps for young people; the European image in education; university co-operation; and vocational training.[53] The proposals, which were endorsed by the European Council meeting in Milan in June 1985, reflected existing areas of co-operation which had been developing since the 1976 Action Programme. Although nothing substantially new was being proposed, the report marks a turning point in the education policy of the Community.

The impression that a turning point had been reached in the education policy of the Community also emerged from the Commission White Paper on the Completion of the Internal Market.[54] Although primarily directed to the removal of impediments to the free movement of goods, persons, services and capital within the confines of the Treaty provisions in these areas, the paper has a social dimension. For example, the section on the free movement of persons concludes by noting that measures to ensure the free movement of individuals would not be restricted to economically active people. It continues:

> Consequently the Commission intends to increase its support for cooperation programmes between further education establishments in the different Member States with a view to promoting the mobility of students, facilitating the academic recognition of degrees and thus diplomas, and helping young people, in whose hands the future of the Community's economy lies, to think in European terms.[55]

A series of measures was to be proposed in these areas by the end of 1985, however most of these measures, but not all of them, related to the first Adonnino Report.[56] Although not included within the Single European Act in the years that followed it a number of new educational programmes would be introduced and greater urgency would be given to existing co-operation in the educational area.

This new sense of urgency is evident in the conclusions of the Council and of the Ministers of Education meeting within the Council in September 1985 on the enhanced treatment of the European dimension to education.[57] The European dimension was seen as a necessary part of the education of all the peoples of the Community and as a contribution to the building of an ever closer union among the peoples of Europe. The action to be taken to give 'a fresh impetus' to this European dimension included the promotion of the teaching of foreign languages, the promotion of measures designed to encourage contacts between pupils from different Member States and the highlighting of the European dimension in curricula, in teacher training courses and in teaching materials. The conclusions of the Council and the Ministers of Education meeting within the Council in 1985 on the European dimension in education were transformed into a resolution of that Council in 1988.[58] The purpose of the resolution was to strengthen the European dimension in education in the period 1988–92 by launching a series of measures which would promote a series of objectives. These related to strengthening the sense of European identity in young people by making them aware of the advantages of the Community through improving their knowledge of the Community and the Member States. The end result of these measures would be to prepare young people to take part in the economic and social development of the Community.

The action necessary to achieve these objectives involved a strengthening of measures at the level of both the Member States and the Community. For the former, this included the incorporation of the European dimension in educational systems, school programmes, teaching material and teacher training. The final group of measures in this area included the promotion of contacts between pupils and teachers from different Member States.[59] At the level of the Community the action to be taken included the exchange of information and the preparation of teaching material on the Community.[60] A report on the development of both sets of measures was to be submitted by the Education Committee by 30 June 1991.

The move towards a People's Europe and the creation of a deadline in the Single European Act to complete the Internal Market, as noted above, gave a new impetus to education and training policies. As the Commission noted in its 1988 report on a People's Europe:

> From now on systems of education and training must contribute to the Community's economic and social cohesion. A Europe which fails to invest in its human resources, in its skills, in its adaptability and in its entrepreneurial spirit will find its capacity for innovation, its competitiveness and its ability to create wealth and prosperity have been undermined.[61]

As part of its investment in human resources a scheme for co-operation between universities and industry in technology training (Comett) had been adopted as had a scheme promoting the mobility of university students (Erasmus).[62] Thus to the existing areas of co-operation in education a new objective–assisting the process of constructing the single market–would have to be added. In one sense, this was merely a reaffirmation of the 1974 resolution of the Ministers of Education meeting within the Council, educational co-operation was to be viewed as making a contribution to the economic and social policies of the Community. In another sense, it marked a new point of reference: co-operation in the future would be more coherent and co-ordinated.

This co-ordination was to be provided by the Conclusions of the Council and the Ministers of Education meeting within the Council in October 1989 on co-operation and Community policy in the run-up to 1993.[63] After discussing the Commission communication on the guidelines for education and training in the medium term (1989–92),[64] the Conclusions identify five objectives as the basis for future co-operation activities. Such objectives were necessary in the words of the Conclusions:

> In view of the fundamental role that education and training play in the economic, social and cultural development of the States of the Community and in the development of the Community itself, [and] in view of the consequences of the establishment of the internal market which will affect the educational policies of the Member States and mark a new stage in the Community

cooperation initiated in this field by the resolution of 9 February 1976.[65]

Education was to be placed in the context of the economic, social and cultural policies of the Community just as the Janne Report had recommended. Thus the 'new' objectives would promote a multicultural Europe, a mobile Europe, a Europe of training for all, a Europe of skills and a Europe open to the world. Going through each of these objectives gives some idea of the future development of Community policy in education.

In relation to a multicultural Europe, this was to be based on four areas of co-operation. The first area was the strengthening of young people's sense of belonging to a European community. In this area reference can be made to the 1988 resolution of the Council and Ministers of Education meeting within the Council on the European Dimension in education.[66] The second area was the promotion of foreign language teaching in school, university and vocational training systems. This was to be achieved through the Lingua Programme designed to promote foreign language competence which was established in July 1989.[67] The third area was taking a variety of cultural approaches into account in education and training systems. In this area reference can be made to the impact of the mobility of university students and staff through the previously adopted Erasmus and Lingua Programmes. These programmes, with the addition of the Comett Programme, would also be used to achieve the objective of the fourth area–the drawing closer together of educational and training establishments.

To promote a mobile Europe, three areas of co-operation were identified. The first was the implementation of a system for the recognition of diplomas and the equivalence of professional qualifications. This had been identified in the first Adonnino Report and in the Commission White Paper as an area for action and such action was eventually taken. Directive 89/48 introduces a general system for the recognition of higher education diplomas awarded on completion of at least three years' professional education and training.[68] (The scope of this directive was extended by Directive 92/51 which established a second general system for the recognition of professional education and training.[69]) The second area was support for the organization of youth exchanges and for training periods abroad. This objective would be promoted through the Youth for Europe Programme adopted in 1988 which was designed to promote youth exchanges throughout the Community[70] and through such programmes as Erasmus and Lingua. These schemes and the conclusions of the Council and Ministers of Education meeting within the Council in May 1987 on the in-service training of teachers[71] would promote the final area–the introduction of procedures providing teachers with the opportunity to teach temporarily in educational establishments in other Member States.

The third objective of co-operation was to create a Europe of training for all. In this area the three objectives would be promoted through such programmes as Erasmus. In addition reference could be made to the 1989 resolutions of the Council and the Ministers of Education meeting within the Council on school provision for children of occupational travellers and for Gypsy and traveller children.[72] Finally, there is also the 1989 resolution on measures to combat failure at school.[73] The fourth objective of promoting a Europe of skills would be achieved through programmes such as Comett. Other programmes relevant in this area include Petra,[74] an action programme for the vocational training of young people and their preparation for adult and working life, Eurotecnet,[75] an action programme to promote innovation in the field of vocational training resulting from technological change, Force,[76] an action programme for the development of continuing vocational training, and Iris,[77] a European network of vocational training projects for women.

The final objective of a Europe open to the world was achieved by the Tempus Programme,[78] which extends to the countries of Central and Eastern Europe, and by the European Economic Area agreement which, on its entry into force, will extend most of the programmes noted above to the countries of the European Free Trade Area.[79]

The net result of the 1989 resolution on the co-operation and Community policy in education in the run-up to 1993 has been to extend significantly the activities of the Community in this area. However, the conclusions make clear that this co-operation: 'must be based on two fundamental principles – respect for linguistic and cultural diversity and affirmation of the subsidiarity of Community activities – and must respect the fundamental powers of the Member States in matters of general education policy'.[80] Education, therefore, remains an area of joint responsibility despite the significant extension of Community competence in this area since 1976. Educational policy now has to promote a series of objectives beyond co-operation in the promotion of the free movement of persons. This policy now has to promote the Community's regional policy, industrial policy, employment policy and research and technology. This is a marked change from the role of information-gatherer and disseminator assigned to the Community by the 1976 Action Programme on Education.

Notes

2

Specific Programmes

Having discussed the origins and development of the educational policy of the Community, this section will examine the specific programmes within that policy. Most, but not all, of these programmes have their origin in the 1976 Action Programme and have been adopted as a result of the renewed impetus arising from the Adonnino Report and the Commission White Paper on the completion of the Internal Market. The programmes can be viewed as the concretization of Community involvement in particular areas of education and vocational training and as an attempt to promote the concept of a People's Europe. Of the nine programmes which have been adopted since 1986 only four programmes have been chosen for further discussion. These are Erasmus, Comett, Lingua and Tempus. Discussion of these four programmes will, hopefully, give some insight into the scope and development of the educational policy of the Community.

ERASMUS

Co-operation between institutions of higher education was one of the priority areas established by the 1974 Resolution of the Ministers of Education meeting within the Council.[1] As part of the Action Programme in the field of education, the following action was considered appropriate to increase contacts between higher education institutions:

(a) the encouragement of the development of links with and between organizations representing higher education institutions;
(b) the encouragement of short study visits for specific purposes for teaching and administrative staff and for researchers;

(c) the promotion of joint programmes of study or research between institutions in several Member States.[2]

In order to promote the mobility already noted, the Community was given the responsibility of arranging discussions between higher educations institutions in the Member States. These discussions would encompass the admission of students, scholarship and other funding arrangements and the development of proposals to eliminate obstacles to the mobility of students, staff and researchers. The final area of Community action related to the recognition of diplomas and study periods. Thus co-operation in higher education was tied to the implementation of Article 57 of the Treaty.

In their report to the Council and Ministers of Education meeting within the Council in 1980, the Education Committee was able to report that various activities had been carried out in implementation of the Action Programme.[3] For example, a scheme of grants to support short study visits by teaching, research and administrative staff to other Member States had been launched in 1977. A total of 210 grants had been awarded since the inception to the scheme allowing its participants to spend a period of up to six weeks in another Member State examining such areas as students admissions and the assessment of academic qualifications. Likewise the grants scheme extended to the promotion of joint programmes of study between institutions of higher education in different Member States.[4] Despite the success of these measures, other areas of the Action Programme did not yield similar results. A common approach had not yet been adopted to the question of admission of students from other Member States to higher education establishments. However, as a result of a conference in Bonn in 1977 involving representatives of higher education institutions from the Member States, the Education Committee was able to propose a common approach to this issue. The objectives and principles of the approach recognized that national policies should take account of the objective of promoting mobility of students by ensuring that admission criteria are applied in a non-discriminatory fashion.[5]

The common approach to admission of students from other Member States was not free from problems. For example, it had to recognize that in several Member States admission criteria were the responsibility of the higher education institutions rather than the government. Equally, numerical limitations for certain courses existed in certain Member States. The Education Committee resolved that a reasonable number of places should be made available to students from other Member States: the interpretation of 'reasonable' was left to the competent national authorities in each Member State. The thorniest issue relating to admission of students from other Member States was that dealing with the financial aspects of their admission. In recognition of the principle of non-discrimination, the Committee considered that that principle should operate so that students from other Member States would not be charged higher fees than national students.[6] On the question of maintenance grants, the Education Committee concluded that the host Member State should not be responsible for awarding grants to foreign students.

The Council adopted the conclusions of the Education Committee: it seemed that co-operation in higher education was flourishing within the Community. By 1983 the Council and the Ministers of Education meeting within the Council returned to the issue of promoting mobility in higher education.[7] In 1982 this Council had established a working party to present a report on the social and material situation of students studying in other Member States. Coupled with the demands of the European Council that mobility between Member States should be facilitated, the 1983 conclusions are directed towards the 'intensification and extension of mobility in higher education' between the Member States. They recommend that the authorities responsible for recognition of qualifications obtained in another Member State and courses attended in other Member States should be guided by the principle of 'greatest possible generosity and flexibility'.[8] To promote mobility an intensification of information was called for on matters such as academic recognition, admission and evaluation of foreign educational qualifications. [9]

Special efforts were called for from the Member States to promote short study periods abroad where this would be relevant to the qualification sought by the students. To support these measures, the conclusions recommend the continuation of the Commission's grant schemes for the support of joint study programmes and short study visits. After the expiry of these grants the Member States were urged to support their continuation.[10] To solve this and related questions, the twinning of higher education institutions was recommended as one way forward.[11] This would solve the problem of tuition fees and further measures were to be taken to alleviate the financial problems arising from student mobility. The principle of non-discrimination endorsed by the Council and Ministers of Education meeting within the Council in 1980 was thus reaffirmed in 1983.

The Adonnino Report on a People's Europe requested the Council and the Ministers of Education to promote further inter-university co-operation by establishing a programme for student exchanges.[12] This would be supplemented by the introduction of a European system of academic credits transferable throughout the Community. These requests were endorsed by the European Council meeting in Milan in June 1985 and further reaffirmed by the Council and Ministers of Education meeting within the Council. At the latter meeting it was also noted that the Commission was to submit proposals to intensify existing co-operation between higher education institutions in the Community by the end of 1985.[13] Erasmus was about to be born.

Decision 87/327 adopted a European Community action scheme for the mobility of university students. The objectives of the scheme are laid down in Article 2:

> to achieve a significant increase in the number of students from universities . . . spending an integrated period of study in another Member State, in order that the Community may draw upon an adequate pool of manpower with first hand experience of economic and social aspects of other Member States, while ensuring equality of opportunity for male and female students as regards participation in such mobility.[14]

In addition the scheme would promote a 'broad and intensive cooperation' between universities by promoting the increased mobility of teaching staff.[15] This would not only improve the quality of education provided by universities, thereby contributing to the competitiveness of the Community, but also consolidate the concept of a People's Europe, by having a pool of graduates with direct experience of intra-Community co-operation.[16]

The Erasmus scheme would, therefore, support and complement the measures agreed by the Council and the Ministers of Education meeting within the Council in 1983 which would still need to be implemented if Erasmus were to be successful.[17] Moreover, the years of pilot funding by the Commission had succeeded in establishing experience in co-operation and would be the basis for the implementation of Erasmus. The Annex to the decision sets out four types of measures to be promoted with the 85 million ECU which were allocated for the programme.[18] The first of these measures is the establishment and operation of a European university network. The network would involve those universities which have concluded agreements for the exchange of students and staff. These agreements would allow students from one university to spend a recognized period of study in at least one other Member State as an integrated part of their qualification. To support such students, the second measure outlined in the Annex is the Erasmus student grants scheme. Such grants would support the mobility costs of students undertaking courses in another Member State and would be additional to any maintenance grants received by students in their own Member State. The remaining action area consisted of measures to promote mobility through the academic recognition of diplomas and periods of study (for example, the European course credit transfer system) and complementary measures to support student mobility in the Community. All decisions on funding were to be taken by the Erasmus committee established under Article 3 of the decision.[19]

Decision 87/327 was passed on 15 June 1987 to be implemented from 1 July 1987, but on 7 August 1987 the Commission brought an action under Article 173 of the Treaty for the annulment of the decision.[20] The final recital of the Decision states:

> Whereas this action programme includes aspects relating to education which, at the present stage of development of Community law, may be regarded as falling outside the scope of the common vocational training policy as provided for in Article 128 of the Treaty; whereas these aspects of the programme can, together with the vocational training objectives to which they are closely linked, contribute to the harmonious development of economic activities throughout the Community; whereas to this extent the Treaty has not provided the necessary powers, and action for this purpose appears necessary to attain, in the course of the operation of the common market, one of the objectives of the Community.

The decision was therefore based on Articles 128 and 235 whereas the Commission had argued that Article 128 by itself was sufficient as a legal basis of the decision.[21]

The Commission maintained that university education should be regarded as vocational training within the meaning of Article 128. This conclusion was not affected by the fact that Article 128 did not list the specific measures which could be adopted.[22] To counter these arguments, the Council maintained that as the Erasmus Programme was not solely concerned with vocational training,

Article 235 was necessary to make up for the lack of powers attributed to the Council by Article 128.[23] In the opinion of the Council, Article 128 allowed it to establish the nature of a common vocational training policy but not to adopt any legal instruments. By referring only to general principles, Article 128 could only define the criteria for co-ordinating action between the Member States rather than imposing legal obligations on them. Finally, the concept of vocational training includes most but not all university education, so the Erasmus Programme, by covering all university education, had to use Articles 128 and 235.[24] The parties intervening in support of the Council maintained that the procedural requirements of Article 128 in comparison with other provisions of the Treaty confirmed the limited scope of that Article.[25]

Advocate General Mischo began by noting the contradictions inherent in Article 128; it refers to the development of a common vocational training policy but the competence of the Council is limited to its ability to lay down only the general principles of that policy.[26] The question was whether Article 128 allowed the Community institutions to implement such a policy directly. Looking at the place of Article 128 within the Treaty, a common vocational training policy was to be one of the priority activities of the European Social Fund. However, unlike other common policies no provision was made for consultation with the European Parliament or for the adoption of decisions on a qualified majority basis. Advocate General Mischo concluded:

> In light of the undeniable coherence of that overall picture, it cannot be supposed that the authors of the Treaty forgot or inadvertently omitted, in Article 128, to give the Council the task of adopting, upon a proposal from the Commission, the measures necessary for the implementation of a common vocational training policy. It is not possible to construe that article as conferring by implication a power on the Council to adopt such measures by a simple majority and without mandatory consultation of the Parliament. In the eyes of the authors of the Treaty that implementation was thus left to others, that is to say the Member States.[27]

After examining the scope of the Erasmus decision, the Advocate General concluded that Article 235 had to be added to Article 128 as the proper legal basis for that decision. Article 128 could only be used to establish general principles only and not to undertake and finance concrete measures.[28]

The next question was whether the use of Article 235 was necessary as some of the measures provided in the decision fell outside the scope of the concept of vocational training. Advocate General Mischo noted that the definition of 'university' in Article 1(2) of the decision as including all university education fell outside the scope of vocational training.[29] The purpose of Erasmus extended beyond vocational training and was aimed primarily at the encouragement of greater mobility for university students. The conclusion was that the Commission's application should be dismissed in its entirety.

As in previous cases the Court began by confirming that Article 235 can be used as a legal basis for a measure where no other Community provision gives the necessary power to Community institutions to adopt the measure in question.[30] The question was whether Article 128 gave the necessary powers to the Community institutions. The Court pointed out that the common vocational training policy was being gradually established by the Member States and the Community institutions working in co-operation. The Court continued:

> From an interpretation of Article 128 based on that conception it follows that the Council is entitled to adopt legal measures provided for Community action in the sphere of vocational training and imposing corresponding obligations of cooperation on the Member States. Such an interpretation is in accordance with the wording of Article 128 and also ensures the effectiveness of that provision.[31]

This conclusion was not invalidated by the fact that Article 128 did not provide for the consultation of the European Parliament or contain specific provisions on voting procedures.[32] The inconsistency of the Treaty provisions on consultation of the Parliament was cited in support of this conclusion. The Council was therefore entitled to use Article 128 as the legal basis of the Erasmus decision subject to the question of whether the measure exceeded the scope of vocational training.

On this question the Court began by repeating the definitions of vocational training which it had adopted in the cases of *Gravier*, *Blaizot* and *Humbel*.[33] In essence these confirm that university education can be classified as vocational training and that such education did not cease to be vocational training because it did not directly provide a qualification for a particular profession. The Court continued:

> It follows that in general the studies to which the contested programme applies fall within the sphere of vocational training, and only in exceptional cases will the action planned under the programme be found applicable to university studies which, because of their particular character, are outside that sphere. The mere possibility of the latter cannot justify the conclusion that the contested programme goes beyond the scope of vocational training and that therefore the Council was not empowered to adopt it pursuant to Article 128 of the Treaty.[34]

The fact that the decision was also part of the process of establishing a People's Europe did not change the proper legal basis of the decision.[35] Moreover, the establishment and operation of a European university network under the Erasmus decision did not affect the organization of education, as maintained by some of the parties. The reasoning of the Court was that if the university network was to be established on the basis of agreements concluded between universities, they would participate on the basis of existing provisions governing their status and organization.[36] However, the application was dismissed on the basis that the decision included some aspects falling within the realm of research. By covering both research and vocational training recourse to Article 235 was necessary.[37] It was clear, however, that on entry into force of the Single European Act reference to Article 235 would be unnecessary as the competence of the Community was extended by that Act to cover research and development.

The decision of the Court was referred to when Decision 87/327 was amended in 1989 and in that amendment Article 128 was recognized as the sole legal basis of the measure.[38] An amendment to Article 1(2) made clear that the Erasmus Programme does not cover research and technological development activities. The scheme applies only to vocational training and this is confirmed by amendments to Article 2. The amended Article 2(ii) sets the objective of promoting 'broad and intensive cooperation in vocational training between universities in all Member States'. The scope of the co-operation in the original decision made no reference to vocational training. The amended Article 2(iii) sets the objective of improving the quality of training, rather than 'education and training' in the original decision. The resources available to promote these and the other objectives were increased to 192 million ECU for the first three years of the five year period of the programme.[39] Finally, the programme was to run until 31 December 1993 by which time the Commission would have submitted a report on the operation of the programme and a proposal for adaptation. The Council must decide on this proposal by 30 June 1994.[40]

The decision also introduces slight changes to the types of schemes which would be funded. In relation to the European University Network, provision is now made for a period of language preparation in anticipation of future student exchanges. This preparation is to be completed in the country of origin. In addition finance will be provided to universities who organize short teaching programmes involving students from several different Member States. Within the student grants scheme, the allocation of funds to the Member States has been changed to provide a minimum block grant and a further allocation. This allocation is based on the number of students at university in that Member State, the number of 18–25-year-olds in the general population, travel costs between the home and host universities and the differences in the cost of living between the Member States of the home and host universities. A number of other changes are also made in the area of individual grants for exchange students.[41] Overall, the changes seek to promote greater and more balanced use not only between Member States but also across the range of academic subjects of the Erasmus scheme.

The Erasmus Programme is one of the more visible Community education programmes. In one sense it is a vindication of the co-operation between Member States in education initiated in the 1974 Resolution of the Council and the Ministers of Education meeting within the Council. In another sense, it represents one of the outcomes of the renewed impetus given to co-operation in education by the Adonnino Report and the move to complete the Internal Market. The Erasmus Programme also demonstrates the gradual development and extension of Community competence in the area of education. That process started with the Community authorities playing the role of information gatherer and exchanger. Gradually, through initial pilot funding a more extensive programme emerged. The European Court of Justice has confirmed that the programme comes within the scope of Article 128 and the recent amendment of the programme reiterates this. No element capable of giving rise to a joint legal basis can now be found in the decision. Despite the extension of the competence of the Community, the Erasmus Programme does not interfere with the organization of education by the Member States. The division of competence remains intact.

COMETT

By Council Decision 86/365 a programme of co-operation between universities and industry was established in the area of training in the field of technology.[42] The programme is better known as Comett. The Community had before the adoption of Comett already expressed its concern about the challenge of technology on vocational training and education.[43] For example, in 1982 a Council resolution was passed concerning vocational training measures in the area of new information technology.[44] The resolution established a series of general guidelines to be undertaken to promote the development of a common approach to the introduction of new information technologies. Guideline (a) noted: 'the need to develop a broadly-based form of training which provides for the acquisition of a wide range of specific skills so as to facilitate access to and continuation in employment through greater occupational mobility'. After the seven general guidelines the resolution went on to list the actions to be taken at the levels of both Member States and the Community. Community action was directed towards the implementation of a network of demonstration projects designed to facilitate the exchange of ideas between the Member States on the development of their policies in this area.[45] Such projects would be funded by the European Social Fund.

In 1983 a further Council Resolution was passed relating to the introduction of new information technologies in education.[46] The Resolution urged the Member States to introduce programmes to familiarize young people in education with new information technologies. Once again, the Community dimension of the resolution involved measures to promote the exchange of information between the Member States. These resolutions were the first steps in the development of a Community response to the challenge posed by new information technologies. In 1984 a meeting of the Council and of the Ministers of Education within the Council emphasized:[47]

> the importance of continuing training given the advance of

technological change and the need to define new relationships between general education and technical and vocational education and training. Faced with the need of the economy and of society for highly-qualified manpower familiar with new technology, it is essential to develop innovative approaches to initial and ongoing training.[47]

The Comett Programme can be viewed as a specific development of the 1982 and 1983 resolutions and the development of an 'innovative' approach to training.[48]

The initial programme, Comett I, was designed to 'strengthen and stimulate' co-operation within the Community between universities and industry in the area of training in the field of technology.[49] Essentially, it would build on the existing network of co-operation between the Member States. Article 3 of Decision 86/365 lists the objectives of the programme as being:

(a) to give a European dimension to cooperation between universities and enterprises in training relating to innovation and the development and application of new technologies;
(b) to foster the joint development of training programmes and the exchange of experience, and also the optimum use of training resources at Community level;
(c) to improve the supply of training at local, regional and national level with the assistance of the authorities concerned, thus contributing to the balanced economic development of the Community;
(d) to develop the level of training in response to technological change and social changes by identifying the resulting priorities in existing training arrangements which call for supplementary action both within Member States and at Community level, and by promoting equal opportunities for men and women.

To implement these objectives a budget allocation of 45 million ECU was estimated to be necessary.[50] These funds would be spent in five specific areas.[51] Fifty per cent of the funds were to be spent on the development of transnational exchanges, which would allow trainees, university staff and staff from particular industries to spend a period of time either in universities or at industries in another Member State. Such exchanges also formed part of one of the other schemes to be financed. Funds were to be allocated to the development of a European network of university–industry training partnerships. Such training partnerships would promote inter-Member State co-operation in the organization of training and the exchange of staff and trainees.

By virtue of Article 6 of the decision the initial budget allocation was to be reassessed by 31 December 1988. This reassessment would be the result of a Commission report on the operation of the Comett I Programme[52] and the possibility existed that the programme would be continued. The Commission duly submitted its report and on 16 December 1988 the Council adopted Decision 89/27 instituting the Comett II Programme.[53] The funds allocated to the programme, for the period 1990 to 1994, were substantially increased to 200 million ECU.[54] This funding is available for similar types of projects as Comett I funding was available for. Funding decisions are made by the Comett Committee which is composed of representatives of the Member States and chaired by a Commission representative. It is interesting to note that the objectives of Comett II are more detailed than those of Comett I. To some extent, this reflects the experience gained from the operation of Comett I: increasing emphasis, however, is given to the European dimension of the co-operation between universities and industry and to the research and development potential of this co-operation. Specifically, Article 3 lists as one of the objectives of Comett II the improvement of the contribution which advanced technology training can make to the economic and social development of the Community.

To conclude this section it is, once again, necessary to discuss the legal basis for the programme. The Treaty basis for the adoption of the Comett I Programme was Articles 128 and 235. The Preamble to the decision makes clear the reasons for the use of the latter provision. As it was unclear whether or not the Treaty had provided the necessary powers for the programme, which was considered necessary to achieve the objectives of the Treaty, the Preamble stated that 'it would therefore appear justifiable, in the interest of certainty as to the law, to have recourse in addition to Article 235.'[55] The decision adopting the second phase of the Comett Programme did not refer to Article 235; instead, it was based on Article 128 and on Council Decision 63/266. As a result of this an action was brought by the United Kingdom, France and Germany under Article 173 for the annulment of this decision.[56] The fundamental argument of the applicants was that Article 128 was an insufficient legal basis for this decision.

In their submissions the applicants argued that there were not sufficient differences between the first and second Comett decisions to justify the choice of a different legal basis. The essential question, therefore, was whether Article 128 could by itself form an adequate legal basis for the contested decision. In the applicants' opinion,

> Article 128 of the Treaty, by referring to the establishment of general principles for implementing a common vocational training policy, allows the Community to coordinate to some degree relevant national policy, but does not allow it to administer independent training projects under a programme such as that adopted by the contested decision.[57]

The implementation of a programme which provided for independent Community projects such as the Comett Programme, the French government argued, went beyond the establishment of general principles. This was contrary to Article 128 which did not envisage significant expenditure by the Community but rather the co-ordination of national programmes which left a certain degree of discretion in the Member States. The decision therefore did not respect the division of competence in Article 128.

The United Kingdom government supported this argument through an examination of the Treaty provisions on vocational training.[58] They argued that Article 128 was inappropriate as the voting procedure was that of a simple majority, whereas the other provisions of the Treaty on vocational training, Articles 41 and 125, require a qualified majority. Moreover, unlike these latter provisions, Article 128 makes no reference to the role of the European Parliament: the use of Article 235 was considered more appropriate not only because of the voting procedure but also because that Article would involve the European Parliament. The Council, the United Kingdom concluded, had used Articles 235 and 128 together in the past and should have done so for the Comett II decision. This conclusion was vindicated by the fact that the decision had budgetary implications and Article 128 had never been used as a justification for conferring budgetary powers on the Council.[59]

On the question of the appropriate legal base for the decision, the Council considered that Article 128 was considered acceptable as the objectives of the programme constituted aspects of the implementation of a common vocational training programme.[60] As the European Court had decided since the Comett I decision that university education could fall within the scope of vocational training, there was no need in the Comett II decision to refer to Article 235.[61] Equally, the fact that the programme laid down only general principles and co-ordinates existing programmes within the Member States indicated that the scope of Article 128 had not been exceeded. The Spanish government intervened to support the Council on this point by noting that the Comett II Programme contained no provision which defined what must be included in the Member States' vocational training policies.[62]

The arguments of the parties had to be reconsidered once the European Court of Justice delivered its judgment in Erasmus. In that decision the Court concluded:

> under the scheme of the Treaty the conditions under which legislative powers and budgetary powers are exercised are not the same. Consequently, the requirements of the budgetary procedure laid down for making available the appropriations needed for the implementation of the programme at issue cannot have any implications regarding the procedural requirements for the adoption of the contested decision, since the latter requirements fall under a completely separate provision.[63]

This paragraph was repeated in the judgment of the Court in Comett II.[64] So, the applicants' objections to the use of Article 128 as an appropriate legal basis because of the operational character of the Comett II Programme and its budgetary implications were therefore rejected.

Having been defeated on these arguments, the applicants then attacked the scope of Comett II by maintaining that Article 128 was inappropriate since the programme extended beyond vocational training to include elements of research and development.[65] The German government on this point noted that although a wide definition had been given to the concept of vocational training, measures which related to continuing education could not come within that concept. Equally, only Article 235 could be used as an additional legal basis as the provisions of the Treaty on research and development were not considered appropriate given the nature of the Comett Programme. In reply the Council and the Commission argued that Article 128 covered both basic vocational training and continuing vocational training. Moreover, the Comett II Programme in no way encroached on the area of research and development and the programme makes clear that the objective of co-operation between universities and industry are related to training.[66] This conclusion emerged from an examination of the concrete actions envisaged by the programme and the Treaty provisions on research and development.

Advocate General Tesauro, after noting that the Erasmus decision dealt with the first group of arguments on the use of Article 128 as the sole legal basis of the Comett II decision, went on to discuss the scope of the term 'vocational training'.[67] He began by noting that Decision 63/266 referred to continuing vocational education and that Community programmes in this area had been adopted using only Article 128 as their legal basis.[68] As no challenge had been mounted to these latter decisions, he concluded that Article 128 covered continuing vocational training. This conclusion was not affected by the fact that elements of research and development were included within Comett II. Indeed if the programme were to have a joint legal base, then Article 130q rather than Article 235 would be the other legal base. However, as the Comett II Programme was directed towards vocational training it was acceptable to use only Article 128.[69]

The judgment of the Court begins with the affirmation of its previous case law on the use of Article 235, just as it had in the Erasmus judgement. That provision could only be used, as its wording indicates, where no other provision of the Treaty gives the necessary power to adopt the contested measure. Having rejected the submissions of the applicants on the use of Article 128 as the legal basis for the Comett II decision, the Court proceeded to examine the arguments that the scope of vocational training had been exceeded. After an examination of the provisions of the decision the Court concluded that the programme was directed towards vocational training.[70] This conclusion was not vitiated by the inclusion of elements of research and development within the programme. These elements were considered to reflect the complementary nature of the vocational training envisaged by the programme. On the question addressed by the German government of whether Article 128 covers continuing education, the Court rejected their argument. It continued:

> According to the wording of Article 128, it is directed at a common vocational training policy and does not draw any distinction between initial training and continuing training. Consequently, the latter type of training cannot be excluded from the

> scope of vocational training without restricting that concept in an arbitrary manner.[71]

The applicants' case was thus dismissed in its entirety.

The Comett Programme serves as an excellent example of the gradual emergence of a Community competence in education, which has developed despite the absence of references to the problems posed by technological changes in the 1976 Action Programme on Education. Concern emerged from various Commission documents and these were eventually reflected in resolutions of the Council. These resolutions paved the way for an initial programme of co-operation between universities and industry in the Member States which would be financed by the Community. The continuation of the programme with substantially greater financial resources and a more European dimension was accepted by the Court as falling solely within Article 128 of the Treaty, despite the inclusion of elements of research and development within the programme. Thus an area of educational co-operation which had not existed in 1976 had by 1990 come within the scope of the Treaty, demonstrating the continuing expansion of the competence of the Community in this area.

LINGUA

One of the seven priority areas identified in the 1974 resolution of the Ministers of Education meeting within the Council was improved teaching of foreign languages.[72] This was to be viewed in the context of the encouragement of freedom of movement for teachers and students. This priority area was further highlighted in the 1976 Action Programme.[73] The programme in this area set out a series of objectives which would be encouraged; including, for example, that all pupils should be offered the opportunity of learning at least one other Community language. To promote this objective, the Member States were to organize study periods abroad for their language teachers and encourage student exchanges. The role of the Community was to organize consultations on language training.

The 1980 report of the Education Committee on the Action Programme concluded, given the importance of language training to the right of free movement guaranteed by the Treaty, that:

> foreign-language teaching should accordingly constitute an

> important element in basic and advanced vocational training and thereby assist in the implementation of a common vocational training policy capable of contributing to the harmonious development both of the national economies and of the common market.[74]

The Member States were urged to examine the means by which the opportunities for young people to learn another one, or possibly two, Community languages could be encouraged within the general education system. In addition, there was to be an exchange of information and experience between the Member States on the teaching of another language at the primary level of education. At the higher education level, a review was to be carried out concerning the possibility of combining a foreign language with the student's chosen subject. It was recommended that all teachers of foreign languages should have the opportunity to spend officially recognized periods of study in another Member State. These could be either an exchange of teachers for one school term or an intensive study period.[75]

By 1984 the Council and the Ministers of Education were calling for a fresh impetus to be given to the teaching of foreign languages to pupils, students and adults.[76] No dramatically new initiatives were contemplated. The Council merely reaffirmed the conclusions of the 1980 report of the Education Committee and the importance of the 1976 Action Programme in this area. While respecting variations in the linguistic circumstances of the Member States, they were again urged to take all appropriate measures to ensure the maximum possible number of pupils acquired a practical knowledge of at least two other languages before the end of compulsory education. Measures were to be taken to allow for the continuation of language training in vocational training, higher education and adult education. Likewise the Member States were to increase their co-operation in the training of language teachers. Finally, the Education Committee was requested to make a report every three years on the measures which had been taken by both the Member States and the Community to encourage foreign language teaching.

These conclusions were used by the Adonnino Report on the measures necessary to achieve a People's Europe.[77] In particular, the report highlighted the need for as many pupils as possible to have a practical knowledge of at least two languages, in addition to their mother tongue, before the end of compulsory education. This objective was to be facilitated by future foreign language teachers spending part of their training in the country whose language they intend to teach and by educational visits to another Member State. Once again, no new initiatives were considered necessary to achieve this objective; the European Council at Milan merely approved the Adonnino Report and the 1985 meeting of the Council and of the Ministers of Education meeting within the Council likewise referred back to the conclusions of the 1984 Council.[78]

The recognition that the European dimension in Education was a necessary part of the People's Europe adopted by the European Council and the Single Market project necessitated a new approach to the area of foreign language competence.[79] This new approach was ushered in by Decision 89/489 establishing the Lingua Programme – an action programme to promote foreign language competence in the European Community.[80] As Article 4 makes clear:

> The principal objective of the Lingua programme shall be to promote a quantitative and qualitative improvement in foreign language competence with a view to developing communication skills within the Community. To that end, it shall, by means of Community wide measures, provide opportunities for supporting and complementing Member States' policies and schemes aimed at achieving that objective.

Lingua will therefore be a complementary programme. It will support the activities of the Member States in the area of foreign language teaching; activities which the Community has encouraged since the 1974 resolution on co-operation in education. Article 5 therefore restates the main areas of foreign language teaching from the 1976 Action Programme to the 1984 conclusions of the Council and the Ministers of Education meeting within the Council.

As Article 4 of Decision 89/489 recognizes, there is also a Community dimension to Lingua. The Annex to the decision lists various supporting measures which according to Article 8 will 'give a significant Community impetus to the efforts of Member States to raise the level of foreign language competence'. The funds allocated to this Community dimension are 200 million ECU for the five-year period, 1990–1994.[81] Five measures are listed in the Annex as benefiting from these funds. They include measures to promote the in-service teaching of foreign language teachers. The funding in this area is by means of a block grant to each Member

State. Aid will also be granted for European co-operation between in-service training establishments. Such aid is to be complementary to that provided by the Member State. The second area of funding is for measures to promote the learning of foreign-languages in universities and in particular to develop the initial training of foreign-language teacher. This area overlaps with the Erasmus Programme and consists of the measures available under that programme; it is also comparable with the fourth area of funding which relates to measures to promote the development of exchanges for young people undergoing professional, vocational and technical education within the Community. It is left to each Member State to define the scope of this area. The remaining area concerns measures to promote knowledge of foreign languages used in work relations and in economic life. Funding in this area covers such matters as the development of teaching materials and self-learning methods.

As indicated above there is an area of overlap between Lingua and Erasmus. In recognition of this and other overlaps, Article 11 of Decision 89/489 obliges the Commission to ensure consistency and complementarity between actions under the Lingua Programme and actions under other Community programmes, such as Erasmus and Comett. Like these programmes, Lingua demonstrates the gradual development of Community competence in education. Once again, an expanded role for the Community emerges from an initial role of information-gatherer and exchanger. However, unlike both Erasmus and Comett, the Lingua Programme is based on both Articles 128 and 235. It is accepted that as the Action Programme includes aspects relating to education and training policy, it falls outside the scope of the establishment of general principles for the implementation of a common vocational training policy provided for in Article 128.

TEMPUS

Whereas the programmes discussed so far have their origins in either the Action Programme for education or a Commission inspired response to the problems faced in vocational training, the Tempus programme, has its origins in the collapse of communism in Eastern Europe. Faced with this situation the European Council meeting at Strasbourg in December 1989 requested the Council to adopt measures which would allow for the participation of Eastern European countries in Community educational programmes. The

Commission had previously proposed such an initiative. The Council and the Ministers of Education meeting within the Council in December 1989 took note of the conclusions of the Strasbourg European Council and stressed the need to take decisions as 'a matter of extreme urgency so that specific measures might be initiated as soon as possible'.[82]

On 7 May 1990 the Council adopted Decision 90/233 establishing a trans-European mobility scheme for university studies – Tempus – to begin on 1 July.[83] The Preamble to the decision makes it clear that the scheme will operate as part of the PHARE Programme which assists the economic and social restructuring of the former communist countries of Eastern Europe.[84] Originally devised to assist Poland and Hungary, PHARE now extends to all the countries of Central and Eastern Europe with the exception of the Commonwealth of Independent States and most of the former Yugoslavia. The basic idea of Tempus is to draw on the experience and expertise gained within the Community in the operation of educational programmes to create a companion scheme for the countries of Central and Eastern Europe.[85] This is reflected in the objectives of the scheme which are laid down in Article 4 of the decision. Article 4(d) lists as an objective of Tempus:

> to enable students from eligible countries to spend a specific period of study at university or to undertake industry placements within the Member States of the Community, while ensuring equality of opportunity for male and female students as regards participation in such mobility.

Thus the objectives of the Erasmus and Comett Programmes would apply to the eligible countries. Article 4(c) makes clear that the objectives of the Lingua Programme also apply.[86] So students from the eligible countries are able to move to the Member States to participate in inter-university co-operation and co-operation between universities and industry. Likewise Community students will have similar opportunities in the eligible countries.

The co-operation process does not have a specific budget allocation noted in the decision, rather the Commission is to assess the necessary budgetary expenditure within the limits of the amount of economic aid made available to the eligible countries.[87] Up to the end of 1992, this figure amounted to 194 million ECU.[88] According to the Annex of the decision, this was to finance three types of measures. The first type of measure is joint European projects which link universities and/or enterprises in the eligible countries with partners in the Community. Such projects should comprise at least one university or enterprise in the eligible countries with partner institutions in at least two Member States. The purpose of the projects would be to respond to the specific educational and/or training needs of the universities and/or industry in the eligible countries.

To support these projects, the second type of measure to be financed is mobility grants which allows students, academic staff (teachers and administrators) and industry personnel from the eligible countries to spend a period of time in the Member States of the Community. Grants will also be available for the same categories of individuals from the Community to spend a period of time in the eligible countries. The relevant period of time may be either a short study visit, in the case of administrative staff or teachers, or up to one academic year for students or teaching staff. Complementary activities are the final type of measures to be funded. The funding of these activities must be co-ordinated with the funding of similar activities by countries which are not members of the Community.[89] This recognizes that the assistance to the eligible countries granted through the Tempus Programme is part of a wider effort by the group of twenty-four countries to support the economic and social restructuring of the countries of Central and Eastern Europe.

By virtue of Article 9 of Decision 90/233, the role of co-ordinator is assigned to the Commission. The involvement of third countries, government, universities and/or industry can take various forms. The Tempus projects may be co-financed by such countries, the facilities of Tempus could be used to channel bilateral aid or nationally based initiatives having the same goals as Tempus can be co-ordinated with such projects. To support the Commission in this role, as in other programmes, a committee made up of representatives of the Member States and chaired by a Commission representative is established.[90] This Committee also has the responsibility of ensuring consistency between Tempus and other actions at Community level. Finally, provision exists for the review and adaptation of the scheme.

A review and an evaluation of Tempus have already been conducted.[91] The outcome was Decision 93/246 which adopts the second phase of the Tempus project to run from 1994 to 1998.[92]

The evaluation of the programme leads to a reorientation of the objectives of Tempus so that it could help in the reform of the structure of higher education establishments in the eligible countries. This is confirmed by Article 4, which states: 'The objectives of Tempus II are to promote, . . . the development of higher education systems in the eligible countries, through as balanced a cooperation as possible with partners from all the Member States of the Community'. Three specific areas of higher education are highlighted in Tempus II. These are curriculum development, the reform of structures and institutions and their management and the development of skill-related training to address existing skill shortages. These areas are reflected in the Annex to the decision which lists the type of measures fundable under Tempus II. These measures are similar to those listed in the Annex to the original Tempus decision. However, there are differences. Reflecting the increasing emphasis on higher education, greater attention is given by Tempus II to the funding of joint European projects. This takes the form of a detailed list of activities for such projects. Mobility grants may also be awardable. In the original decision, student mobility grants formed a separate category of measures which could be funded. The remainder of the decision is comparable with the Tempus I decision.

Despite the different origins of Tempus and the fact that third countries may be involved in the financing of Tempus projects, the scheme is broadly similar to those already discussed in this chapter. All the programmes are built on three main principles. First, the idea of networking: all programmes involve the creation of transnational networks of organizations facing similar problems which may be soluble through the exchange of information. Secondly, joint transnational projects: having created a network, projects are undertaken within that network to add a European dimension to the specific education or training to be undertaken. Finally, mobility and exchange: to ensure a European dimension to education and training, all the programmes allow for the possibility of students, academic staff, teachers, researchers or administrators, and industry personnel to gain direct experience in another Member State or third country. These three principles demonstrate the renewed impetus given to educational co-operation since the Adonnino Report and the move to complete the Internal Market. They may be contrasted with the gradual development of the competence of the Community in education since its humble origins in the Action Programme in 1976 to 1984.

A RIGHT OF RESIDENCE FOR STUDENTS

One consequence of the increasing use of action programmes, notably Erasmus and Comett, is that students will spend a period of time in another Member State. A natural extension of this is that a student may wish to study for a degree or diploma in another Member State rather than undertake only a short period of study there. The question which arises in this case is: Is such a student entitled to a right of residence? An examination of Articles 48 to 66 of the Treaty of Rome indicates that all significant economic activity is covered by the free movement of persons provisions. As study appears not to be an economic activity, a student moving to another Member State to study for a degree or diploma may not be covered by these provisions. However, as the Hague Summit of 1969 declared, the Community is more than an economic association of states.[93] In the pursuit of the social goals of free movement in 1979 the Commission submitted a draft directive on the right of residence for nationals of Member States in the territory of another Member State.[94] The rationale of the proposal was to extend the right of free movement to all those who wished to move to another Member State irrespective of the economic purpose of such a move. The proposal was not adopted. In 1989 the Commission tried again and this time it was to be successful.[95] In contrast with the 1979 proposal, this time there were to be three directives: one for persons of independent means; one for retired persons; and one for students. On 28 June 1990 the Council adopted all three proposals.[96]

Directive 90/366 which deals with the right of residence of students is worth examining for the purposes of the education policy of the Community, especially as the Preamble makes clear that the right of residence of students is part of 'a set of related measures designed to promote vocational training'.[97] However, the directive, like the other two directives, is supplementary. It is designed to assist those students who do not already enjoy a right of residence under Community law. Such students may either be workers who have decided to pursue vocational training or the children of migrant workers. In both these cases, rights are available under Regulation 1612/68 on the free movement of workers in the Community.[98] The Preamble to the directive refers to the case law of the European Court of Justice on the interpretation of Articles 7 and 128 of the Treaty. Although these will be discussed in greater detail in the next chapter, it has to be noted that the case law referred to prohibits discrimination on the grounds of nationality and that the scope of Article 7 of the Treaty does not extend to assistance granted by the host Member State to its own nationals.[99]

In relation to the Treaty bases of the measure specific reference is made in the Preamble to Articles 3(c) and 8A of the EEC Treaty. Thus the right to free movement for students is seen as part of the activities of the Community and as a necessary part of the completion of the Internal Market. Despite these references, and the references to Articles 7 and 128, the Preamble notes that 'the Treaty does not provide, for the action concerned, powers other than those of Article 235'. The use of Article 235 as the legal basis of the directive was successfully challenged by the European Parliament.[100] The Parliament argued that the directive should have been based on Article 7 of the Treaty. (The Commission in its proposal had suggested that Article 7 be used.) The result of the failure to select the proper legal basis, the Parliament argued, was that the measure was not subject to the co-operation procedure as it should have been. Instead, as required by Article 235, Parliament had merely been consulted.

The Court considered that the directive could have been adopted under Article 7 and therefore, the Council was not justified in its decision to base it on Article 235. The Preamble to the directive could be of assistance here as it makes clear that the directive was one of a set of measures designed to promote vocational training, covered by Article 128, and to prohibit discrimination as regards access to this training, covered by Article 7. The necessary powers existed within the Treaty so there was no need to refer to Article 235. The Council argument was that the directive conferred rights which went beyond a right of residence for the purposes of vocational training, hence the need to use Article 235. This was rejected by the Court and it was pointed out that the scope of measures which could be adopted under Article 7 can extend to measures which appear necessary to enable the rights derived from that Article to be exercised effectively.[101] The right of residence given to the student's spouse and children was thus seen not as a factor taking the matter outside the scope of Article 7 but rather as an indispensable factor in the exercise of the student's right of residence. The directive was annulled. The effects of the annulled directive were to continue to have force pending the entry into force of a directive adopted on the appropriate legal basis.

The decision of the Court vindicated the approach of the Commission when it submitted its proposals. Access to vocational training, therefore, falls within the competence of the Community and, given the wide definition adopted by the Court of vocational training, a Community competence in education exists. That such a competence is founded on Article 128 underlines the fact that the competence of the Community may vary over time. This emerges from the Erasmus and Comett judgements discussed above. It could not have been envisaged in 1957, or even in 1971 when the Ministers of Education of the Member States met for the first time, that such an outcome was possible. The fact that the Court considered Article 7 of the Treaty to be an appropriate legal basis for the directive opens up the area of education to the principle of equality of treatment. The fact that this principle is a general one and the fact that legislation under Article 7(2) may include areas ancillary to this principle so that it may be effectively exercised, means that the Community competence in education has changed beyond recognition.

On 17 May 1993 the Commission submitted a proposal for a Council directive on the right of residence of students based on Article 7(2) of the Treaty.[102] The Preamble in the proposal makes specific reference to the decision of the Court. It is interesting to note that there is a slight change in other recitals in the Preamble. Once again, reference is made to the case law of the Court on the interpretation of Articles 7 and 128 of the Treaty, the recital then continues to state that access to vocational training in one Member State by a national of another Member State implies for that person a right of residence in the host Member State. The directive is now clearly designed to lay down the conditions 'likely to facilitate the effective exercise' of the right of residence.[103] As for the content of the proposal, there are, as expected, no changes to the substance of the directive.

Having discussed the legal challenge to the basis of the directive and the new Commission proposal on the matter, it is now time to consider the actual contents of the directive. According to Article 1 of the Directive:

> Member States shall, in order to facilitate access to vocational training, grant the right of residence to any student who is a national of a Member State and who does not enjoy this right under other provisions of Community Law, and to the student's spouse and their dependent children, where the student assures the relevant national authority, by means of a declaration or by such alternative means as the student may choose that are at

> least equivalent, that he has sufficient resources to avoid becoming a burden on the social assistance system of the host Member State during their period of residence, provided that the student is enrolled in a recognized educational establishment for the purpose of following a vocational training course there and that they are covered by sickness insurance in respect of all risks in the host Member State.[104]

Thus the student's right of residence is limited. Before exercising the right, the student must satisfy the national authorities of the host Member State that he or she has sufficient resources to live in that state. Furthermore, the student must by covered by medical insurance with respect to sickness in that Member State. These limitations will be exacerbated if the student elects to be accompanied by his or her spouse and children.

Unlike the right of residence granted under the other two directives, to persons of independent means and retired persons, the student's right of residence is limited to the duration of the course of vocational studies undertaken. The issuing of a residence permit provides evidence of the right of residence and the provisions of Article 2 of the directive make clear that the residence permit is limited to the duration of the course of study. Derogation from the provisions of the directive must be on grounds of public policy, public security or public health; in the event of derogation the provisions of Directive 64/221 apply. The final point confirms the case law of the European Court with respect to awards for study. Article 3 of the directive states: 'This Directive shall not establish any entitlement to the payment of maintenance grants by the host Member State on the part of students benefitting from the right of residence'.

The rationale of Directive 90/366 is to abolish obstacles to the free movement of persons between Member States. Now to be based on Article 7(2) of the Treaty, the directive also espouses an equality of treatment between students from other Member States and national students. However, there are limits to this equality. The principle of equality of treatment will apply only in relation to the conditions of access to vocational training. The question that arises is: How do you classify a particular requirement imposed by the directive? Take, for example, the requirement that the intending student (and spouse and children) should have medical insurance. Can this be classified as a condition of access? It seems that it is a condition of access, especially as Article 4 of the directive makes clear that the right of residence remains 'for as long as beneficiaries of that right fulfil the conditions' of Article 1. If such insurance is not required from national students, then the requirements of Article 1 of the directive may be contrary to Article 7 of the Treaty.

The use by the Court of Article 7 as the correct legal basis for Directive 90/366 must imply that the provisions of that directive are consistent with Article 7. The Court has admitted that the scope of Article 7(2) extends beyond the rights in paragraph (1) to cover those ancillary rights which are necessary to allow the rights in paragraph (1) to operate effectively. O'Leary correctly concludes:

> It is argued that recourse to Article 235 was motivated precisely by Member State fears that Community competence in education would be further increased if the general provisions of Article 7 were allowed to apply to the free movement of students. If the Court's decision in Case C-295/90 is brought to its logical conclusion, this should prove to be so, and the vindication of Article 7 in Case C-295/90 should spark off some judicial challenge of the validity of the provisions of the Directive. If not, the Parliament's victory will have been formalistic, since the text of the Directive will not be substantively altered, and the Court of Justice's vindication of the principle of equal treatment may prove to be both selective and shallow.[105]

As noted above, the text of the directive has remained unchanged as a result of the legal challenge to the basis of the directive. It is only a matter of time before a legal challenge to its provisions emerges.

CONCLUSION

There is general evidence of movement from a system of rules designed to liberate those pursuing economic activities from the constraints of national boundaries to one allowing movement across boundaries for 'non-economic' purposes. This is coupled with a nascent attempt by the Community to encourage all citizens to become more Community-minded, in short the European Community is turning its hand to what in former times would have been called 'nation-building'.[106]

This is how Lonbay begins an article on the education law of the European Community. The discussion of the right of residence of students, indeed the entire history of the education policy of the Community, may be seen as a vindication of this viewpoint.

In reviewing the history of the education policy of the Community, it is remarkable that so much has been achieved since the initial resolution on education and the 1976 Action Programme. It is possible to see three periods in the Community's education policy. In the initial period it was uncertain what the exact scope of the policy would be. The recommendations of the Janne Report were considered inappropriate and a much more limited sphere of action was agreed on. Within this more limited sphere, a need existed for greater information. Hence the roles assigned to the Community of information gatherer and disseminator and the sponsor of a series of pilot studies. During this period of learning the Community was confronted with new challenges. In particular, the rise of new information technologies and, more importantly, the challenge to accepted beliefs resulting from the problems caused by youth unemployment. Initially, the Community sought to apply similar techniques as had been applied in the past. For the Community, the role of information-gatherer and disseminator and sponsor of pilot projects would provide a solution to these problems. However, there comes a time when all the information collected, all the pilot projects undertaken would have to be evaluated, and if found wanting, new approaches are needed. This point of transition was reached in 1983 when Community action in education was called on to complement action in the economic, financial and employment areas.

The sphere of action would change as a result of these new challenges and the additional challenges emerging from the desire to promote a People's Europe and the move to complete the Internal Market. The second period would be a much more interventionist one than the first. In the areas identified by the 1976 Action Programme the Council and the Ministers of Education meeting within the Council would no longer be able to act by merely passing resolutions or, as it usually had done, of reaching general conclusions. Instead, in the years that followed progress would be made by directives and decisions – instruments which had largely not had a role in the first period of the history of education policy. By the end of this period, specific programmes would exist in university education, university-industry co-operation, and the teaching of foreign languages. Higher education was acquiring a European Dimension.[107] This would be seen as complementary to the European dimension advocated for many years in primary and secondary education. The scope of the policy would change further as events in Europe led to the extension of these programmes first to the EFTA countries and then to the countries of Central and Eastern Europe. The education policy of the Community has thus acquired a truly international dimension.[108]

Scott summarizes the development of Community competence in education from the Treaty of Paris establishing the European Coal and Steel Community to the 1980s in the following fashion:

> In sum, the Community began without an educational policy as such. The dynamics of economic integration, first in the coal and steel sectors and later in the economy in general drove it to elements of social engineering, originally for certain sectors and for a notionally transitional period only. From this intervention grew a broader and more positive approach to vocational training. The growth of social policy in the 1970s brought a number of interventions in the educational area concerned mainly with problems relating to mobility. Despite some European concern in the 1980s to deregulate the labour market, the increasing pace of economic integration in recent years led to more far-reaching programmes, nearer the core of the educational process. Education is now recognized as being central to the development of European construction.[109]

The centrality of education emerged from a very limited Treaty base. Article 128 on vocational training was used by the Community to invade the previously national domain of education policy. A crucial role was played by the European Court of Justice in the interpretation of Article 128 and the provisions of secondary legislation on the education of migrant workers and their children, the competence of the Community has been consistently extended by the Court. This extension of Community competence will be the subject of the next chapter. What that discussion will demonstrate is that education remains a highly sensitive area of Community competence. Issues of national sovereignty continue to dominate Community discussions of the scope of its education policy and such issues will be of even greater significance in the third period of the education policy of the Community. This period begins with the provisions of the Treaty on European Union because for the first time that Treaty assigns specific competence to the Community in education as distinct from vocational training.

Notes

3

The Extension of Community Competence

Having traced the development of the competence of the Community in the field of education, this chapter is devoted to the consideration of three specific aspects of that policy. The three areas to be examined are: the educational rights of migrants and their children; the concept of vocational training; and the mutual recognition of qualifications. One of the reasons that these areas were chosen was because they reveal the role that the European Court of Justice has played in the development of the education policy of the Community.

THE EDUCATIONAL RIGHTS OF MIGRANTS AND THEIR CHILDREN

Regulation 1612/68 on Freedom of Movement for Workers within the European Community forms one of a series of measures designed to promote the realisation of Article 48 of the Treaty of Rome.[1] The provisions of the regulation are designed to abolish all forms of discrimination based on nationality between workers as regards eligibility for employment, remuneration and other conditions of work or employment. In relation to education, two particular provisions of the regulation are important, Article 7 and Article 12. The purpose of Article 7 is to secure for the migrant worker equality of treatment with the national worker. One aspect of this equality of treatment is according to Article 7(2) access to the 'social advantages' enjoyed by national workers. According to Article 12 of the regulation:

> The children of a national of a Member State who is or has been employed in the territory of another Member State shall be admitted to that State's educational, apprenticeship and

> vocational training courses under the same conditions as the nationals of that State, if such children are residing in its territory. Member States shall encourage all efforts to enable such children to attend these courses under the best possible conditions.

The purpose of the regulation is, as noted above, to encourage the free movement of workers within the Community and Articles 7 and 12 can be seen as a necessary ingredient of the decision of a worker to exercise the right of free movement. As the Preamble of the regulation makes clear, the provisions of the regulation are designed to aid the integration of migrant workers and their families into the host state. The Articles are significant as they are examples of the few Community provisions which give an explicit right to education. Indeed Article 12 is the most significant of these two provisions as it extends beyond the narrow focus of vocational training and retraining. Given this significance, it will be discussed first.

Article 12 of Regulation 1612/68

The right to education guaranteed to the children of migrant workers by Article 12 of Regulation 1612/68 has been subject to further legislation, namely Directive 77/486.[2] By virtue of Article 1 the Directive applies to:

> children for whom school attendance is compulsory under the laws of the host State, who are dependants of any worker who is a national of another Member State, where such children are resident in the territory of the Member State in which the national carries on or has carried on an activity as an employed person.

The host state is obligated under the directive to take appropriate measures to facilitate the initial reception of such children, in particular by the teaching of the official language of that state.[3] The teaching of the language and the culture of the country of origin of the child are also to be promoted.[4] The desire is to integrate the child as smoothly as possible into the host state's educational system without neglecting the background of the child. The main source of the interpretation of Article 12 is not this particular piece of legislation but the case law of the European Court of Justice (ECJ).

The first case to come before the ECJ in the education area was that of *Casagrande*.[5] Casagrande lived in Munich since his birth, his parents were Italian and had exercised their rights under the free movement of persons provisions of the Treaty. He applied for an educational award under the Bavarian Promotion of Education Act but this was refused since the Act restricted the category of persons entitled to an award to German nationals, stateless aliens or those entitled to political asylum. The plaintiff began an action in the administrative courts to recover the award claimed. The Bayerisches Verewaltungsgericht referred the question of whether the eligibility criteria under the Act were compatible with Article 12 of Regulation 1612/68. In his opinion, Advocate General Warner began by discussing the history and rationale of Regulation 1612/68. After citing Article 12 he noted that:

> It is not difficult to see that the requirement of the first paragraph of that Article that the children of a migrant worker are to be admitted to the host State's educational courses 'on the same conditions' as nationals of that State is intended to secure the 'integration' which the preamble envisages. Nor is it difficult to detect from the second paragraph of the Article a broad intention on the part of the authors of the regulation that in the field of education . . . everything possible should be done to facilitate that integration.

In the light of this remark it is not difficult to predict the likely opinion of the Advocate General. He stated that in any interpretation of the first paragraph of Article 12 a wide approach should be adopted.[7] This wide approach meant that the phrase 'under the same conditions' included on the same financial terms as nationals of the host state. This would achieve the equality of opportunity which lies at the heart of Regulation 1612/68. The ECJ would reach a similar conclusion. It declared:

> In providing that the children of a citizen of a Member State who is employed or has been employed in the sovereign territory of another Member State can participate in education 'on the same terms as the citizens' of the host country, Article 12 of Regulation 1612/68 has in mind not only the conditions of admission, but also the general measures designed to facilitate participation in education.[8]

The Court was anxious in *Casagrande* to ensure that difficulties faced by the worker and, in particular, members of the worker's family did not act as an impediment to the exercise of their rights under the Treaty and secondary legislation.

On the more general point of the role of educational policy, the ECJ admitted that 'as such' it was not to fall within the competence of the Community. However, should the application of rules which do fall within the competence of the Community affect the implementation of educational policy, then the latter is to be implemented in accordance with the principles of the Treaty.[9] The principle involved in this case was that of non-discrimination. Although not directly relevant to the judgement in this case, this principle, deriving from Article 7 of the Treaty, would assume increasing significance in future cases, especially those in which Regulation 1612/68 was not at issue. Finally, the ECJ did not discuss, as fully as the Advocate General had discussed, the impact of their adoption of a wide interpretation to Article 12. The Advocate General had noted the legislative position of most of the Member States in relation to the award of grants to children of migrant workers. In the end, he did not consider the diverse nature of the position in the Member States, and even within some Member States, as a ground for adopting a narrow approach to the interpretation of Article 12.[10] The Court limited itself to remarking on this point that according to Article 189 regulations were binding in their entirety and apply directly in all Member States, it did not matter which particular body, whether central or local government or even bodies exercising powers conferred on them by law, was responsible for ensuring the conditions referred to in Article 12 were applied.[11]

The proper interpretation of Article 12 was raised again in the following year in the case of *Alaimo*.[12] In this case, having failed some examinations, the plaintiff, (the daughter of an Italian national working in France) was refused a grant on her transfer to a different school. The reason for the refusal was that given the large number of applications for grants, financial assistance was to be limited to pupils of French nationality. The Administrative Court referred the following question to the ECJ:

> whether the phrase in Article 12 of Council Regulation 1612/68 'the children of a national of a Member State ... shall be admitted ... under the same conditions as nationals of that State' can be interpreted as reserving for the children of nationals of Member States only an equality limited to eligibility to register for courses; can also be interpreted as guaranteeing them further

an equality of status with regard to the whole of the rights arising out of admission.

The opinion of the Advocate General, once again Advocate General Warner, and the judgment of the Court are extremely short. They repeat their opinion and decision from *Casagrande*.

Further issues concerning the proper interpretation of Article 12 of Regulation 1612/68 arose in the joined cases of *Echternach and Moritz*.[13] The facts of the cases are extremely involved. In the case of Echternach, a resident of the Netherlands since 1966 when his father moved there from Germany to work, he was refused finance for his studies on the ground that he could not be treated as a Dutch resident. His father worked for the European Space Agency; the status of the Agency, and its employees, was the subject of an international agreement between the Netherlands and the Agency. As a result the Dutch Aliens Act did not apply; had it applied he may have been entitled to a grant. In Moritz, he had lived in the Netherlands from 1972 to 1985 at which time his father was reassigned to Germany. Moritz had started college in the previous year and he re-enrolled in 1985. In 1986 he took up residence again in the Netherlands and was granted a temporary residence permit. As a holder of such a permit his application for study finance was also refused: only those foreign students possessing a residence permit for an indefinite period were treated in the same way as Dutch nationals with respect to study finance. Both applicants appealed the refusal to give them finance to the Appeals Committee.

In both cases the Appeals Committee referred questions of interpretation to the ECJ. These questions were distilled to four questions by Advocate General Darmon.[14] First, to what extent does a system of providing public financial assistance to students fall within the scope of Regulation 1612/68 in general and Article 12 of the regulation in particular? Secondly, and specifically for the case of Echternach, is a Community national who is an official of an agency governed by an international agreement to be deprived of their status as workers and their consequent rights under EC law as a result of that agreement? Thirdly, and specifically in the case of Moritz, do the rights which a child derives in a host Member State from their parents' status as migrant workers disappear on the departure of the parents from the Member State? Finally, may the child of a migrant worker be prevented from claiming any financial assistance from the host Member State by reason of the requirements relating to his right to reside in that state?

The issue of financial assistance can be easily resolved as the ECJ had already dealt with this point in both *Casagrande* and *Alaimo*. The Court merely confirmed that financial assistance for the cost of study and maintenance during study were to be regarded as social advantages to which the children of migrant workers are entitled under the same conditions as apply to the nationals of the host Member State. The Court confirmed that such financial assistance would promote the integration of the student into the host Member State. The ECJ continued: 'For such integration to come about, a child of a Community worker must have the possibility of going to school and pursuing further education in the host country, as is expressly provided in Article 12 of Regulation 1612/68, in order to be able to complete that education successfully'.[15] In light of this conclusion, when the Court came to deal with the issues raised in the Moritz case, it could be predicted that the Court would decide that the child of a migrant worker must be entitled to continue his/her studies after their parents' return to their home state. The Court did indeed decide the third question in this manner pointing out that Article 12 refers to the parent who 'is employed or *has been* employed in the territory of another Member State'.[16] In addition, they stressed that education was a continuous process and, at present, there was a lack of co-ordination between educational systems in the Member States.

In relation to the question specifically referred in the case of Echternach the Court stated:

> it must be stated that a Community national working in a Member State other than his State of origin does not lose his status as a worker within the meaning of Article 48(1) of the Treaty though occupying a post within an international organization, even if the rules relating to his entry into and residence in the country in which he is employed are specifically governed by an international agreement concluded between the international organization and the State in which it is established.[17]

So, like Moritz, Echternach's rights under Community law were superior to the rights which he might have had under any more specilized agreement. It is, therefore, not surprising that on the final question the Court would rule that the enjoyment of the rights of the children of migrant workers under Community law could not be made subject to conditions relating to residence.[18]

In the case of *Humbel*,[19] of the three questions referred to the

ECJ one related to Article 12 of Regulation 1612/68. In this case, the defendants and their son lived in Luxembourg; they were French nationals. The son enrolled in a Belgian institute and was required to pay an enrolment fee (a minerval). He refused to pay this and the Belgian authorities brought an action against the defendants. The defendants argued *inter alia* that as the child of a migrant worker their son should come within the scope of Article 7 of Regulation 1612/68. The opinion of the Advocate General, Advocate General Slynn, began by noting the strange nature of Belgian legislation on this issue. The minerval was not payable by Belgian students or by the children of French nationals residing in a French commune which is within 15 kilometres of Belgium. Furthermore, the minerval was not payable by Luxembourg nationals who chose to study in Belgium. In these circumstances, the Advocate General noted that Article 7 of the Treaty would only be relevant if discrimination was 'practised in circumstances which fall within the scope of the Treaty'.[20] As this could not be shown, he concluded by stating that Article 12 cannot require 'a Member State to make education available to migrant workers resident in another State on the same basis as it makes it available to nationals of that other Member State'.[21] Therefore he rejected the argument advanced by the Italian government that Article 12 is not limited to education provided in the territory of the host Member State.[22]

The ECJ on this question stated that the situation would only arise in cases which do not involve vocational training within the meaning of Article 128. It concluded:

> Article 12 of Regulation 1612/68, properly construed, does not preclude a Member State from imposing an enrolment fee, as a condition for admission to ordinary schooling within its territory, on children of migrant workers residing in another Member State even when nationals of that other Member State are not required to pay such a fee.[23]

Despite this ruling in the case of *Di Leo* the ECJ reached a different conclusion.[24] Di Leo, the daughter of an Italian national who had worked in Germany for twenty five years, decided to study medicine. Due to *numerus clausus* provisions in German medical schools she decided to study medicine in Italy. She applied for a grant under the Federal law on Grants for Training and Further Education. Her application was refused on the grounds that a grant for study abroad could only be awarded to German nationals, stateless persons or foreigners entitled to asylum. On appeal to the Administrative Court a question was referred to the ECJ in the following terms:

> Is Article 12 of Regulation 1612/68 to be interpreted as meaning that children who come within the scope of its provisions are to be treated in the same way as nationals, not only where the education or training is pursued in the host State, but where such children receive their education or training in another Member State of which they are nationals?

The Court began its judgment by making reference to its decision in *Echternach and Moritz*. It did not refer to the decision in *Humbel*. It continued:

> According to its actual wording, Article 12 is not confined to education or training within the host country. The condition of residence, laid down by Article 12 of Regulation 1612/68, is designed to restrict equal treatment as regards the advantages referred to in the Article solely to the children of Community workers who reside in their parents' host country. However, it does not mean that the right to equal treatment depends on the place where the child concerned pursues his studies.[25]

The Court, therefore, ruled that Article 12 could be invoked if the child studied abroad and the parents resided in a Member State which granted financial assistance to national students studying abroad. The argument presented by the Italian government in *Humbel*, which was unsuccessful, was adopted by the Court. This is despite the fact that both the German and Netherlands governments stressed the residence requirement in Article 12 and the fact that if allowed to study abroad this would not promote the objective of integration of the child in the host Member State. In the end the Court chose to ignore these arguments, based as they were on the previous case law on Article 12. Instead it sought to promote equality of opportunity across the educational systems of the Member States. In the opinion of the Court, if the arguments of the German and Netherlands governments had been accepted a new form of discrimination would have emerged.

It is interesting to note that in coming to this conclusion the Court made reference to Article 7(2) of Regulation 1612/68. This requires Member States to extend to migrant workers all the social advantages which it gives to national workers. Arguing from this the Court held that the same principle must apply to the children of migrant workers covered by Article 12. This conclusion was not invalidated by the fact that Di Leo was an Italian national who wanted to study at an Italian university. The principle of integration which for so long had formed the basis of the case law of the Court on Article 12 gave way to the principle of non-discrimination.[26]

Article 7 of Regulation 1612/68

This provision of Regulation 1612/68 has been invoked in several cases, both before national courts and the ECJ. As an example of its use in national courts, there is the English case of *MacMahon* v. *Department of Education.*[27] The plaintiff was an Irish national who after working for over a year in England decided to undertake a teacher training course. He applied for an award to his local Education Authority. The application was refused on the basis of the relevant regulations which provided the Authority was not under a duty to make an award if the applicant had not been ordinarily resident in the United Kingdom for the three years preceding the first year of the course. In addition the plaintiff was required to pay fees at a higher rate as an overseas student. The plaintiff instituted proceedings for a declaration that the decisions of the Education Authority were contrary to Article 7 of Regulation 1612/68. It was admitted that the plaintiff was a worker within the meaning of Article 7 and the plaintiff's argument was based on Article 7. First, he argued that under Article 7(2) he was entitled to the social advantages which were available to national workers. Secondly, using Article 7(3) he argued that he was entitled to access to vocational training 'by virtue of the same right and under the same conditions as national workers'. Therefore, the three-year residence requirement was discriminatory and he should be entitled to an award and should not be required to pay higher fees.[28]

Leaving aside the question of the definition of 'vocational training' until the next section, Dillon J. adopted the ECJ case law on the definition of a social advantage emerging from cases such as *Cristini*[29] and *Reina*[30]. These cases show that the term social advantages cover all advantages which would be granted to national workers by reason of their residence in the particular Member State and their status as workers. It is not necessary, however, that such advantages should be connected with a contract of employment. The question to be answered was whether MacMahon was a worker at the time of his application. Dillon J. concluded that the plaintiff could not succeed on this argument: 'The relevant time for the purposes of paragraph (2) is the time when the advantage is to be enjoyed; that, with these benefits, was during the continuance of his position as a student and he was not then a "worker".'[31] The plaintiff did succeed on the basis of his arguments on Article 7(3) and the principle of non-discrimination in Article 7 of the regulation. The residence requirement was an example of covert discrimination which impeded the goals of the Treaty with respect to the free movement of workers.[32] Dillon J. did not consider it necessary to refer any question to the ECJ, however, questions were referred in the cases of *Lair*[33] and *Brown*.[34]

In *Lair* the plaintiff was a French national who moved to Germany to work. She was employed for two years and was then made redundant. She enrolled in the University of Hannover to study Romance and Germanic languages. Previously she had applied for an education grant from the university. This application was later rejected on the grounds that foreigners could not receive training grants unless they had completed five years' employment for which they had paid taxes and social security charges. The plaintiff instituted proceedings against this decision and the administrative court then referred several questions to the ECJ. These asked whether Community law allowed an individual to claim a grant on the same basis as nationals and whether the residence requirement was contrary to Article 7 of the Treaty.

The first question to be considered by Advocate General Slynn in his opinion was whether Lair was a worker.[35] Using the previous case law of the Court, he had little difficulty in establishing that Lair had exercised her rights under Article 48 of the Treaty.[36] So she was entitled to exercise the rights given to her by Regulation 1612/68 unless there was some reason to deny her these rights. The reason why her rights were denied in this case was the five year residence requirement. Advocate General Slynn did consider that it was reasonable to impose a residence requirement but five years was considered to be excessive; one year was thought by the Advocate General to be a reasonable period.[37] Having disposed of this question, the Advocate General proceeded to discuss the scope of Article 7 of the regulation. The German and Danish governments submitted that once Lair became a student she ceased to be a worker and, therefore, for the period which she was a student she ceased to have rights under the regulation.[38] Speaking to this submission, the Advocate General stated:

> It seems to me plain that such right, whether of access or training, is given to the worker. He can exercise it, and he is entitled to the full benefit of it, even if it means that during the period of training he ceases to work. To say that he can exercise the right by going to a vocational training school but that, the moment he does so, he loses all the benefits conferred on national workers deprives the provision of all content, indeed of all sense.[39]

Therefore by ceasing employment to take up vocational training a worker does not lose his rights under the regulation. Article 7(3) is not limited to workers who take part-time courses. Equally, the Advocate General refused to concede that there was a limitation in Article 7(3) which would limit the application of the provision by linking the training with the previous employment.[40] The next question to be addressed was whether Article 7(3) excluded the application of Article 7(2). The Advocate General considered that it did not.[41] As a result Lair was entitled to a grant under Article 7 of the regulation.

In their consideration of the interpretation of Article 7 of Regulation 1612/68, the Court began by examining the concept of social advantage in Article 7(2) and concluded that this provision entitled workers who had exercised their right of free movement to all the advantages of 'improving their professional qualifications and promoting their social advancement' as were available to national workers.[42] So a grant was a social advantage within Article 7(2).[43] This conclusion was not limited by the fact that Article 7(3) provides for a more specific social advantage.[44] The crucial question for the Court was whether Lair was a worker at the relevant time. The Court in line with its previous case law pointed out that the fact that Lair was unemployed did not mean that she had lost her status as a worker and that she would continue to have certain rights linked with her status as a worker. One of these rights is contained in Article 7(3). However, the Court continued:

> In the field of grants for university education, such a link between the status of worker and a grant awarded for maintenance and training with a view to the pursuit of university studies does, however, presuppose some continuity between the previous occupational activity and the course of study; there must be a relationship between the purpose of the studies and the previous occupational activity.[45]

This restriction, which was rejected by the Advocate General in his opinion,[46] was tempered by the rider that such continuity may not be required where the worker becomes involuntarily unemployed and conditions on the job market necessitate retraining in another area.

It is interesting to note at this point that in the English case of *MacMahon* v. *Department of Education*, Dillon J. rejected the argument that there should be a link between previous employment and training. Such a link, in his opinion, would be a major obstacle to the free movement of workers, as it would prevent an unskilled migrant worker 'from ever learning a trade or acquiring craft skills'.[47] Obviously the ECJ in *Lair* did not consider this be so. An obvious question to ask is: Why did the Court rule in this manner? In the submissions of the German, Danish and United Kingdom governments a certain disquiet was expressed concerning the possibility that if grants were freely available to workers this right would be abused.[48] For example, by persons moving to a particular Member State with the sole purpose of being awarded assistance after a very short period of employment. The Court pointed out that 'such abuses are not covered by the Community provisions in question'.[49] The decision of the Court to bow to pressure from the Member States is to be regretted.[50] It is arguable that Dillon J.'s approach was more in keeping with the wording and spirit of Community law in this area than that of the Court.[51]

The facts of *Brown* are slightly different. The plaintiff had lived since birth in France. His father was British and his mother French, they had last worked in the United Kingdom in 1965. Having passed all his school examinations, Brown began a degree course in Electrical Engineering at the University of Cambridge in October 1984. Prior to this for nine months he was involved in 'pre-university industrial training' with a company in Scotland. This company later awarded him a scholarship involving a grant and further training in the summer vacations. Brown also applied for a grant from the Scottish Education Department but was refused on the grounds that he did not fulfil the conditions laid down in the relevant regulations. He had not been resident for three years in the British Isles; his parents had not been employed in Scotland for the previous three years; and, finally, the course he was intending to study was not a vocational course at a vocational training establishment. He then applied for judicial review of this decision. The Court of Session referred a number of questions to the ECJ. These asked whether a course of full-time study at a university amounted to vocational training within the scope of the Treaty and/or Regulation 1612/68. The Court was also asked to give an interpretation of the potential application of Article 7 to the situation in the case.

Advocate General Slynn on the issue of vocational training repeated the remarks which he had made in *Gravier*. (These will be discussed in the next section.) On the question of the application of Article 7 of Regulation 1612/68, the Advocate General began his consideration by examining whether Brown was a worker.[52] Part of the problem with this question was the fact that Brown had secured employment as a part of his university studies. The Commission in its submissions considered that Brown's intention in taking up employment was irrelevant to the question of whether or not he was a worker.[53] Yet in the submissions of the United Kingdom, Germany and Denmark, the regulation requires employment for a substantial period. In their opinions, Brown could not be covered by Article 7 as he had taken up employment as a means of supplementing his income before he went to university.[54] The Advocate General in considering these submissions concluded that Brown did not satisfy the definition of a worker. He stated:

> A person who has the fixed intention of going to a Member State in any event as a student, and who has a place in a university or school for a fixed date and period, but who in order to gain useful experience does a short term job, does not in my view qualify under Article 7(2) and (3) as a person who can claim a grant in his capacity as a worker.[55]

As the work was purely ancillary to the course of study it could not be said to be genuine and effective employment. Despite agreeing with the submissions of the United Kingdom, Germany and Denmark, the Advocate General did not consider that a worker had to be employed for a substantial period to be covered under Article 7. The period of work must be reasonable and he repeated his opinion from *Lair* that one year was considered as a 'reasonable' period.[56] However, the Advocate General did consider that Article 7 of the Treaty would cover discrimination in the payment of tuition fees but not the payment of maintenance.[57]

On the question of the applicability of Article 7 of Regulation 1612/68, the Court, like the Advocate General, began its consideration with the question of whether Brown was a worker. They considered that he was a worker.[58] The question then became whether Brown was entitled to the social advantage of a grant. After referring to its decision in *Lair*, the Court continued:

> it cannot be inferred from that finding that a national of a Member State will be entitled to a grant for studies in another Member State by virtue of his status as a worker where it is established that he acquired that status exclusively as a result of his being accepted for admission to university to undertake the studies in question.[59]

As the employment relationship was purely ancillary to the education to be pursued, Brown could not be covered by Article 7 of Regulation 1612/68. As his parents had ceased to reside in the United Kingdom before Brown was born, he could not rely on Article 12 of the Regulation to secure a grant.

The decision of the Court in *Brown* is, like that of *Lair*, not beyond reproach. It seems strange that the Court classified Brown as a worker, even though he acquired that status as a result of his admission to university, and then used that fact to deny him a benefit which he was entitled to as a worker. The more sensible approach would have been to follow the opinion of the Advocate General; Brown was not a worker because he acquired that status as a result of his acceptance into university: as he was not a worker, he was not entitled to use Article 7 of Regulation 1612/68. To decide as the Court decided means that Article 7(2) must now be read as referring to 'genuine' workers, a limitation neither explicitly nor implicitly contained in Article 7.

Finally in this section, there is the case of *Matteucci*, where both Article 7(2) and Article 12 of Regulation 1612/68 were considered.[60] In this case, Matteucci was born and educated in Belgium, her parents were Italian nationals working in Belgium. After she completed her studies she attained a job as a teacher. Two years later she applied for a scholarship to complete her training at a German educational establishment, as no suitable educational establishment existed in Belgium. Her application was refused on the ground that scholarships, under the existing Cultural Agreement between Belgium and Germany, were only available to Belgian nationals. She brought an action alleging a breach of Articles 7 and 48 of the Treaty and Articles 7 and 12 of Regulation 1612/68. A question was referred to the ECJ concerning, in essence, the relationship between the provisions of the Treaty and the Cultural Agreement between Belgium and Germany. Two sets of arguments were raised;

one dealing with the application of Article 7 and the other with the possible application of Regulation 1612/68.

In relation to the possible application of Article 7 of the Treaty, Advocate General Slynn pointed out that the question had been resolved by the judgment of the Court in the cases of *Lair* and *Brown*. In relation to the second set of arguments on the possible application of Regulation 1612/68, the first question addressed by the Advocate General was whether Matteucci was a worker.[61] Although this was for the national court to decide, it did not affect the question of whether she could claim under Article 7 of the regulation. Assuming that she was not a worker, her father could claim the advantage under Article 7(2) of the regulation as he was a worker. Assuming that she was a worker, Advocate General Slynn concluded that the decision in *Lair* meant that she would be able to have access to the scholarship system.[62] The Advocate General then turned to the question of whether Matteucci could claim under Article 12 of the regulation. He concluded that the child of a migrant worker could rely on Article 12 if the child was not eligible under Article 7, even though the child has been employed before the start of the further education. The Court chose not to deal with this question and limited itself to the consideration of Article 7 of the regulation.[63]

The Court began its consideration of the arguments by pointing out the provisions of Article 11 of Regulation 1612/68.[64] This allows the child of a migrant worker to take up activities as an employed person. Once they have done so the migrant worker's child can rely on the provisions of Community law providing for equality between migrant workers and national workers. The Court assumed that Matteucci's job satisfied the definition of a worker under Community law. Turning to the question of the relationship between the rights of the worker under Community law and the bilateral agreement, the Court stated:

> Article 5 of the Treaty provides that the Member States must take all appropriate measures whether general or particular, to ensure the fulfilment of the obligations arising out of the Treaty. If, therefore, the application of a provision of Community law is liable to be impeded by a measure adopted pursuant to the implementation of a bilateral agreement, even where the agreement falls outside the field of application of the Treaty, every Member State is under a duty to facilitate the application of that

> provision and, to that end, to assist every other Member State which is under an obligation under Community law.[65]

The argument of the French government that Article 7 of Regulation 1612/68 is not binding on the host state where the training in question is provided in the territory of another Member State was rejected by the Court.[66] The bilateral agreement could not prevent the application of the principle of equality of treatment in Article 7 of Regulation 1612/68 between national and Community workers established in Belgium.

A Summary:
To conclude this section it might be useful to summarize the position reached so far in relation to the educational rights of migrant workers and their families.

1) Under Article 12 of Regulation 1612/68 all forms of education are covered and discrimination in relation to access to education is forbidden. The children of migrant workers will have access to education even if their parents are no longer resident in the particular Member State.
2) Such children must not be subject to discrimination in relation to maintenance grants, even where such grants are provided for study outside the host state.
3) Grants have also to be made available to workers, as a social advantage under Article 7(2) of the regulation, pursuing vocational courses. The only limitation which may be imposed is that the vocational course pursued must have some connection with the previous employment unless the conditions on the job market necessitate retraining in another area.
4) The principle of non-discrimination applies irrespective of the source of the financing of such grants; such financing may be either from the Member State or through bilateral agreements between Member States.

THE CONCEPT OF VOCATIONAL TRAINING

In this section of the Chapter the case law of the Court on rights within the sphere of education which fall outside the scope of Regulation 1612/68 will be examined. However, it is not possible to draw a sharp distinction between the cases which come within the regulation and those which fall outside. The cases in this section are bound together by their discussion of vocational training, a discussion which took place in a few of the cases noted above. The most significant of the cases to be discussed is that of *Gravier*[67] where the Court tackled the question of the definition of the concept of vocational training. This concept was subsequently extended in several cases which followed *Gravier*, where the implications of the judgment were fully discussed. For example, in *Humbel* the Court finally resolved the question of whether education was a service within the meaning of the Treaty. In *Gravier* it chose not to answer this question.

Towards a Definition

The section begins with the case of *Forcheri* which was the first in a series of judgments of the ECJ which sought to define, and even extend, the competence of the Community in education.[68] The facts of the case are relatively straightforward. Mr Forcheri was an Italian national employed in the Commission on Brussels. His wife wished to attend a vocational course (for social workers) and she was asked to pay an additional charge not payable by nationals, the soon to be famous 'minerval'. This fee was required from all foreign students since 1976 and the rules for applying it were laid down in circulars issued by the Ministry of Education. According to the relevant circular only Belgian students and certain other categories of students were exempt from this fee. Mrs Forcheri did not fall within this latter category as her husband although a worker in Belgium did not pay taxes to the Belgian Treasury. Mr and Mrs Forcheri brought an action for a declaration that the payment of the fee was contrary to Community law. The judge referred the question to the ECJ.

Before discussing the opinion of the Advocate General or the decision of the ECJ it is interesting to speculate on the application of Regulation 1612/68 to the facts of the case. Had the husband wished to take the course then Article 7 of the Regulation, as interpreted by the ECJ in *Lair* and *Brown*, may have allowed him to take the course on the same basis as Belgian nationals. Equally had the children of Mr and Mrs Forcheri chosen to take the course then Article 12 of Regulation 1612/68 would have allowed them to do so on the same basis as nationals. Therefore, on the basis of previous case law, such as *Casagrande*, it could be suggested that the ECJ would merely rule that the spouse of a worker was included within the scope of the educational provisions of the regulation. However, the ECJ adopted a different approach. To some extent this may have been predicted as the question referred invoked Article 7 of the Treaty in addition to Regulation 1612/68.

After an outline of the facts and the legislative position with respect to the fees, Advocate General Rozes considered that before answering the questions referred, a preliminary question had to be answered. This question was whether or not the payment of an enrolment fee in a further education establishment fell within the scope of the Treaty. The Advocate General considered that it was apparent from the decision in *Casagrande* that:

> the effective exercise of the powers of the Community may be hindered by the effects of national measures adopted in a sphere, such as that of education and training policy, in respect of which the Treaty has not as such conferred power upon the Community institutions. In so far as such national measures constitute an obstacle to the full exercise of the powers properly delegated to the Community they can no longer, in my opinion, have effect except in so far as they observe the Community legal system.[69]

Despite this observation, Advocate General Rozes considered that 'there was no rule or principle of Community law' which would affect the validity of the fee system at issue in the case.[70] The ECJ in its decision were not so sympathetic to the validity of the system.

The Court began by recalling the purpose of Article 7 of the Treaty. The relevant Belgian rules did involve discrimination between the nationals of the Member States as only Belgian and Luxembourg nationals were exempt from the relevant fee. Article 7 therefore appeared to have been breached. In relation to the preliminary question, asked by Advocate General Rozes, whether access to educational courses fell within the scope of the Treaty, the Court examined Article 128 of the Treaty and Council Decision 63/266 laying down general principles for the implementation of a common vocational training policy. It concluded:

> It follows that although it is true that educational and vocational training policy is not as such part of the areas which the Treaty has allotted to the competence of the Community institutions, the opportunity for such kinds of instruction falls within the scope of the Treaty. Consequently if a Member State organises educational courses relating in particular to vocational training, to require a national of another Member State lawfully established in the first Member State an enrolment fee which is not required of its own nationals in order to take part in such courses constitutes discrimination by reason of nationality, which is prohibited by Article 7 of the Treaty.[71]

It has been noted that the decision in *Forcheri* was the first time that the Court had relied exclusively on Article 7 of the Treaty in the area of the free movement of persons.[72] The ECJ seized the opportunity afforded by the question referred to them of establishing the competence of the Community in relation to education. In essence, although the organisation of education remained a matter for the discretion of the Member States, the application of that discretion was subject to Community law. A way had thus been found for the general principles of Community law to influence the educational systems and policies of the Member States. However, the ruling was limited. It related only to the situation where the student was 'lawfully established' in the particular Member State. What does 'lawfully established' mean?[73] More fundamentally, as the above quotation makes clear, the ruling applies 'educational course relating in particular to vocational training': if Article 128 was the basis for the Court's decision that Article 7 of the Treaty is applicable, then as Article 128 relates solely to vocational training Article 7 applies only in relation to discrimination in vocational training. The definition of vocational training, therefore, became crucial as that definition would determine the extent of the Community's competence in education.

The opportunity to give further guidance on vocational training arose in the English case of *R* v. *Inner London Education Authority ex parte Hinde*,[74] however, Taylor J. did not consider it necessary to refer any questions to the ECJ as he believed the matter was already clear as a result of *Forcheri*. The case arose as a result of the refusal by the defendants to give grants to the plaintiffs on the ground that they had not been resident in the United Kingdom for the required three-year period prior to the start of their course and the courses they wished to study were not vocational courses. The plaintiffs, one of whom was French, the other two being Irish, sought judicial review of this decision. In his decision, Taylor J. considered that: 'if an educational establishment provides a vocational training course on a substantial and continuing basis it is a vocational school, whatever else it may do. Not so, if the provision of vocational training were *ad hoc*, intermittent or *de minimis*'.[75] Taylor J. concluded that this definition covered a medical school, a teacher training college and the Bar's School of Law and the Law Society's College of Law. It did not cover a university law degree course, since such a course trained lawyers but not legal practitioners.[76] On this basis, two of the applicants succeeded. Hinde, who was studying for the degree of LLB failed in his application.

Although the decision may be criticized on other grounds,[77] in relation to the free movement of workers it is beyond reproach.

A Definition

The ECJ were given another opportunity to rule in this area in the case of *Gravier*.[78] Essentially, it is a continuation of its reasoning from *Forcheri*, as it afforded the Court the opportunity to define what was meant by 'lawfully established' and to give substance to the concept of vocational training. Gravier, a French national, registered for a four-year course on the art of strip cartoons at the Royal Academy of Fine Arts in Liege. As a foreign student she was charged an enrolment fee, the minerval. The applicant applied for exemption from this fee, but this was refused. As she did not pay the minerval, her enrolment for the next academic year was refused and her residence permit was not extended. She brought an action claiming exemption from the minerval and for the issuance of the documents necessary for her stay in Belgium. She argued that the requirement to pay the minerval amounted to discrimination prohibited by Article 7 of the Treaty and, in the alternative, that she must be free to go to Belgium to study as a recipient of services under Article 59 of the Treaty. The questions referred to the ECJ mentioned only the first of these arguments. They asked whether vocational training fell within the scope of Article 7 and whether the particular course followed by Gravier was vocational.

Advocate General Slynn began his opinion by noting that Belgium and Greece were the only remaining Member States to charge higher fees to foreign students, even though the majority of such students were exempted.[79] The Belgian government, supported by the Danish and United Kingdom governments, argued that the minerval was not contrary to any rule of Community law. They admitted that the position would be different had Gravier been a migrant worker or a dependant of a migrant worker as in both cases Regulation 1612/68 would apply. Article 7 of the Treaty, they contended, was much too general to be used in this case.[80] In reply, Advocate General Slynn began by considering whether education fell within the scope of the Treaty. In light the decisions of the Court in *Casagrande* and *Forcheri*, he concluded that access to education and vocational training fell within the scope of the Treaty, so discrimination based on nationality in relation to access in these areas was covered by Article 7.[81] The Advocate General did note that Gravier did not fall within the precise category of persons considered in *Forcheri*. However, he did not consider that the right to undertake a particular vocational course was dependent on a pre-existing right of residence.

The issue of what was included in the phrase 'vocational training' was then addressed by the Advocate General. He concluded that education which prepared for a particular qualification or provided the necessary training and skills, where no formal qualification is required, fell within the scope of vocational training.[82] On the basis that the Court would conclude that Article 7 did not apply, the Advocate General went on to consider the argument that education was covered by Article 59.[83] The argument for its coverage was that those who provide education are paid so the services they provide are 'normally provided for remuneration'. Advocate General Slynn did not consider this to be the right approach as it divided education into the categories of publicly and privately funded. Instead regard should be paid to the economic nature and the intrinsic nature of the particular service. Having regard to the intrinsic nature of education, Advocate General Slynn concluded that it could not be classified as a service within the meaning of Article 59.[84]

The Court began its consideration of the questions by asking whether the fee constituted an infringement of Article 7. In their submissions to the Court, the Danish and United Kingdom governments had argued that Article 7 allowed a Member State to treat its own nationals more favourably in the area of education. The Court, although noting these arguments, did not expressly disagree with them. They concluded, given that the inequality of treatment was based on nationality, that Article 7 had been breached.[85] The reason for this was that although the organization and financing of education were the responsibility of the Member States, access to such education fell within the Treaty. Article 7 of Regulation 1612/68 and Article 128 of the Treaty were used to vindicate this conclusion. The Court stressed that access to vocational training would promote the free movement of persons throughout the Community as it would enable such persons to obtain a qualification in the host Member State and so allow them to complete their training and/or develop their particular talents. Having established that access to vocational training did fall within the Treaty, it only remained for the Court to define vocational training. They defined it as follows:

> any form of education which prepares for a qualification for a particular profession, trade or employment or which provides

> the necessary training and skills for such a profession, trade or employment is vocational training, whatever the age and the level of training of the pupils or students, and even if the training programme includes an element of general education.[86]

Therefore, the course being pursued by Gravier was vocational training and it was contrary to Article 7 of the Treaty to subject her to a charge which was not payable by Belgian nationals. The issue of whether or not education was a service within the scope of Article 59 of the Treaty was left unresolved by the Court. They would eventually resolve the issue in the case of *Humbel*.

As noted above, the decision in *Gravier* is a continuation of the reasoning of the Court in *Forcheri*. Further weight was added to the explicit use of Article 7 of the Treaty in this area.[87] It now seems clear that a Community national may enter another Member State to pursue vocational training there. Moreover, the concept of vocational training had been given greater precision, yet it still remained uncertain as to what factors should be used to differentiate vocational training from general education, especially as elements of the latter could be included in vocational training. For example, it was not clear to what extent university education was covered by the definition of vocational training.[88] In both *MacMahon* and *ex parte Hinde* the English courts considered that some university courses could be classified as vocational training.[89] Further guidance on the question of what constituted vocational training, which had occupied part of the ECJ's time in *Gravier*, would therefore be needed. It was to be provided in three subsequent judgments on the minerval. Before discussing these cases, the case of *Commission* v. *Belgium*[90] needs to be discussed as it arose out of the judgment of the Court in *Gravier*.

After the decision in *Gravier* the Commission considered that the relevant Belgian law on education was a breach of Article 7 of the Treaty and incompatible with the decisions of the Court in *Forcheri* and *Gravier*. It had a meeting with the relevant Belgian authorities and later sent them a letter stating that the provisions of its law were contrary to Community law. The letter requested a response from the Belgian authorities within eight days. No response came within this period although several days later the Belgian government requested an extension of this eight day period. The Commission did not respond to this letter. It then issued a reasoned opinion, as required by Article 169 of the Treaty, requesting Belgium to take the necessary measures within fifteen days. With the failure of Belgium to respond to the reasoned opinion, proceedings were instituted against Belgium and an application was lodged for interim measures. The Court dismissed the Article 169 action as inadmissible as Belgium has not been fully informed of the views of the Commission before the proceedings were brought against it. The main interest of the case lies in the submissions of the parties and the opinion of the Advocate General on the substance of the case.

Advocate General Slynn in his opinion after considering the arguments of the parties on the admissibility of the proceedings turned to the substance of the case. One of the issues related to the provision on Belgian law allowing for the charging of the minerval for foreign students at Belgian universities. The question was thus raised as to the extent to which vocational training can be undertaken at universities. The Commission considered university education always to be vocational training.[91] Belgium considered that such education was never vocational.[92] Advocate General Slynn began his discussion of this conflict of views by looking at Article 128 and the judgment of the Court in *Gravier*. He pointed out that the important factor was not the place of training but rather the content of such training.[93] To decide otherwise could open the door to discrimination between and within Member States. Universities could therefore not be automatically excluded from the scope of the *Gravier* decision. Having rejected the argument of the Belgian government, the Advocate General turned his attention to the Commission argument. As the most important factor was content rather than location, the Commission's argument could not be accepted.[94] 'The essential task as I see it is to look at the course as a whole and to ask whether, in the first place, it provides a qualification recognized for admission to a particular profession, trade or employment. If it does that is enough for the course to qualify'.[95] In those cases where a university degree is a necessary but not sufficient condition for qualifying for a particular profession, the university degree will be covered by the *Gravier* decision if it is an integral and necessary part of the final qualification. On this basis the decision of Taylor J. in *ex parte Hinde* that an LLB degree was not vocational in nature would be incorrect as it provides exemption from certain subjects in professional examinations.

On a further issue the Advocate General refused to draw a distinction between workers who undertake vocational training and those who have not yet become workers who wish to undertake vocational training.[96] The Court limited its judgment to the question of admissibility and decided that the application was inadmissible.[97] By refusing to rule on the substance of the issues raised in the case, the Court lost the opportunity to develop the ruling in *Gravier*.[98] However, it would have this opportunity as a result of a further trilogy of cases on the minerval.

Refining the Definition

The first of these cases was that of *Barra*.[99] In this case Barra and the sixteen other plaintiffs were all French nationals pursuing gunsmithing studies at the Municipal Technical Institute for Precision Engineering, Gunsmithing and Clockmaking in Liege. Each year they were obliged to pay the minerval. After the decision of the ECJ in *Gravier*, they applied for the repayment of the minervals they had previously paid. Several months later the Belgian law on education was changed and Article 63 provided that fees charged since the introduction of the minerval in 1976 to 31 December 1984 'will in no event be reimbursed'. However, the Article went on to state that for those students who were nationals of a Member State of the Community and who had taken vocational training courses, the minerval would be refunded if proceedings for repayment had been brought before the courts before 13 February 1985. Barra's summons was issued on 7 March 1985. The questions referred to the Court asked whether the refusal to refund the minerval in this case was compatible with Community law.

Once again the Advocate General was Advocate General Slynn. He began with the question of vocational training and repeated the remarks he had made in the case of *Commission* v. *Belgium*. He stated that it was the course rather than the institution where the course was conducted that was crucial to the question of vocational training.[100] The Belgian government considered that the course was not vocational as it was conducted at a secondary level and was not available in the plaintiffs' home state. In response, the Advocate General pointed out that neither of these limitations appeared in the judgment of the Court in *Gravier*.[101] In relation to the question of whether the refusal to refund the minervals paid was compatible with Community law it was pointed out that only the Court can limit the effects of its judgments. No such power exists in the Member States. He did suggest that although the judgment in *Gravier* did not impose any limitations, a temporal limit should be imposed. This limit related to those who were undertaking vocational training at, or after, the date of the *Gravier* judgment or who had instituted proceedings for repayment before the delivery of this opinion.[102]

The Court began by agreeing with the Advocate General that it was not for the Member States to limit the temporal effect of its judgments. As an exceptional measure the Court recognized that it had the power to impose temporal restrictions on its judgments. However, as the Court did not limit the temporal scope of its judgment in the actual case of *Gravier*, it considered that 'such a restriction could not be made in this judgment'.[103] On the question of whether or not national law could deprive those who had paid the minerval of the right to bring legal proceedings for repayment, the Court declared that as the national court was obliged to apply Community law in its entirety it could not apply a provision of national law which deprived individuals of their rights under Community law.[104] The Court therefore brushed aside the arguments of the Belgian government: they had argued that as *Gravier* constituted a new development in Community law and that no Article 169 actions had been brought against it, not to restrict the temporal effect of the *Gravier* judgment would be both contrary to legal certainty and financially disastrous.[105]

The second case of the trilogy is that of *Blaizot*.[106] Like Barra the plaintiffs in this case were seventeen French nationals following courses at four Belgian universities. Each of them were studying veterinary medicine, the course involving three years' study for a preliminary degree followed by a further three years leading to the award of a doctor's degree. For each year Blaizot and the sixteen other plaintiffs were all required to pay a minerval. As a result of the decision of the ECJ in *Gravier*, they instituted summary proceedings in April 1985 for repayment of the minervals already paid. As in *Barra*, the plaintiffs had to contend with Article 63 of the Belgian Education Act. The Belgian Court referred two questions to the ECJ: whether the study of veterinary medicine at university fell within the scope of the Treaty and whether the right to repayment of the minervals paid was affected because the claim was against the universities involved.

Advocate General Slynn considered that the question referred covered two issues namely, whether university courses in veterinary medicine fell within the definition of vocational training and whether Article 63 of the Belgian law could limit the rights of the plaintiffs arising from the *Gravier* decision. As the Advocate General made clear in his opinion in the direct action, university education was capable of constituting vocational training, although not all university education was vocational.[107] The problem in this case was the division of the study of veterinary medicine into two degrees. In accordance with his previous opinion, noted above, the Advocate General concluded that the course was vocational training for the purposes of Article 7 of the Treaty.[108] On the question of the temporal effect of the interpretation of the phrase vocational training, Advocate General Slynn referred to the opinion, noted above, which he gave in the case of *Commission* v. *Belgium*.

The Court in its judgment also considered that the question referred raised two issues. The first issue involved a definition of vocational training and the Court began its consideration of this by repeating its definition of vocational training from *Gravier*. It considered that in order to decide whether university studies fulfil the criteria from Gravier, a distinction had to be drawn between whether such studies by their very nature constitute vocational training and the circumstances in which these studies prepare for a qualification. The Court noted that according to Article 10 of the European Social Charter university education was to be treated as a form of vocational training. It continued:

> With regard to the issue whether university studies prepare for a qualification for a particular profession, trade or employment or provide the necessary training and skills for such a profession, trade or employment, it must be emphasized that that is the case not only where the final academic examination directly provides the qualification for a particular profession, trade or employment but also in so far as the studies in question provide specific training and skills, that is to say where a student needs the knowledge so acquired for the pursuit of a profession, trade or employment, even if no legislative or administrative provisions make the acquisition of that knowledge a prerequisite for that purpose.[109]

The Court considered that university studies generally fulfil these criteria. The fact that the study was divided into two stages was not considered to affect this conclusion, so the requirement for foreign students to pay the minerval for study at university constituted discrimination contrary to Article 7 of the Treaty.

On the question of the temporal effect of this decision, the Court adopted a different attitude than it did in *Barra*. Although an exceptional measure, the Court considered that as this judgment dealt for the first time with the question of whether university education constituted vocational training, the demands of legal certainty meant that the judgment would only have prospective effect.[110] As a justification for so limiting the temporal effect of the judgment the Court pointed to the attitude of the Commission who until 1985 did not believe that the imposition of the minerval with respect to university education to be contrary to Community law. This attitude the Court indicated would have led the Belgian authorities to believe that their legislation was acceptable. The decision to restrict the temporal effect of this judgment is regrettable; although having the power to do so, the Court has exercised it sparingly.[111] The reason for exercising it in this case is acceptable, yet it could be argued that Belgium should have foreseen this ruling. In essence, it is merely a continuation of the Court's approach to vocational training evident in *Forcheri* and *Gravier*. Moreover, English courts had already come to the conclusion that some university education was encompassed in the concept of vocational training.[112]

The final case of the trilogy of cases on the minerval is that of *Humbel*, the facts of which have been already noted.[113] One of the questions referred to the ECJ asked whether the course of study in the case amounted to vocational training. The particular course of study was a course of general secondary education provided for pupils of compulsory school age. Naturally, the defendants maintained that the course was vocational in nature as it allowed for access to a stage where more technical training would be provided. Advocate General Slynn considered that in the light of the definition of vocational training offered by *Gravier*, it was up to the national court to determine whether or not the course was vocational in nature.[114] Both the Advocate General and the Court in its decision reviewed the decisions noted above. In the end the Advocate General was not satisfied on the information available that the particular course was vocational training.[115] The Court contented itself with stating that:

> a year of study which is part of a programme forming an indivisible body of instruction preparing for a qualification for a particular profession, trade or employment or providing the necessary training and skills for such a profession, trade or employment constitutes vocational training for the purposes of the EEC Treaty.[116]

One consequence of the decisions discussed above was a further

Article 169 action against Belgium.[117] The Commission claimed that Belgium had breached Community law, in particular Article 7 of the Treaty and Article 12 of Regulation 1612/68,

> by failing to exempt students who are nationals of Member States other than Belgium and . . . Luxembourg from the category of students ineligible for financing by the State . . . who apply for registration for and admission to courses provided by higher education establishments not of university level which has already filled the 2% quota set in respect of vocational training by imposing conditions involving discrimination on the grounds of nationality.[118]

The Belgian government did not submit any formal conclusions in this case and indeed did not contest the Commission's basic point of view. The case, as Advocate General Slynn pointed out, was not concerned with a direct financial barrier to access to education.[119] However, as it may not be economically feasible for educational institutions to accept more than 2% of students from other Member States, the law could be a barrier to free movement. It seemed obvious that discrimination contrary to Article 7 of the Treaty existed as there would be no numerical limitations on Belgian nationals wishing to undertake vocational training. In relation to the argument that the relevant law concerned the financing of education and so not subject to the provisions of the Treaty, the Advocate General pointed out that the numerical limitation was a financial barrier within the meaning of *Gravier*, and thus within the scope of the Treaty.[120]

In its judgment, the Court began by stressing that it had already held in *Gravier* the conditions of access to vocational training fell within the scope of the Treaty. The Court therefore concluded:

> it should be noted that the legislation in question, in so far as it limits . . . the financing of vocational higher educational establishments, has the direct effect of excluding, in practice, students who are nationals of other Member States from such vocational training once the quota of 2% is attained, whereas such a restriction is not provided for in respect of Belgian students. Consequently this restriction constitutes discrimination on grounds of nationality prohibited under Article 7 of the Treaty.[121]

In relation to the second argument on Article 12 of Regulation 1612/68 both the Advocate General and the Court considered that the actual wording of Article 12 and the previous case law of the Court meant that the legislation was also contrary to Community law.

Education as a Service

The case of *Humbel* also finally resolved one of the arguments raised in *Gravier*, that education was a service within the terms of the Treaty. One of the questions asked in *Humbel* was whether the Defendant's son was to be regarded as a person for whom services was intended within the meaning of Article 59 *et seq.* of the Treaty. The defendants argued that Education was to be regarded as a service in the situation prevailing in this case. The United Kingdom, as an intervening party, repeated the arguments it had advanced in *Gravier*. They argued that a Community national travelling to another Member State to study could not be regarded as a recipient of services within the meaning of the Treaty. Two conditions would have to be satisfied, the United Kingdom argued, before education could be regarded as a service. First, the person providing the service must do so for a profit. This, it was argued, was implicit in the Treaty definition of services and other provisions. Secondly, the recipient of the services must pay for them and such payment could not be supplementary to payments from other sources; in this case, the national treasury.[122] The Commission in its observations rejected these arguments: education was, in their opinion, a service. Their reasoning was that the list of examples in Article 60 was not exhaustive and they pointed out that education fell within the definition of economic activities previously adopted by the ECJ. Remuneration was equally not as significant as the United Kingdom considered it to be. Furthermore, once it was shown that teaching activities constitute the provision of services of an economic nature, the distinction between public and private educational establishments was unnecessary.[123] In support of the Commission's argument, the judgment of the ECJ in *Luisi and Carbone* was enlisted. In this case the ECJ noted:

> the freedom to provide services includes the freedom, for the recipient of services, to go to another Member State in order to receive a service there, without being obstructed by restrictions, even in relations to payments . . . tourists, persons receiving medical treatment and *persons travelling for the purpose of*

> *education* or business are to be regarded as recipients of services.

Advocate General Slynn began with the above quotation, arguing that it was not relevant as that case concerned restrictions on freedom to make payments for services received abroad imposed by the home state on the recipient of those services.[125] He had little difficulty in accepting that education was not a service as he had previously adopted this opinion in *Gravier*. He admitted that the arguments advanced by the United Kingdom had great force. He argued that education was not provided by the State for remuneration and concluded:

> The State is not a commercial organization seeking a profit or indeed to recover its costs and break even. If an organization which does not seek profit (not having a 'but lucratif') cannot take advantage of the freedom to establish and to provide services in other Member States conferred by this Treaty (as is clear from Articles 58 and 66), it seems to follow that would-be recipients of services provided by such an organization cannot rely on the Treaty either.[126]

In its consideration of this question the Court began by examining Articles 59 and 60 of the Treaty. They emphasized that remuneration was crucial as it constituted 'consideration for the service in question, and is normally agreed upon between the provider and the recipient of the service'. This characteristic, the Court noted, was absent from courses provided under a national educational system. Moreover, the public funding of education outweighs the private contributions of parents or pupils. The Court drew the logical conclusion from these points, namely that secondary education is not a service within the meaning of the Treaty.[127] It should be stressed that the decision relates to publicly funded educational services. So, a private school or university may fall within the provisions of the Treaty on the freedom to provide and receive services.

A Summary

To conclude this section, it is possible to summarize the present state of the law:

1) A national of one Member State may move to another Member State to attend a vocational course in that Member State. It is

contrary to Article 7 of the Treaty to discriminate against nationals of other Member States in relation to access to such courses.

2) In the current state of Community law it is not contrary to Community law to deny a maintenance grant to nationals of other Member States, not covered by Regulation 1612/68, attending vocational courses in other Member States.
3) Vocational training includes any education that prepares to a qualification or that provides the necessary training and skills for such a trade or profession whatever the age and level of training of the students. General education is excluded from the scope of vocational training although it is possible to have vocational training which contains elements of general education. University education may, and usually will, constitute vocational training.
4) It is a breach of Article 7 of the Treaty for national legislation to provide a disincentive to the admission of nationals of other Member States in vocational training institutions.
5) Publicly funded educational establishments are not covered by the service provisions of the Treaty.

THE MUTUAL RECOGNITION OF QUALIFICATIONS

According to Article 57(1) of the Treaty of Rome, as amended by Article 6(6) of the Single European Act:

> In order to make it easier for persons to take up and pursue activities as self employed persons, the Council shall, on a proposal from the Commission and in cooperation with the European Parliament, acting unanimously during the first stage and by a qualified majority thereafter issue directives for the mutual recognition of diplomas, certificates and other evidence of formal qualifications.

It is essential that once a Community national has received a qualification that that national should be free to move to work, or provide services, in other Member States and have their qualification recognized in those states. This section is concerned with the efforts of the Community authorities to implement Article 57 of the Treaty. After discussing the specific directives implementing Article 57, consideration is given to the general principles of

Community law applicable in the absence of specific directives, before the discussion concludes with an analysis of the general directive on higher education qualifications.

Specific Directives

In relation to the specific directives on the mutual recognition of diplomas, certificates and other evidence of formal qualification, one starting point is the 1974 resolution on this matter.[128] The purpose of the resolution is to lay specific principles and guidelines for the implementation of Article 57(1). The resolution recognizes that specific directives on the recognition of qualifications were of importance in connection with education policies. Such policies were considered as making a potentially positive contribution to freedom of establishment, yet it was recognized that the directives which were to be adopted should not hinder the educational reform efforts of the Member States.[129] The Council agreed on the following guideline for future work on a flexible and qualitative approach to mutual recognition:

> Given that, despite the difference existing between one Member State and another in training courses, the final qualification giving access to similar fields of activity are in practice broadly comparable, directives on the mutual recognition of professional qualifications and on the co-ordination of the conditions of access to the professions should resort as little as possible to the prescription of detailed training requirements.[130]

To implement this guideline, a specific list of diplomas and other evidence of formal qualifications were to be drawn up and advisory committees were to be established.

As a result of this resolution a series of directives covering a significant number of areas was passed in subsequent years. For example, there are directives on the mutual recognition of qualifications in nursing,[131] midwifery,[132] dentistry,[133] pharmacy,[134] veterinary medicine[135] and architecture[136]. The objectives of these and other directives is to assist the process of persons having the relevant qualifications from one Member State establishing themselves in another Member State. The directives apply irrespective of whether the person having the qualification wishes to pursue the relevant trade or profession as either an employed or self-employed person. The pattern of the legislation can be ascertained from an examination of the measures adopted in relation to medicine; due to frequent amendment these directives have now been consolidated by Directive 93/16.[137]

The first title of the new directive on medicine contains provisions on the reciprocal recognition in the Community of qualifications awarded in any Member State. Articles 2 and 3 of Directive 93/16 lists the qualification for each Member State and Articles 23 and 24 go on to specify what must be covered by the course leading to this qualification. Minimum periods of study are established; Article 23(2) of the Directive states that the course must comprise a minimum of 5,500 hours of theoretical and practical instruction given in a university or under university supervision. In addition to basic medical training, the directive also covers specialized training. In the implementation of the flexible and qualitative approach advocated by the resolution noted above, the specifications of course content are extremely general. Articles 11 and 12 of Directive 93/16 lays down the conditions for the exercise of medicine, covering such matters as proof of good character, membership of professional bodies and linguistic knowledge. So a medical practitioner, either general or specialized, who satisfies the conditions of the directives must be given the right to practise medicine in another Member State. However, the directive does not contain a definition of what activities are to be regarded as those of a doctor of medicine or a specialist.[138]

The directives on the mutual recognition of qualification in medicine were raised in *Broekmeulen*.[139] In this case, the plaintiff, a Dutch national, had qualified in medicine at a Dutch-language University in Belgium. He wished to return to the Netherlands to practise as a general practitioner. The General Practitioner's Committee in the Netherlands refused to allow the plaintiff permission to practise in the Netherlands. The reason for their refusal was that the Netherlands authorities insisted that graduates wishing to practise as general practitioners had to undergo a further training period of one year. This requirement would be waived in the case of nationals of other Member States but it would not be waived in the plaintiff's case as he was a Dutch national. The plaintiff applied to the Appeals Committee for a review of the decision and the Committee referred a question to the ECJ on the interpretation of Directives 75/362 and 75/363.

In it's consideration of the matter, the Court began by noting that the provisions of the directives could be invoked by individuals. The basis for this interpretation was the provisions of the Treaty dealing with the freedom of movement of persons, a freedom which had been exercised by Broekmeulen. Moreover, this freedom prevented a Member State from denying the benefits of Community law to one of its nationals who had exercised the right of free movement to attain a professional qualification in another Member State. As general practice was not recognized by the directive as an area of specialized medicine, it was not possible for the Dutch authorities to impose an additional training period on those doctors who had attained a recognized diploma in medicine in another Member State.[140] The Court therefore concluded:

> Directive 75/362 is to be interpreted as meaning that a national of a Member State who has obtained a diploma listed under Article 3 of the directive in another Member State and who, by that token, may practise general medicine in that other Member State is entitled to establish himself as a general practitioner in the Member State of which he is a national, even if that Member State makes entry to that profession by holders of diplomas of medicine obtained within its own borders subject to additional training requirements.[141]

As this makes clear, reverse discrimination is acceptable but discrimination against those who have qualified in other Member States is not.[142]

General Principles

In the absence of specific harmonizing measures, an individual wishing to pursue an activity in another Member State has to rely on the provisions of the Treaty and the general principles of Community law. The extent of this assistance is illustrated in the following set of cases. In the case of *Patrick*[143], the plaintiff, a British architect, wished to practise in France. He did not have a French qualification but a 1964 decree of the French Minister for Cultural Affairs recognized the British qualification in architecture as equivalent to the French qualification. His application for authorization to practise was refused on the ground that there was no reciprocity in recognition between the United Kingdom and France. Patrick brought an action, based on Article 7 of the Treaty, challenging this refusal.

The Court began by reiterating its decision in *Reyners*[144] that the rule of equality of treatment in freedom of establishment was one of the fundamental legal provisions of the Community. It was not possible to argue against the direct effect of that rule by pointing to the failure of the Council to adopt the appropriate directives. The Court concluded:

> Nevertheless, the fact that those directives have not yet been issued does not entitle a Member State to deny the practical benefit of that freedom to a person subject to Community law when the freedom of establishment provided for in Article 52 can be ensured in that Member State by virtue in particular of the provisions of the laws and regulations already in force.[145]

The refusal to authorize Patrick to practise architecture was therefore contrary to the Treaty as national law provided a means of recognizing his qualification.

One question which emerges from *Patrick* is: Would the situation be different if the recognition of the qualification emerged not from national laws or regulations but from a more limited source? Such a situation arose in *Thieffry*.[146] In this case the plaintiff, a Belgian national, obtained a doctorate in Law from the University of Louvain. After a period of practise in Belgium and London, he established himself in Paris. The University of Paris recognized his diploma as equivalent to the degree of licence in French law. Having passed the qualifying certificate for the profession of avocat, Thieffry applied to take the oath so that he could be registered for training at the Paris Bar. His application was refused on the grounds that his Belgian diploma offered no evidence of a French diploma, either a licence or a doctorate, in French law. On appeal from this decision, a question was referred to the ECJ.

The Court began its consideration of the question by pointing to the purpose of Article 57. It was, in their opinion, designed to reconcile the freedom of establishment guaranteed by the Treaty with the application of national rules for the conduct of professions in such a way as to eliminate discrimination between nationals of the Member States. Article 5 of the Treaty, the Court insisted, could be used to attain this reconciliation if there was not a specific directive already issued. This article imposed an obligation on public authorities, and legally recognized professional bodies, to ensure that their legislation and practice was applied in accordance with the objective of freedom of establishment.[147] As Thieffry had his diploma recognized as an equivalent qualification by a competent authority in the Member State in which he wished to establish himself, the rejection of his application on the ground that he did not have a French diploma was contrary to Article 52 of the

Treaty. The situation was complicated in this case by the fact that recognition of Thieffry's diploma for academic purposes was distinct from recognition for professional purposes. The Court left this question to be resolved by the appropriate national authorities.[148]

In both *Patrick* and *Thieffry* there was some element of recognition, the final question relates to the situation where there is no recognition. In such a situation, what are the rights of the person wishing to establish themselves in another Member State? This question was addressed in the case of *Heylens*.[149] Heylens was a Belgian national possessing a diploma for football trainers. He was employed by the French club, Lille, and French law required the holders of such positions to have a French diploma or a diploma recognized as equivalent. His application for recognition of the equivalence of his Belgian diploma was refused. No reasons were given for this refusal. Heylens was prosecuted for continuing to practise as a trainer and in his defence he raised issues of Community law. A question was then referred to the ECJ asking whether it was possible for the refusal to recognize the equivalence of his diploma to be the subject of judicial proceedings.

Relying on its decisions in *Patrick* and *Thieffry*, the Court pointed out that in the absence of harmonization, the Member States remain free to lay down the conditions of access to a particular profession.[150] On the question of recognition of foreign qualifications, the national authorities were required to ascertain, on an objective basis, that that qualification covered knowledge and training at least equivalent to that provided by the national diploma.[151] As this decision related to one of the fundamental rights of individuals under Community law – free access to employment – there must be a judicial remedy against any decision which refuses the benefit of that right. This was a general principle of Community law.[152] So that such judicial review can be effective the Court stated that it must cover the reasons for the refusal. The applicant must, therefore, be given reasons so that a decision, based on full knowledge of the relevant facts, can be made as to whether or not to pursue a judicial remedy.[153]

In the absence of harmonization, individuals therefore possess certain rights. If national legislation or the practise of professional bodies allows for the freedom of establishment of nationals of other Member States, then such laws and rules have to be administered to promote the objectives of the Treaty. In any decision refusing recognition, reasons must be given so that the applicant may exercise their right to a judicial remedy. Having established that nationality can no longer be a barrier to the freedom of movement guaranteed by the Treaty, these sets of cases seek to lessen the impact of the limited legislative activity under Article 57. A new approach to the question of mutual recognition of diplomas was needed to ensure the benefits of the right of free movement did not depend on judicial activity.

The General Directive

This new approach was signposted by the European Council at its meeting in Fontainbleau in 1984 calling on the Council to take measures to respond to the expectations of the peoples of Europe.[154] One particular area noted was a general system for ensuring equivalence of university diplomas so as to bring about the effective freedom of establishment within the Community. In the following year the Commission proposed a directive on a general system for the recognition of higher education qualifications.[155] The new flexible approach would replace the individual directives on mutual recognition on qualifications in particular areas. There would therefore be no need to harmonize education and training within degrees as allowances would be made to recognize professional experience. The new system would have five characteristics: it would be general; would be based on the comparability of training courses; it would call for mutual confidence between the Member States, it would include procedural and individual guarantees; and it would be evolutionary.[156]

The proposal was eventually translated into legislative form by the enactment of Directive 89/48 on a general system for the recognition of higher education diplomas.[157] The Preamble makes clear the specific purpose of the directive:

> in order to provide a rapid response to the expectation of nationals of Community countries who hold higher-education diplomas awarded on completion of professional education and training issued in a Member State other than that in which they wish to pursue their profession, another method of recognition of such diplomas should also be put in place such as to enable those concerned to pursue all those professional activities which in a host Member State are dependent on the completion of post-secondary education and training, provided they hold such a diploma preparing them for those activities on completion of a

> course of studies lasting at least three years and issued in another Member State.[158]

This recital of the Preamble also makes clear the key concepts of the directive. It is designed to benefit 'nationals of Community countries' holding 'diplomas' which enable them to practise in a 'regulated profession'. Each of these concepts and the basic rule of the directive will be examined in turn.

According to Article 2 the directive applies only to nationals of a Member State who wish to pursue a regulated profession in another Member State either as an employed or self-employed person. A recommendation adopted at the same time concerning nationals of Member States who hold diplomas conferred in a third state recommends that the governments of the Member States should recognize these diplomas and so allow these nationals to take up and pursue regulated professions within the Community.[159] The final limitation in Article 2 of the directive is that it applies only to those professions which are not covered by a separate directive on the mutual recognition of qualifications.

The next key concept is that of diploma. This is defined in Article 1(a) as anything which amounts to evidence of a formal qualification or set of formal qualifications meeting the following three characteristics:

- which has been awarded by a competent authority in a Member State, designated in accordance with its own laws, regulations or administrative provisions;
- which shows that the holder has successfully completed a post-secondary course of at least three years duration, or of an equivalent duration part-time, at a university or establishment of higher education or another establishment of similar level and, where appropriate, that he has successfully completed the professional training required in addition to the post-secondary course; and
- which shows that the holder has the professional qualifications required for the taking up or pursuit of a regulated profession in that Member State.

It is further provided in the second paragraph of Article 1(a) that the education and training received in the Community and not fulfilling the second characteristic noted above will be treated as a diploma, certificate or other evidence of formal qualifications if recognized by a competent authority in the Member State concerned as allowing the person to take up and pursue a regulated profession. Thus the scope of the directive extends beyond the study for a diploma at a university to studies at equivalent institutions. As a matter of interest, given the third characteristic noted above, it appears unlikely that an ordinary law degree would qualify as a diploma as a further period of study is necessary before the holder of that degree can practise law. Only after this period of study will there be a diploma in the sense envisaged by Article 1(a).

Having defined diploma the directive goes on to define in Article 1(c) and (d) what is included within the scope of a 'regulated profession'. By virtue of these paragraphs if the pursuit of any professional activity is subject by the laws of the Member State to the possession of a diploma, as defined in Article 1(a), then that profession is considered to be regulated. Equally, should the use of a professional title be dependent on the possession of a diploma, then that profession is considered to be 'regulated'. In the event that the laws of a Member State do not cover a particular profession, Article 1(d) makes clear that if there is a professional organization responsible for the activities of the particular profession, which is recognized by the Member State, then that profession will be covered by the directive. A list of such bodies is provided in the Annex to the directive and is limited to professional bodies in Ireland and the United Kingdom.

Having defined the key concepts of the directive, the next question relates to the rule for recognition. This is laid down in Article 3. This states that if the pursuit of a regulated profession in a host Member State is subject to the possession of a diploma, the national authorities of that state may not refuse to authorise a person from another Member State if that person wishes to pursue that profession and possesses a diploma from his/her own Member State. If the particular profession is not regulated in one Member State, the other Member States which do regulate that profession must accept the person from the former Member State where that person has pursued the profession full-time for two years and possesses evidence of formal qualifications. The provisions of Article 3 will not apply where there are differences between the Member States with respect to the duration or content of the studies for a particular diploma or where the activities covered by the profession differ.

If the period of training is at least one year shorter in the Member State of which the person is a national than the period of study in the Member State in which that person wishes to pursue the profession, the latter Member State may refuse to recognize the qualification unless the person has actually practised the profession. According to Article 4(1)(a) the evidence of professional experience may not exceed four years and will usually be for the period of difference in training between the Member States. If there is a difference in the content of training, or where the profession covers different activities, the Member State in which the national of another Member State wishes to pursue a regulated profession may require that person to undergo an adaptation period or take an aptitude test. An adaptation period is defined in Article 1(f) as a period of supervised practice, with the possibility of further training, which is subject to an assessment. The adaptation period may not exceed three years. An aptitude test is defined in Article 1(g) as a test of the professional knowledge of the applicant assessing their ability to pursue the particular profession. Normally, it is up to the applicant to decide which of these options will be chosen. An exception to this principle is made if the profession requires precise knowledge of national law and/or the provision of advice on national law. In these cases it is up to each Member State to chose the appropriate mechanism, either adaptation period or aptitude test, for nationals of other Member States who wish to give legal advice or practise law.

The remaining provisions of the directive seek to ensure the integration of the national from another Member State into the host state. For example, Article 6 of the directive allows the host Member State to impose certain constraints on the admissions of nationals from other Member States who wish to pursue a regulated profession. The competent authorities of the Member State may require evidence of good character or physical or mental health; the evidence from the Member State of origin is considered acceptable. Article 7 of the directive allows those nationals of other Member States who fulfil the conditions for taking up a regulated profession to use the professional title of the host state corresponding to that profession. In relation to the legal profession, this is in marked contrast to the provisions of Directive 77/249 which states that lawyers who provide services in another Member State must use the title of their host state.[160] Article 8 of the directive provides the Member State with the power to assess qualifications. Decisions in this area are to be reached quickly and be capable of judicial review, thus adopting the principle from *Heylens*.

Other Issues

As holders of the appropriate title for the profession in the host Member State, the nationals of other Member States must comply with the normal rules of the host state in relation to the conduct of that profession. The Court has made clear that such rules will be incompatible with Community law where they hinder the free movement of persons and cannot be justified. This emerges from cases such *Auer* (*No.2*),[161] *Reinks*[162] and *Commission* v. *France*.[163] In the first of these cases, Auer was born in Austria and in 1957 he obtained a degree in veterinary medicine from the University of Parma in Italy. In 1958 he moved to France and since 1961 he has been a French national. He practised for a period with another veterinary surgeon before setting up his own practice. He was continually refused the registration necessary to do this and as a result was prosecuted for unlawful practice. The prosecution in issue occurred after the time limit for the implementation of the directives on mutual recognition of qualifications in the field of veterinary medicine.[164] Auer relied on these directives claiming that the French authorities could no longer refuse to recognize his degree and so he must be registered as entitled to practise.

The Court noted that the laws of the Member States which require compulsory registration in order to practise a particular profession are not, as such, incompatible with Community law. The Court continued:

> However . . . the conformity of that obligation with Community law is subject to the condition that the fundamental principles of that law, and in particular the principle of non-discrimination, are respected. It is not permissible to refuse to enter a person on the register of the professional society on grounds which disregard the validity professional qualifications obtained in another Member State, when that qualification is one of those which all the Member States, and the professional societies, as bodies entrusted with a public duty, are required to recognise under Community law.[165]

As the refusal to register Auer was contrary to Community law, there were no grounds for his prosecution for practising without being registered. A similar conclusion was reached, again with respect to veterinary surgeons, in *Reinks*.[166]

A variation on the above situation occurred in *Commission* v. *France*. This Article 169 action related to a provision of the French

Public Health Code and a Decree which required doctors and dentists established in another Member State to cancel their registration in that State in order to be able to practise in France. France maintained that this was justified on public health grounds, namely that doctors and dentists should be accessible to their patients as medical care should be continuous. The Court pointed out that nationals of other Member States must comply with the national rules governing the conduct of that profession. Where these rules have the effect of restricting the free movement of persons they will be compatible with the Treaty only where they are justified 'in view of the general obligations inherent in the proper practise of the professions in question and apply to nationals and foreigners alike.'[167] The Court considered the French prohibition on registration was too absolute and general to be justifiable under Community law.

The principle of respecting the national rules for a professional conduct applies irrespective of whether or not there is a harmonizing directive. This was established in the case of *Klopp*.[168] Klopp, a member of the Dusseldorf Bar, applied to take the oath as an avocat and to be registered for the period of training at the Paris Bar. He wished to establish chambers in Paris while remaining resident in Dusseldorf. His application was refused on the basis that the law required Klopp to be registered and resident in Paris. The ECJ answered the question referred by stating:

> Even in the absence of any directive coordinating national provisions governing access to and the exercise of the legal profession, Article 52 *et seq.* of the Treaty prevent the competent authorities of a Member State from denying, on the basis of national legislation and the rules of professional conduct which are in force in that State, to a national of another Member State the right to enter and to exercise the legal profession solely on the ground that he maintains chambers simultaneously in another Member State.[169]

The Court recognized that the special nature of the legal profession allowed a Member State to establish rules to ensure the proper administration of justice. Such rules should not, however, prevent the nationals of other Member States from the proper exercise of the right of establishment.[170] Klopp was therefore entitled to establish himself in Paris despite having offices in Dusseldorf.

The obligation to respect the professional rules of conduct as outlined in the cases above also applies to a national of one Member State who moves temporarily to another Member State to provide services under Articles 59–66 of the Treaty. However, there may be rules against other Member State inhibiting such a provision of services. To use the example discussed; does the person providing services in another Member State need to register in that state? A distinction has been drawn by the Court between regulated and less regulated professions.[171] In relation to medical practitioners, Article 17 of Directive 93/16 confirms that there is no need for registration.[172] Article 4(1) of Directive 77/249 which was designed to facilitate the freedom of lawyers to provide services, does not require the registration of lawyers in the Member State in which the services will be provided.[173] However, according to Article 7(1) of the same directive, the lawyer may be requested to establish 'his qualifications as a lawyer'. The directive does contain further limits on the rights of a lawyer from one Member State to provide services in another Member State.

Under Article 1 of the directive, a Member State may reserve to 'prescribed categories of lawyers the preparation of formal documents for obtaining title to administer estates of deceased persons, and the drafting of formal documents creating or transferring interests in land'. A further limitation is provided in Article 5 which states that the Member State may require the lawyer when representing a client in legal proceedings to be introduced to the presiding judge and the President of the relevant Bar and to work in conjunction with a local lawyer entitled to appear in the court in question. This latter obligation does not apply where national legislation does not require representation by a lawyer.[174] Finally, under Article 4 of the directive, the lawyer must respect the professional rules of conduct of both the Member State in which the service is provided and their home Member State.[175]

In concluding this section it is worth repeating the history of the issue of the mutual recognition of qualifications under the Treaty. After a considerable lapse of time, movement towards mutual recognition began through a process of issuing specific directives for particular professions. In the absence of specific directives certain general principles were held to apply to the area by the ECJ either as a result of the provisions of the Treaty or the general principles of Community law. The case law of the Court lessened the impact of the absence of specific directives and indeed obviated much of the need for such directives. However, the judicial route to recognition of qualifications was eventually, and rightly, replaced by further legislative intervention. The approach of the general directive was based on establishing confidence and mutual trust between the Member States in relation to their professional training. The need for harmonization could be viewed as an impediment to mutual recognition. The approach of the general directive mirrors the approach taken by the Community with respect to the free movement of goods; harmonization being restricted to that which is considered to be essential to fulfil the objectives of the Treaty. The remaining restrictions on the freedom of establishment and the right to provide services imposed by particular provisions of the national law of the Member States exist only in so far as they do not impede the exercise of the right to free movement within the Community.

CONCLUSION

The above survey of the three areas of the educational rights of migrant workers, the concept of vocational training and the mutual recognition of qualifications demonstrates the important role played in the educational policy of the Community by the European Court of Justice. They have given an expansive interpretations to the provisions of Regulation 1612/68 with respect to the educational rights of both migant workers and their children. Their decisions in *Lair* and *Brown* represent something of a retreat prompted by the concerns of the Member States. While respecting the autonomy of the Member States, the Court has generally asserted that the Community does have a role in education. This role emerges from both Regulation 1612/68 and Article 128. With respect to the latter, the second section demonstrated the gradual approach of the Court to the interpretation of this provision. Once again, the definition was expansive.

The final section presents a somewhat different picture. The problem of mutual recognition was seen to be one capable of legislative solution. The Court played a role in those areas where specific legislation was absent, however, eventually the Court's role here was supplanted by further legislation. The only role for the Court now relates to the restrictions of national law which have not yet been harmonized but which must be applied in accordance with the general principles of the Treaty. This whole chapter is evidence of the importance of general principles in Community law, especially Article 7 of the Treaty. The Court has given that Article a role which the Member States had never assumed it could have. This will be a cause of celebration for an individual seeking to rely on Community law but a source of concern to the Member States, as more areas of national competence are subjected to the rigours of Article 7.

Perhaps, this is the most disquieting aspect of the Court's development and extension of the Community's competence in education. The Court has always stressed its desire to respect the division of competence between the Community and the Member States in relation to education. However, the principle of non-discrimination by applying to all aspects of education and vocational training, from access to funding, certain problems have arisen for the Member States. Hartley identifies these issues as relating to goverment funding of education to admission policies[176] He concludes:

> These problems illustrate the danger of policy-making by judicial decision. It would have been better if the European Court had left it to the Council to adopt a policy on migrant students. Such a policy would no doubt take time to develop, but the end result would probably have been preferable from an educational point of view.[177]

The question which now needs to be answered is: will the provisions of the Maastricht Treaty allow for an education policy to emerge as a result of the Council's endeavours rather than the Court's? This is the question which will be addressed in the final section of this part.

Notes

4
From Maastricht to the Future

Having previously discussed the development and extension of the competence of the Community in the area of education, the focus of this chapter is the specific provisions of the Treaty on European Union on education. By virtue of the amendment of Article 3 of the Treaty of Rome, the Community now has as one of its activities 'a contribution to education and training of quality'. In any consideration of how the Community will make a contribution to quality education, a review or evaluation of the history of the Community policy on education will be central. This will help in the interpretation of the new provisions of Article 126 of the Treaty on education, and give some insight into the likely development of those provisions. So before considering the provisions of the Maastricht Treaty it is essential to conduct a brief review and evaluation of Community policy in Education from its origins in the 1976 Action Programme.

A REVIEW: 1976–93

When discussing the history of the education policy of the Community, it is possible to discern two distinct periods of activity; from 1976 to 1985 and from 1985 to 1993. The first period began with the Action Programme. That programme, drawing on the 1974 resolution on co-operation in education,[1] listed seven priority areas for further action:

(i) better facilities for the education and training of nationals and the children of nationals of other Member States of the Community and non member countries;
(ii) the promotion of closer relations between educational systems in Europe;

(iii) the compilation of up-to-date documentation and statistics on education;
(iv) increased cooperation between institutes of higher education;
(v) improved possibilities for academic recognition of diplomas and periods of study;
(vi) the encouragement of freedom of movement and mobility of teachers, students and research workers in particular by the removal of administrative and social obstacles to the free movement of such persons and by the improved teaching of foreign languages;
(vii) the achievement of equal opportunity for free access to all forms of education.[2]

The Education Committee established by the Action Programme was able to report four years later that substantial research had been conducted in all areas and possibilities existed for further co-operation between the Member States.[3] In only one area, that of the educational rights of the children of migrant workers, was the Committee able to point to a concrete legislative outcome.[4]

Despite this limited legislative output, co-operation in education was being gradually accepted by the Member States. As the Commission itself recognised:

> The progressive development of the 1976 Education Action Programme sowed the seeds for the introduction of a range of specific action programmes launched at Community level from 1986 onwards. The range and character of the action programme reflected the common concerns already identified in 1976 but were a clear development out of them in so far as they were responding to a Community which was developing with a new dynamism and purpose.[5]

The 'new dynamism and purpose' was the impetus created by the drive to complete the Internal Market. Other factors were also significant. For example, greater co-operation was considered necessary as a result of the social problems arising from youth unemployment and the challenge of new technology. Equally, the desire to create a People's Europe was an additional factor. Of course, the role of the Court of Justice must not be neglected as a factor promoting greater co-operation in education and, specifically, the introduction of the action programmes.[6] Each of the action programmes can be viewed as responding to a particular educational or training need.

A more recent factor and one which has not yet been discussed is the emergence of the social dimension of the Single Market – the Social Charter. In December 1989, the European Council meeting at Strasbourg adopted the Community Charter of Fundamental Social Rights of Workers, the Social Charter.[7] Just as co-operation in education was inspired by the realization that the Community was more than an economic association of states, so the Social Charter emerged from a similar background. The Single European Act in addition to setting a deadline for the completion of the Internal Market, an area within which there would be free movement of goods, persons, services and capital, also stressed the need to reinforce the economic and social cohesion of the Community.[8] Despite this emphasis in the Single European Act, progress towards agreement on the content of the Charter was very slow. In the end, the Charter was signed by only eleven of the Member States. The United Kingdom chose not to adhere to the Solemn Declaration constituting the Charter.

The Charter contains fundamental principles relating to twelve main areas.[9] The relationship between the Charter and education and training is made clear in Article 15 which states:

> Every worker of the European Community must be able to have access to vocational training and to benefit therefrom throughout his working life. In the conditions of access to such training there may be no discrimination on grounds of nationality. The competent public authorities, undertakings or the two sides of industry each within their own sphere of competence, should set up continuing and permanent training systems enabling every person to undergo retraining more especially through leave for training purposes, to improve his skills or to acquire new skills, particularly in the light of technical developments.[10]

The responsibility for implementing the provisions of the Charter fell within the powers of the Member States. However, there were areas which fell within the competence of the Community and the Commission was invited to present initiatives in these areas. The resulting social action programme was divided into thirteen chapters.[11] However, the proposed measures can be seen to relate to five areas: freedom of movement; the social security of migrant workers; employment and working conditions; the improvement of the working environment; and vocational training.

In relation to vocational training various measures were

proposed.[12] With respect to legislative measures, three particular proposals were envisaged. There was to be a proposal for a Community instrument on access to vocational training. A proposal would also be made to update Decision 63/266 which laid down the general principles for the implementation of a common vocational training policy. Finally, there would be a proposal concerning a joint programme for the exchange of young workers and youth exchanges. Other action envisaged related to the submission of Commission communication on the rationalization and co-ordination of Community action programmes in the area of initial and continuing vocational training. The communication was submitted and will be discussed further below. By virtue of Decision 91/387 amendments were made to the Petra Programme which relates to the transition of young people from school to adult and working life.[13] The Preamble to the decision makes specific reference to the Social Charter. In addition Decision 89/657 establishing Eurotecnet seeks to promote innovation in vocational training, especially in the area of technology.[14] Finally, Decision 90/267 introducing the Force Programme is designed to encourage greater investment in continuing vocational training.[15] All of these measures are based on Article 128 whereas the Youth for Europe which promotes youth exchanges for young people aged 15 to 25 who are outside the educational system is based on Articles 50 and 235.[16] The action contemplated in the Commission's response to the Social Charter in relation to vocational training is already well under way.[17]

One factor which must now be considered is the attitude taken to the Social Charter by the Treaty on European Union. On the insistence of the United Kingdom, the Social Chapter of the Maastricht Treaty was removed from the Treaty and was made subject to a separate Protocol. The Protocol on Social Policy notes that eleven of the Member States 'wish to continue along the path laid down by the Social Charter of 1989'.[18] The objections of the United Kingdom to the adoption of the Social Charter continued and it will not take part in the deliberations and the adoption of proposals to implement the Agreement on Social Policy attached to the Protocol. It must be noted that, although part of the Social Charter, the Agreement on Social Policy contains no explicit reference to vocational training. It does list as an area for decision the 'integration of persons excluded from the labour market', proposals in this area are to be 'without prejudice to the provisions of Article 127' of the Treaty.[19] Article 127 of the Treaty is a new provision dealing more specifically than its predecessor (Article 128) with the implementation of a vocational training policy.[20] As Article 126 lays down specific Community competence in education as distinct from vocational training, it appears that henceforth a distinction may have to be made between action programmes whose primary goals are related to vocational training and those programmes which relate more to education.

To take the examples of the specific programmes already discussed, Erasmus, Comett, Lingua and Tempus may be considered primarily to serve educational goals, although it is not possible to divorce completely the education and training objectives of each programme. Erasmus has among its objectives the promotion of co-operation between institutions of higher education and the encouragement of greater student mobility. One consequence of such co-operation and mobility would be greater mutual recognition of qualifications. The Comett Programme, in addition to student mobility, also seeks to promote co-operation between universities and industry to assist training in the area of technology. The principle of exchanges was extended beyond universities to include placements in industry in another Member State. The Lingua Programme attacked one of the most important areas where action was necessary to promote a People's Europe – the ability of individuals to communicate in at least another Community language other than their native language. Finally, there is the Tempus Programme: this is designed to assist the process of educational restructuring, especially in higher education, as part of the economic and social reforms necessary in Central and Eastern Europe. As previously noted, despite the different problems which each of these and the other Action Programmes seek to address, a common framework for Community action exists.

The central element of this framework is the establishment of networks between organizations facing comparable or similar problems. Within such networks the collection and dissemination of information can help in potential solutions to these problems. The following are just some examples of the success of this particular measure.[21] For the Tempus scheme there are 637 joint european projects between the eligible countries and the Member States of the Community involving a total of 1,800 institutions as part of the restructuring of higher education in Central and Eastern Europe. Within the Lingua Programme there are 200 Inter-University Co-operation Programmes and a network of national agencies to promote the objectives of the programme. In comparison with these more recent programmes the Comett scheme involves a network of 205 University-Industry consortia which have 10,000 members covering all the regions of both the Community and EFTA and most of the advanced technology areas. Finally, within Erasmus there are over 1900 Inter-University Co-operation Programmes involving 1,200 higher education institutions throughout the European Community. In addition to problem solving these programmes also provide the structure for the second common measure: exchanges.[22]

The persons involved in such exchanges are usually students. The number of students benefitting under Erasmus is estimated to be about 40,000. Lingua exchanges for language students are between 6,000 and 7,000 every year and Tempus has so far managed to send about 6,500 students, mostly from the eligible countries to the Community. Although the main beneficiaries of the mobility schemes are students, the four programmes also provide for the mobility of both university staff (either academic or administrative) and industry representatives. Comett mobility actions, which cover both university students, staff and industry representatives, are estimated to have involved over 30,000 persons for an average period of six months. Lingua mobility actions which covers training placements for language teachers are estimated to be 4,000 per annum and around 30,000 young persons in vocational, professional and general education have benefited from brief exchanges and meetings every year. The staff mobility programme under Erasmus currently benefits up to 5,000 university staff each year.

The final element of the framework is the establishment of joint transnational projects.[23] In this area, Tempus has established over 600 projects, mostly in the area of curriculum development, upgrading of facilities and the encouragement of university–industry linkages. Lingua has helped in the training of over 4,000 language teachers and compiled language training packages for industry. Comett has financed 1,000 training projects which will train around 150,000 people through the courses developed within such projects, this figure stands at 7,000. Finally, under Erasmus there are currently 170 projects on co-operation in the joint development of new curricula. The statistics appear to be impressive but they provide only a partial answer to the question of how effective these, and the other, programmes have been. Only an evaluation of whether the programmes have achieved their objectives will provide a complete answer and give some indication of the future of these programmes after the entry into force of the new Article 126.

The Commission report on the results and achievements of Community education and training programmes divides these achievements into five areas.[24] Some indication has already been given above of the first area of achievement – increased mobility and co-operation in education and training. In total, over a quarter of a million students and trainees have benefited from the mobility provisions of the programmes. To this figure must be added a further 26, 500 persons, either young people or teacher and training personnel, who have also benefited from the mobility provisions. Despite the apparent success in this area, the figure set for Erasmus exchanges of 10 per cent of students studying abroad has still not been attained.[25]

It is essential to realise that the impact of the mobility provided under the schemes is not limited to the time spent abroad. For example, Erasmus, Lingua and Comett all provide for education and/or training prior to the period spent abroad. Increasingly, therefore, university education and training is acquiring a European dimension. This is significant as such a dimension has already been the subject of a resolution of the Council and the Ministers of Education meeting within the Council with respect to primary and secondary education.[26] The European Dimension which the Community programmes are seeking to promote also emerges from other aspects of the mobility provisions of these programmes. This is especially the case as most student exchanges take place within the structure provided by Inter-University Co-operation Agreements. Mobility cannot, therefore, be seen as an end in itself rather it is part of a larger framework for the promotion of quality education. For example, under Erasmus the exchange of students takes place within a degree programme. If the period spent abroad is recognized for degree purposes this indirectly promotes the mutual recognition of higher education qualifications. Equally suitable arrangements for exchange students have to be made with the result that a better framework for mobility is created.

The most important factor in the exchange of students is the provision of adequate finance for the period spent in another Member State. This can be achieved not only through an Erasmus mobility grant but also through the recognition of the period abroad by the national grant awarding authorities. Further arrangements may include the provision of accommodation, academic guidance and language preparation. The provision of such services will improve the reception of the exchange student and will also benefit the home students as well. In the light of experience gained from the mobility provision of the Community's programmes policy development within the Member States is encouraged and this may even lead to changes in national legislation.[27] The Tempus Programme is an excellent example of where co-operation will lead to positive legislative changes as one of the objectives of the scheme is to promote the restructuring of higher education.

In this first area of achievements for the Community's education and training programmes it is possible to point to tangible results: for example, a set number of students going to another Member State or changes in the education legislation of a Member State. The remaining four areas are: contributing to increased European competitiveness;[28] economic and social cohesion in the Community;[29] bringing Europe closer to the citizen;[30] and transnational transfer of knowledge and expertise.[31] For these remaining areas the results appear to be less tangible. In particular, how is it possible to assess whether or not the progress has made in these areas? To take the area of increasing the competitiveness of the Community, all the programmes have this as a common aim. But will the improvement in the quality and quantity of professional and vocational qualifications increase the competitiveness of the Community? The programmes will undoubtedly promote a better trained workforce but this alone may be insufficient to increase the competitiveness of the Community.

To take the area of economic and social cohesion in the Community, the Commission argue that:

> Economic and social cohesion has been identified as a fundamental condition for the balanced development of the Community, and education and training have been identified as a crucial factor in achieving balanced social and economic development in all the Member States. No grouping of nations can nowadays claim to have achieved a high quality of growth if significant elements of its human potential remain untapped, redundant or underutilised.

It is impossible to argue with the general tenor of this argument. The education and training programmes of the Community will promote a better trained workforce. By providing a Single Market in training and qualifications the programmes will allow for greater free movement of persons within the Community. Such free movement rights will be exercised in the search for employment in other Member States if none is available in the home state. To hope that the education and training programmes will eliminate regional disparities within the Community is to assign to education and training programmes an objective which they alone are incapable of achieving. It may be achievable if the education and training programmes are part of a wider scheme, involving all aspects of Community policy, to tackle particular issues. A People's Europe, for example, will not grow out of the education and training programmes. The concept is too broad to be achieved by such a narrowly focused set of programmes.

In its conclusion to the review of the education and training programmes, the Commission does seem to realize the limited nature of these programmes. It states: The combined achievements of the programmes put in place since 1986 can clearly be seen to have been considerable, in terms of the numbers of people who have participated; the trans-national activities generated; and their impact on policy thinking in different Member States.[33] These achievements emerge from the mobility and co-operation in education and training provisions of the programmes. No reference is made to the loftier aims, and less tangible achievements, of the programmes. It may be wrong to criticize the programmes for their attempt to confront a range of economic and social issues which fall outside the scope of the traditional definition of education and training. However, some redefinition of the objectives of the programmes will have to be undertaken as a result of the Treaty of Maastricht. This will introduce for the first time specific Community competence in education, in addition to various reforms to the existing Treaty provision on vocational training. By building a policy on education through the provision on vocational training the Community has tied these two areas together. It is an open question as to whether separate provisions on these matters will lead to a distinction being made between action programmes whose primary goals are related to vocational training and those programmes which relate more to education. This question can only be answered after an assessment of the likely future shape of education policy in the Community under Article 126 of the Treaty.

THE MAASTRICHT PROVISIONS

Before considering the specific provisions on education, it is instructive to examine the thinking of the Commission prior to the Maastricht Treaty on the future of the existing education and training programmes. One reason for this is that although the Maastricht Treaty separates education and vocational training, there will be a need for continuity to be maintained in the programmes after 1993. Equally, if there is to be a distinction between education and training it is important to determine within which category the existing programmes come. Education will fall within Article 126 and vocational training within Article 127. If it is not possible to draw a distinction between the education and training aspects of the existing programmes, then in the future a joint legal base, of Articles 126 and 127, will be needed for these programmes. However, a basis for a distinction between 'education' and 'training' can be divined from various Commission documents which discuss the future of the Community's programmes in the 1990s.

One starting point could be the 1990 document on the rationalization and co-ordination of vocational training programmes.[34] This document has its origin in the Action Programme of the Commission on the implementation of the Social Charter. Included within the objectives of the communication was the concern for greater transparency and coherence in the management of Community vocational training measures. Further objectives included:

> to permit a clearer identification of the relationship between Community measures and the vocational education and training policies carried out within the Member States and of the added value contributed by the Community measures; to clarify the options for future development either through the extension or diversification of existing programmes or through the integration of measures which respond to new demands and which contribute to the overall impact of the Commission's action.[35]

One of these new demands is the need to provide a framework for future Community actions in the field of education as a result of the inclusion of a new Treaty provision in that area.

In the Framework for Action the Commission identified five fields of activity into which existing Community action fell. These were: initial vocational education and training of young people; higher education and advanced training; continuing education and training; language training; and co-operation with third countries. The existing Community policies were then located within these five fields of activity. If a distinction is to be drawn in the future between education and vocational training then it appears likely that field 2, higher education and advanced training, and elements of field 5, international co-operation, will come within the sphere of education, and hence Article 126. The remainder will fall within the sphere of vocational training, and hence Article 127. In field 2 the specific Community programmes at issue are Erasmus, Comett, Lingua and Tempus. As the analysis of these programmes in Chapter 1 indicated, they are primarily concerned with education. It is not possible, and indeed may not be desirable, to draw such a sharp distinction between the education and training programmes. For example, the Comett Programme involves university–industry co-operation with the objective of improving the quality of training provided. However, a distinction must be drawn if the separation of education from vocational training effected by the Treaty of Maastricht is to have any content.

Within the existing scope of the education and training programmes of the Community it would appear that future legislation in these areas would require the use of both Article 126 and 127. If the Community wishes to proceed using Article 126 as a single legal base for existing measures in education, it appears that such measures may be limited to the promotion of higher education and advanced training. Thus the areas where the Community can take action will include measures encouraging mobility of students and teachers, promoting co-operation between educational establishments and developing exchanges of information and experience between the Member States. These areas are consistent with the objectives of the Erasmus, Comett, Tempus and Lingua Programmes. One consequence of these programmes is that higher education is acquiring a European Dimension and this was one aspect of a Commission paper which was discussed at a meeting of the Council and Ministers of Education meeting within the Council on 27 November 1992.

The Commission Memorandum on Higher Education in the European Community emerged from the 1989 resolution of the Council and Ministers of Education meeting within the Council on co-operation in education and training in the run-up to 1992.[36] The Memorandum begins by tracing the growing requirements for higher education and the contribution which higher education can make to various Community policies.[37] Taking both of these factors into account, the memorandum identifies the challenges facing higher education which call for new educational policies. Four critical areas for higher education in the future were identified.[38] These include the question of access to higher education, partnerships with economic life, continuing education and open and distance learning. In relation to the first of these areas, the Commission points out that problems arising from increased access to higher education may be solved more easily if the Member States exchange information on these problems. Such information exchanges can occur within the framework of existing Community programmes.[39] Of these programmes, Comett will be able to assist in the process of establishing much closer links between universities and industries.[40] For the remaining areas greater cooperation between the Member States was requested by the Commission, especially as both areas would contribute to increased participation in higher education.[41] While each of these four issues is discussed in detail, the centrepiece of the Memorandum is the development of a European Dimension in higher education.

The Commission Memorandum maintained:

> The willingness to cooperate, to exchange experience and to take Community considerations into account in formulating their responses to the challenges of the nineties and beyond, will not, however, make full impact unless accompanied by a firm statement of a European Community Dimension in Higher Education.[42]

Such a statement would cover nine areas of activity. The first area of the statement would be student mobility.[43] In this area a more comprehensive policy would be promoted so that impediments to mobility would be removed and incentives to mobility would be enhanced. In addition, the second area envisaged more intensive co-operation between institutions at the European level leading to joint programmes of teaching and curriculum development.[44] This would involve staff exchanges as a mechanism which would extend the 'European' experience of those students who could not participate in the mobility programmes. In a sense if the students could not go to Europe, Europe would be brought to the students. Within this area it was also envisaged that exchanges between higher education institutions and industry would contribute to the European dimension of higher education.

The sixth area of the statement called for a flexible approach to the issue of recognition of qualifications and periods of study so as to promote not only the mobility of students but also the mobility of graduates throughout the Community.[45] The success of the measures anticipated in the areas so far noted depends on adequate language competence, for this is a major impediment to student mobility. The central importance of language was the fourth area of the European dimension.[46] The Lingua Programme was seen as an important element in the promotion of language competence in higher education institutions. In addition there was the indirect contribution of having students from other Member States within the higher education institution. Once again staff exchanges were considered important in the development of this area. Such exchanges would be extended to secondary levels of education as the fourth area of the European dimension involved the training of teachers at this level.[47] Although the effect of this measure will be felt at the secondary level, it qualifies as part of a European dimension in higher education given that the training of teachers is conducted within higher education institutions. The net result of all these measures would be that the European Community would be on the curricula of both secondary and higher education; this was the third area of the European dimension in higher education.[48] The final three areas stressed the international role of higher education, the role of information and policy analysis and, finally, the need for dialogue within the higher education sector.[49]

The Commission memorandum makes it clear that it is designed to stimulate discussion. The Council and the Ministers of Education meeting within the Council having discussed the memorandum identified areas of special interest for the future development of the European dimension in higher education.[50] Four particular areas were highlighted as potential contributors to the European dimension in higher education.[51] These included the further development of inter-institutional links, especially to promote collaboration over the curriculum. In both of these areas it was recognized that the mobility of teaching staff could make an important contribution to the European dimension. The existing programmes, with their provisions on student and staff mobility, which had already contributed to the flowering of a European dimension, would be used to develop that dimension further. However, the number of students who could benefit from the existing programmes is limited. For those students and staff who could not benefit from the mobility provisions of the programmes other measures were to be developed in favour of the European dimension. Perhaps as an example of these other measures, the Council and Ministers of Education urged that specific measures should be developed to incorporate distance learning into the education programmes.[52]

The Council and the Ministers of Education meeting within the Council recognized that debate on the issue of the European

Dimension in Higher Education was not yet complete. Further issues for consideration arose from the 1992 Commission Report on Higher Education-Industry Cooperation, subtitled 'Advanced training for competitive advantage'.[53] Whereas the Commission memorandum on higher education had concentrated on Erasmus, this report concentrated on the contribution of the Comett Programme. What the report demonstrates is that Comett is on the dividing line between education and vocational training. In terms of the future the report states:

> A fundamental recommendation is that higher education institutions should adopt cooperation with industry as part of their fundamental mission, especially in the continuing training field, and that companies themselves should have an explicit education and training strategy as well as an organised interface with higher education which will facilitate access and dialogue.[54]

Community action in the implementation of this recommendation would be directed towards the Europeanization of existing networks for university–industry exchanges. A new mechanism would be needed to develop these exchanges. Specifically in relation to education, it was considered that measures promoting continuing education should form part of higher education efforts and that productivity within higher education should be improved. One mechanism to achieve this latter goal would be the promotion of distance learning.[55]

In the context of the question of what is to be covered by Article 126 of the Treaty, it appears that the Comett Programme will require a joint legal base if it is to be renewed or replaced by a Europeanized mechanism for university–industry exchanges. Article 127 will be the other legal basis for action in this area. Thus the areas where the Community may take action under Article 126 will include measures encouraging mobility of students and teachers, promoting cooperation between educational establishments and developing exchanges of information and experience between the Member States. These areas are consistent with the objectives of the Erasmus, Comett, Tempus and Lingua Programmes which also promote a European dimension in higher education. It must be noted that only Erasmus and Tempus belong fully within the scope of Article 126; Comett and Lingua will straddle the division between education and training effected by the Maastricht Treaty. The discussion so far has been limited in the sense that the documents on which it was based have not concerned themselves with the impact of the Maastricht Treaty. The discussion of the various fields of activity of the Community in education and training points to a meaningful distinction between these areas. It is now time to determine whether this distinction is effected by the new provisions on education.

As already noted, according to the amended Article 3 of the Treaty of Rome the Community now has as one of its activities 'a contribution to education and training of quality'. Some indication of how this is to be achieved is provided in Article 126 of the Treaty which states:

1) The Community shall contribute to the development of quality education by encouraging cooperation between Member States and, if necessary, by supporting and supplementing their action, while fully respecting the responsibility of the Member States for the content of teaching and the organisation of education systems and their cultural and linguistic diversity.
2) Community action shall be aimed at:
   - developing the European dimension in education, particularly through the teaching and dissemination of the languages of the Member States;
   - encouraging mobility of students and teachers, *inter alia*, by encouraging the academic recognition of diplomas and periods of study;
   - promoting cooperation between educational establishments;
   - developing exchanges of information and experience on issues common to the education systems of the Member States;
   - encouraging the development of youth exchanges and the exchange of socio-educational instructors;
   - encouraging the development of distance education.
3) The Community and the Member States shall foster cooperation with third countries and the competent international organisations in the field of education, in particular the Council of Europe.
4) In order to contribute to the achievement of the objectives referred to in this Article, the Council:
   - acting in accordance with the procedure referred to in Article 189b, after consulting the Economic and Social Committee and the Committee of the Regions, shall adopt incentive measures, excluding any harmonisation of the laws and

regulations of the Member States;
- acting by a qualified majority on a proposal from the Commission, shall adopt recommendations.

Before any assessment of this provision can be undertaken it is essential that the principle of subsidiarity be discussed, as this principle will inform future Community initiatives.

According to the new Article 3b, introduced by the Maastricht Treaty:

> The Community shall act within the limits of the powers conferred upon it by this Treaty and of the objectives assigned to it therein. In areas which do not fall within its exclusive competence, the Community shall take action, in accordance with the principle of subsidiarity, only if and in so far as the objectives of the proposed action cannot be sufficiently achieved by the Member States and can therefore, by reason of the scale or effects of the proposed action, be better achieved by the Community. Any action by the Community shall not go beyond what is necessary to achieve the objectives of this Treaty.

Thus subsidiarity will be a general principle of Community action. As the Preamble to the Treaty recognizes, the process of building an ever closer union among the peoples of Europe requires decisions to be 'taken as closely as possible to the citizen in accordance with the principle of subsidiarity'. The final paragraph of Article B of the Treaty also recognizes that in achieving the objectives of European Union, the principle of subsidiarity will be respected. Two questions need to be addressed: What does this principle mean? And what will be its impact on Community action in the field of education?

The exact meaning of the principle of subsidiarity has been the subject of much debate within the Community.[56] The core of the principle is contained in the second paragraph of Article 3b. It is not clear from this paragraph which areas of the Treaty fall within the exclusive competence of the Community. The case law of the Court of Justice indicates that the exclusive competence of the Community is not a static concept.[57] Indeed the Court of Justice has consistently striven to extend the powers of the Community.[58] From a legal point of view, subsidiarity may be a concept of diminishing importance. As the Community legislates in a new area for the first time, it will have to respect the principle of subsidiarity; future legislation by the Member States will have to respect the doctrine of occupied field. The approach of the Court of Justice to the powers of the Community in the past clearly informed the Commission when it identified a number of areas of exclusive Community competence.[59] These include the free movement of goods, persons, services and capital; the common organization of agricultural markets; the conservation of fishery resources; the essential elements of transport policy; the general rules on competition; and the common commercial policy.

However, subsidiarity is more than a legal principle, it is also a political principle or, as one commentator has stated, it is the legal formulation of a political principle.[60] It is this aspect of the principle of subsidiarity which is the most significant. For some of the Member States it is viewed as a means of restricting the competence of the Community, thus preventing an exercise of power by the Community in those areas where national regulation is considered to be more appropriate.[61] There would, therefore, be less regulation at Community level. In a situation where there is a disagreement on the exact scope over the scope of the principle, an agreed interpretation is essential to allow for the smooth functioning of the Community. An agreement emerged at the Edinburgh European Council meeting in December 1992 in the form of guidelines for the application of Article 3b(2). These guidelines state that action by the Community will be justified if three conditions are satisfied:

- the issue under consideration has transnational aspects which cannot be satisfactorily regulated by action by the Member States; and/or
- actions by the Member States alone or lack of Community action would conflict with the requirements of the Treaty (such as the need to correct distortion of competition or avoid disguised restrictions on trade or strengthen economic and social cohesion) or would otherwise significantly damage Member States' interests; and/or
- the Council must be satisfied that action at Community level would produce clear benefits by reason of its scale or effects compared with action at the level of the Member States [the reason for that conclusion must be substantiated by qualitative or, wherever possible, quantitative indicators].[62]

As to whether these guidelines will resolve the conflict between the Commission and some of the Member States as to the exact scope of the principle of subsidiarity remains an open question.[63] It is hoped that the inter-institutional agreement giving fuller effect to the guidelines will give further substance to the principle of subsidiarity. At least a start has been made on the definition of the principle.

As for the impact of the principle of subsidiarity on the Community's activities in the field of education, the answer is much more definite. Article 126 makes clear that the primary responsibility for the organization and content of education remains with the Member States. The role of the Community is to be supportive of the Member States' actions and to supplement these actions. Community measures will not be aimed at the harmonization of the legislation of the Member States on education. The Commission maintain that respect for the principle of subsidiarity will limit the Community to action at three levels, namely:

- the encouragement of well-structured cooperation between education and training systems;
- the promotion of quality through innovation by exchanges of information and experience; and
- the launching of specific direct actions on a Community-wide basis, where there is a clear advantage over action only at the national level.[64]

As the discussion of the development of the education policy of the Community in Chapter 1 demonstrated, these three levels are already the basis of existing Community policy. However, a distinction can be drawn between education and vocational training, as assumed above.

This assumption is vindicated in the Commission's guidelines for Community action in the fields of education and training. These guidelines consider the future of existing Community activities in the field of education and training while taking into account the impact of the Treaty of Maastricht on existing Community programmes.[65] The document is divided into three sections; 'Situation and Challenges'; 'The Contribution of the European Community'; and 'Proposed Action Lines'. The first of these sections reviews the development and achievements of the Community's education and training policy[66] and, as this has already been considered, no further discussion is considered necessary. In the second section, the Commission elaborates on the contribution which the Community can, and does, make in the areas of education and training. In the elaboration of the Commission's approach to the future, it has already been noted that it will have to respect the principle of subsidiarity. The future is, therefore, one of co-operation with Member States. As the guidelines state:

> Cooperation should be designed to promote ever closer relations between the different systems so that the planning of future reforms in individual Member States is illuminated by a comparative understanding of developments throughout the Community, as well as ensuring the necessary adaptation of national systems to contribute to the purpose and functioning of the European Community.[67]

Note that Article 126(4) excludes the possibility of harmonization of the education laws of the Member States. In addition to subsidiarity and co-operation, the main guiding principles of future Community action in education and training will include the need for specific direct actions, interaction with structural policies and the participation of all concerned parties.[68]

The final section of the guidelines contain two proposed 'Lines of Action' for the next phase of the development of existing programmes: Action Line A for actions in relation to higher education and schools and Action Line B for actions relating to training and qualifications. As suggested earlier, the former will fall within Article 126, whereas the latter will fall within Article 127. The aim of Action Line A is:

> To encourage innovation and improve quality of education through strengthening cooperation at Community level involving the active participation of universities and other higher education institutions. The action programme would provide for the exchange of persons, ideas, know-how and experience, strengthen links between research and higher education and training, and develop a European Dimension to education.[69]

To implement these principles, the three principal methods used in past education and training programmes will continue to be used; namely, networking, mobility and exchange and joint transnational projects.[70] However, such programmes will need to be rationalized so as to avoid any problems or appearances of fragmentation.

The Commission had earlier discussed the possibility of rationalizing the existing range of programmes. In relation to the Erasmus, Comett, Lingua and Tempus Programmes, it concluded that it 'would be premature to merge the programmes at this stage'.[71]

Instead, a single advisory committee was recommended to promote the harmonious implementation of the programmes. In the guidelines, the Commission repeated its earlier recommendation for a single advisory committee.[72] However, the Commission also goes further by advocating a single coherent framework for the future development of these programmes.[73] The framework will include the inter-university co-operation and exchange programmes under Erasmus; the Erasmus course credit transfer system; action under Lingua relating to university language tuition; student placements in industry under Comett; co-operation in the area of teacher training; and the development of a European dimension in higher education. As part of this European dimension, distance learning is to be encouraged for those students who do not have an opportunity to study abroad. To remove the greatest impediment to study abroad – finance – the Member States will be requested to give greater financial resources to support student exchanges.[74] The role of the Community in the future is to be complementary.

Outside the scope of higher education, the guidelines also point to action by the Community at the level of school education.[75] Once again, the Commission envisages instituting a wide-ranging co-operation scheme. In addition, language competence will be catered for through the Lingua scheme and greater efforts will be made to promote a European dimension in school education. For young people outside both secondary and higher education, the guidelines call for the further development of the existing Youth for Europe scheme.[76] Finally, and in recognition of the areas of common concern between the Member States, not only in relation to school education but also higher education, the Commission advocates a more systematic transfer of information and experience.[77]

Intended to stimulate debate, the Commission communication on the guidelines for the future development of education and training within the Community effects a separation of existing programmes in accordance with the new provisions in these areas. Further documents will emerge given that most of the programmes are due for renewal in 1994. In this process of renewal, as Article 126(4) makes clear, not only will the Commission and the Council be involved, but a formal role will be given for the first time to the European Parliament and the Committee of the Regions. In all their discussions the principle of subsidiarity will have to be respected and this will, given the differing interpretations of this principle, serve to restrict the future activities of the Community to the areas of encouraging existing co-operation, the promotion of information exchanges and experience and certain specific direct actions. It seems that the Community with respect to education has returned to the situation it found itself in 1974 with respect only to the question of the division of competence between the Member States and the Community. The major difference is that since 1974 an acceptable role had been carved out for the Community in education.

A CONCLUSION

According to Article 60 of the Draft Treaty establishing European Union:

> In order to create a context which will help inculcate in the public an awareness of the Union's own identity and to ensure a minimum standard of training, creating the opportunity for free choice of career, job or training establishment anywhere in the Union, the Union shall take measures concerning:
>
> - the definition of objectives for common or compatible training programmes;
> - the Union-wide validity and equivalence of diplomas and school, study and training periods;
> - the promotion of scientific research.[78]

This was how the European Parliament viewed the future development of education in the European Community. Events since the Draft Treaty have shown that education has assumed a role far greater than that anticipated by the Parliament.

Despite the urging of some Member States, education was not included within the scope of the Single European Act (SEA).[79] In one sense, the absence of education from the SEA served the development of the educational competence of the Community. The Commission considered that action on education was necessary to complement the movement towards the completion of the Internal Market. The Parliament was already a supporter of such complementary action. Further support also emerged from the European Council's desire to create a People's Europe. In the creation of the Single Market and a People's Europe, the European Court of Justice has rendered great assistance, thus promoting the role of the Community in education. Indeed all the institutions, including the Member States, have played their part in the development of the competence of the Community. As a result, the provisions of the Treaty of Maastricht on education appear to represent a balance between the powers of the Member States and those of the Community.

Having developed in a period when Community competence in the area was uncertain, the eventual competence of the Community was bound to respect the principle of subsidiarity. Action taken originated in intergovernmental co-operation, from this the Community assumed the role of collator of information. From this limited role other developments led to the gradual emergence of a more developmental role. What Article 126 of the Treaty of Maastricht does is to confirm those areas where the Community adds value to the educational policies of the Member States and the economic and social policies of the Community. As Article 126 makes clear, the Community will take action to develop the European dimension to education, while respecting the responsibility of the Member States for their educational policies. To promote the free movement of persons, student and staff mobility is to be encouraged and this will promote co-operation between educational establishments in the Member States. The principle of exchange will also extend to information, ensuring that the Member States do not enact legislation which would frustrate the objectives of the Community.

The future of the education policy of the Community is therefore assured by Article 126 of the Treaty of Maastricht. The initial reluctance of the Member States to allow discussions of education at the Community level has been overcome and the desire of the Community to be involved in all areas of the Member States' educational policies has also been curtailed. In this respect the period between the SEA and the Treaty of Maastricht has served to identify those aspects of the educational policies of the Member States where action needs to be taken in consideration of developments in other Member States and those aspects of the integration of the Community where action on education is desirable to complement the agreed goals of the Community. The Treaty of Maastricht, therefore, concluded the discussion which had been ongoing since 1976 on the proper scope of the role of the Community in education. What will emerge in the future is a Community policy which respects the different traditions of the Member States in the area of education, and, at the same time promotes the goals of the Community. What will also emerge is a series of policies in the Member States which respect the contribution which the Community can make to the achievement of national goals in education. This will be subsidiarity and integration in harmony.

Part 2
Culture

Notes

5
The Emergence and Development of Community Competence

The original Treaty of Rome contains few references to culture. Whereas Articles 30 and 34 of the Treaty prohibit quantitative restrictions or measures having equivalent effect on imports or exports, Article 36, *inter alia*, allows for prohibitions or restrictions 'justified on grounds of the protection national treasures possessing artistic, historic or archaeological value'. Thus the competence of the Community in relation to culture emerges from an even narrower legal basis than Community competence in education.

Indeed the development of Community competence in culture bears considerable similarities with the development of educational policy within the Community. However, there are important differences. The Ministers of Education first met within the Council in the early 1970s, the equivalent meeting for the Ministers of Culture did not occur until the early 1980s. The basis for the early meetings of the Council on Education was a report called for by the Commission (the Janne Report) followed by a Commission Communication. In relation to culture there was to be no outside report but rather several Commission Communications before there was a meeting within the Council. The desire to create a People's Europe and the drive to complete the Internal Market were factors leading to greater Community involvement in education and a similar picture emerges with respect to culture. As discussed above, just as the amendments to the Treaty of Rome effected by the Maastricht Treaty brought education within the sphere of Community action, cultural action by the Community was granted a specific Treaty basis. This will be discussed in greater detail in the next chapter; this chapter will concentrate on the history and scope of the policy of the Community in relation to culture up to the completion of the Internal Market.

TAKING THE FIRST STEPS

One starting point for the emergence of a Community policy on culture is the 1974 resolution of the European Parliament calling for Community action on culture.[1] It is also possible to point to a series of statements made at several meetings of the heads of state and of government of the Member States. For example, the 1969 meeting at The Hague recognized the need to preserve Europe as 'an exceptional seat of development, culture and progress'.[2] The idea that the Community was more than an economic association of states which emerged from The Hague meeting was further endorsed at the 1972 meeting in Paris.[3] Finally, in the communique on European identity adopted at the Copenhagen meeting in 1973, culture was seen as being one of the fundamental elements of that Identity.[4] In the wake of all this encouragement the Commission finally produced a document entitled 'Community Action in the Cultural Sector'.[5]

The Commission began by identifying the scope of the phrase 'cultural sector' as including those persons and undertakings involved in the production and distribution of cultural goods and services. The Commission continued:

> Community action in the cultural sector is therefore necessarily centred on solving the economic and social problems which arise in this sector as in all others – sometimes, even in more acute form. Firstly, it aims to support culture by gradually creating a more propitious economic and social environment.[6]

The areas identified as falling within the scope of the Community's action on culture included the following: freedom of trade in cultural goods; combating theft of cultural goods; freedom of movement and establishment of cultural workers; training periods for young cultural workers; harmonization of taxation in the cultural sector; harmonization of laws on copyright and related rights; social aspects; and other action.

In most of these areas, as the Commission itself recognized, Community action in the area of culture involved no more than the application of the Treaty to this sector of activity.[7] For example, with respect to the freedom of trade in cultural goods, the

Commission urged that formalities to the movement of cultural goods should be simplified. The majority of this section was devoted to the problem of combating thefts of cultural goods; the Commission recommended the institution of a system of record cards for cultural goods.[8] No reference was made to the scope of the exception in Article 36 relating to the protection of national treasures. This omission is to be regretted as the European Court of Justice had not yet ruled on the scope of this exception to Article 36. The possibility to do so arose in the 1968 case of *Commission v. Italy* concerning the legality of a duty imposed by the Italian authorities on the export of art treasures.[9] The Italian government argued that the products subject to the measures were not goods within the meaning of the Treaty and, in the alternative, that the exception in Article 36 covered the particular measure.

The Court began by pointing out that although the Treaty did not define goods, except to the extent that it covered everything which was not an agricultural product, it must be that anything capable of monetary valuation and being the subject of commercial transaction would constitute a 'good' for the purposes of the Treaty.[10] Having dismissed the first argument of the Italian government, the Court did not proceed to examine the scope of Article 36. That provision was not at issue, according to the Court, as the measure at issue was a tax and Article 36 could not be relied on to justify a tax.[11] An opportunity to pronounce on the scope of the exception in Article 36 was therefore lost and, again, this is regrettable as the exact scope of the exception is by no means clear. For example, although the English version of the Treaty referees to 'treasures', other versions of the Treaty refer to 'artistic heritage'. What, if any, is the significance of this difference in wording? Indeed, what is included within the phrase 'treasures'? Is there a distinction between treasures which are the products of the particular civilization and culture of a Member State and treasures which are accumulated by the Member State from other countries?

These questions of interpretation of Article 36 are addressed and answered by Oliver. He submits that there are three questions which must be asked in approaching this issue:

- is the object of such historical or archaeological value to *this* Member State or any of its regions as to qualify as a 'treasure'? If so, then the Member State is entitled to retain it without more, regardless of whether it has any artistic value. If not, then;
- can the object be described as an artistic treasure? If not then it

falls outside this limb of Article 36. If it is an artistic treasure then;
- is it a product of the civilization or culture of this Member State? If so, then it may be retained under this part of Article 36. If not, then one has to decide the point of principle whether the Member State concerned may retain the object nevertheless.[12]

This approach appears straightforward, yet it still leaves a 'point of principle' to be resolved. It would have been helpful had the Commission chosen in the Communication to discuss the possible scope of the exception in Article 36 and to offer guidance on its interpretation and the point of principle recognized by Oliver.

In relation to other areas which involved the extension of the Treaty to the field of culture, the Commission, for example, called for greater information to facilitate the freedom of movement and establishment of cultural workers.[13] In the area of harmonization of taxation, the Commission advocated significant action being taken by the Member States.[14] For example, it was recommended that the tax system should be altered to allow for the development of cultural foundations and patronage. Further measures included a reasonable application of indirect taxation to cultural goods and a more generous application of direct taxation rules to cultural workers to take into account periods of employment and unemployment. Another area for harmonization related to the laws of the Member States on copyright and related rights.[15] A number of problem areas were identified in this area. For example, a survey of the copyright legislation of the Member States revealed variations in the duration of copyright, from seventy years in Germany to fifty years in other Member States. The use of copyright was recognized as an impediment to the free flow of goods between the Member States. It is interesting to note that the Commission did not consider the emerging case law of the European Court of Justice in the area of intellectual property rights.

The Treaty of Rome states in Article 222 that it shall 'in no way prejudice the rules in the Member States governing the system of property ownership'. Intellectual property rights, including copyright, may be viewed as a form of property ownership and it is obvious that the exercise of such rights may affect trade between the Member States. In the case of *Parke Davis v. Centrafarm,* which concerned patents, the Court recognized:[16]

The national rules relating to the protection of industrial

> property have not yet been unified within the Community. In the absence of such unification, the national character of the protection of industrial property and the variations between different legislative systems on this subject are capable of creating obstacles both to the free movement of the patented products and to competition within the common market.[16]

The particular rules of the Treaty which were at issue in *Parke Davis* were the rules on competition, contained in Articles 85 and 86 of the Treaty. Article 30 on the free movement of goods was the next provision against which the exercise of intellectual property rights would be tested and this occurred in the case of *DGG v. Metro*.[17] In this case a question was referred from a German Court concerning the exercise of a 'neighbouring right' of a sound-recording enterprise, DGG, under German law. DGG sought to invoke this law to prevent Metro from selling DGG's records in Germany; these records had previously been marketed in France by a subsidiary of DGG. The Court drew a distinction between the existence of intellectual property rights, which remained unaffected by the Treaty, and the exercise of such rights, which was subject to the rules of the Treaty. Thus the neighbouring right could not be enforced against Metro.[18]

A turning point in the development of the approach of the Court to issues of the exercise of intellectual property rights was the case of *Centrafarm v. Sterling Drug*.[19] In this case, concerning the exercise of patent rights to prevent imports of products from one Member State to another, the Court reaffirmed the distinction between the existence and exercise of intellectual property rights. The Court continued:

> Whereas an obstacle to the free movement of goods of this kind may be justified on the ground of protection of industrial property where such protection is invoked against a product coming from a Member State where it is not patentable and has been manufactured by third parties without the consent of the patentee . . . a derogation from the principle of the free movement of goods is not however justified where the product has been put onto the market in a legal manner by the patentee himself or with his consent in the Member State from which it has been imported.[20]

This principle, which would become known as the doctrine of

exhaustion of rights, would be applied to other forms of intellectual property rights. The Commission communication on culture can be criticized in that it failed to consider the possible implications of the doctrine on copyright, especially as this is significant from the viewpoint of the free movement of cultural goods.

In 1981 the doctrine of exhaustion of rights was applied to copyright in the case of *Music-Vetreib v GEMA*.[21] The case is significant in that it was the first time that the Court ruled expressly that copyright fell within the scope of the free movement of goods provisions of the Treaty. In Germany, GEMA, a collecting society, sought to collect the difference between royalties payable in Germany (8 per cent) and those in the United Kingdom (6.25 per cent) as a condition of allowing parallel imports. The Court concluded:

> National legislation whose application results in obstructing trade in sound recordings between Member States must be regarded as a measure having an effect equivalent to a quantitative restriction within the meaning of Article 30 of the Treaty. That is the case where such legislation permits a copyright management society to the distribution of sound recordings originating in another Member State on the basis of exclusive exploitation right which it exercises in the name of the copyright owner.[22]

In contrast to other areas of intellectual property, the Court avoided defining the specific subject-matter of copyright, although it did give some indication of what was covered.[23] The fact that the records were produced in the United Kingdom under a compulsory licence was not considered a factor in finding against GEMA.[24]

GEMA also confirms the decision of the Court reached in the case of *Coditel v. Ciné Vog* which was not concerned with the free movement of goods but the free provision of services under Article 59 of the Treaty.[25] The case concerned the licensing of a film to a company in Belgium, Ciné Vog, with the stipulation that the film could not be shown on television until forty months after the first performance in Belgian cinemas. A licence was also granted for Germany with no stipulation as to broadcasts on television. When broadcast on German television, it was picked up by Coditel and retransmitted directly in Belgium. Ciné Vog brought an action for infringement of copyright. The Court concluded that Ciné Vog's copyright had been infringed. The Court continued:

> Whilst Article 59 of the Treaty prohibits restrictions upon freedom to provide services, it does not thereby encompass limits upon the exercise of certain economic activities which have their origin in the application of national legislation for the protection of intellectual property, save where such application constitutes a means of arbitrary discrimination or a disguised restriction on trade between Member States. Such would be the case if that application enabled parties to an assignment of copyright to create artificial barriers to trade between Member States.[26]

The Court seemed to draw a distinction between the free movement of artistic works (for example, books) and cases where the essence of the copyright was to control a series of performances. In this latter case the relevant articles appear to be the provisions on the free movement of services rather than the free movement of goods.

Beyond the areas of copyright the Commission identified a number of areas of related rights, including a public lending right and a resale right for artists. In the area of public lending rights the Commission recommended the extension throughout the Community of the system applicable in Denmark and Germany. The system would allow additional resources to authors and publishers and provide a contribution to the literary sector in each Member State.[27] The Commission did not consider the negative effects of the proposal in that the system would require a charge to be made on libraries and borrowers. In spite of these problems at least one of the Member States introduced a public lending right after the Commission communication. The United Kingdom Public Lending Right Act of 1979 applies to all books, of at least thirty-two pages, written by authors who are EEC nationals lent out to the public by local library authorities.

The other proposal concerned resale rights benefitting 'creative artists in the plastic arts sector following the original sale of their works, where the selling price exceeds a certain level'. The payment arising from such rights would be a percentage of either the price obtained on successive sales of the work or the capital gain from one sale to the next. The Commission recommended a directive, to be issued under Article 100, to ensure the harmonization of the laws of the Member States in this area; only six of the then nine Member States at the time recognized resale rights. In the United Kingdom the Whitford Committee had refused to recommend the introduction of a resale right for primarily practical reasons.[28] The goal of the Commission proposals in this area was to improve the material situation of cultural workers so as to allow them to fulfil their cultural role. As a further indication that the Community valued the contribution of its cultural workers, the final area where the Treaty could be applied related to social problems of cultural workers, in particular protection by the social security system.[29]

For those areas which fell outside the application of the Treaty, the Commission envisaged specific Community contributions in the following areas: the preservation of architectural heritage; the development of cultural exchanges; increased co-operation between the cultural institutes of the Member States; and the promotion of socio-cultural activities at a European level.[30] Specific measures within these areas included such measures as the promotion of specialist training for restorers[31] and Community patronage for a youth orchestra.[32] These were to be areas where a specific Community contribution would be made to European culture and this was recognized in the draft Council resolution which concludes the communication. In addition, the Preamble to the draft resolution states the conviction that:

> the economic and social difficulties of the cultural sector can be progressively overcome by stricter application thereto of the EEC Treaty, and in particular the provisions of thereof regarding free trade, freedom of movement and establishment, tax harmonization, the harmonization of laws, and social measures.[33]

As for the substance of the draft resolution it merely called for Community action in the cultural sector to be based on the guidelines identified and discussed above. The resolution was not passed and no other action was taken in response to the communication, despite the favourable reaction of both the European Parliament and the Economic and Social Committee.[34]

The Commission communication emphasizes that a cultural policy is not being developed, rather there is to be Community action in the cultural sector. The majority of this action consists of the application of the Treaty rules to the particular problems facing trade in cultural goods and cultural workers. So attention would be paid to the free movement of cultural goods and services, the free movement of cultural workers plus associated rights and the harmonization of the laws of the Member States in these areas. Community competence in the cultural sector was thus seen as an extension of the economic and social provisions of the Treaty to this sector. As for additional action by the Community, this was to be limited to the four identified areas, for which the Parliament set aside a specific budgetary allocation. Action would therefore be complementary to that of the Member States and, as the Commission also recognized, complementary to that of other international organizations such as the Council of Europe.[35] As the Commission recognised in its 1982 assessment of its activities in the cultural sector:

> The Commission considered, and still considers, that Community action in the cultural sector should be both complementary and subsidiary to what is already being done internationally. There is therefore no duplication with the efficiently run activities of organizations like the Council of Europe, for which the development of culture is a prime objective.[36]

Community action in the Cultural sector, according to the 1977 communication, would be limited to highlighting the cultural dimension of existing Community policies and any additional measures would build on the activities of the Member States and the Council of Europe.

TOWARDS STRONGER ACTION

The 1982 assessment of Community action in the cultural sector is significant in that it resulted in proposals for stronger action in this area by identifying a number of priority areas of concern.[37] The four areas of concern are; freedom of trade in cultural goods; improving the living and working conditions of cultural workers; enlarging the audience; and conservation of the architectural heritage. What is interesting about the identification of these priority areas is that they mix the extension of the Treaty provisions to the cultural sector with the additional measures identified by the 1977 communication. Action is therefore both general – the application of the provisions of the Treaty – and specific – the application of specially designed measures.

In the area of freedom of trade in cultural goods, the Commission recognized that there may be justified restrictions on the free movement of goods under Article 36 of the Treaty. The traditional concept of 'national heritage' inherent in this exception, the Commission argued, should be expanded to become the new concept of

'Community heritage'.[38] For barriers to trade which could not be justified under Article 36, the Commission recognized that such barriers run counter to the interests of cultural workers, so a group of experts would be set up to examine national measures which could constitute barriers to trade.[39] The focus of concern in this area was not these barriers to trade but rather the administrative formalities of movement of cultural works from one Member State to another. Two regulations were proposed which would eliminate the negative effects of these formalities.[40] To ensure that this would not lead to a greater flow of trade in stolen works of art, the Commission returned to the idea floated in the 1977 communication of a record card for works of art.[41]

Just as the 1977 communication had failed to consider the scope of Article 36, the 1982 communication failed to discuss developments in the area of the free movement of goods since 1977. The most notable of these developments was the decision of the European Court of Justice in the *Cassis de Dijon* case.[42] The case concerned a requirement under German legislation that fruit liqueurs, like the Cassis which was to be imported in this case, could only be marketed if they contained a minimum alcohol content of 25 per cent. Cassis de Dijon has a minimum alcohol content between 15 and 20 per cent. The Court concluded:

> Obstacles to movement within the Community resulting from disparities between the national laws relating to the marketing of the products in question must be accepted in so far as those provisions may be recognised as being necessary in order to satisfy the mandatory requirements relating in particular to the effectiveness of fiscal supervision, the protection of public health, the fairness of commercial transactions and the defence of the consumer.[43]

The significance of this conclusion was that the Court made no reference to the issue of discrimination which had informed most of its previous decisions on the interpretation of Article 30. As a consequence of the decision, the non-discriminatory trade measures of the Member States will breach Article 30 unless they are necessary, and no more than is necessary, to satisfy one or more of the mandatory requirements. Furthermore, the Court made clear that the category of mandatory requirements was not limited to the four it had mentioned.

This case marked a major turning point in the approach of the

Court to the interpretation of Article 30 and in the approach of the Commission to the issue of harmonization. From the point of view of the free movement of cultural goods, the case raises the question whether or not the protection of culture could be classified as a mandatory requirement and so be used to restrict the free movement of such goods. The 1982 communication does not address this point and the Court, when presented with the question, also failed to give a direct answer. The Court was faced with the question in the case of *Cinéthèque*.[44] At issue in this case was a 1982 French law on audio-visual communication which provided that no film shown in the cinema could be simultaneously sold or hired as a video until twelve months after its release in the cinemas. The question facing the Court was whether this amounted to a breach of Articles 30, 34, 36 and 59 of the Treaty. According to the Court, no issue was raised under Article 59, so the problems relating to the law fell within Articles 30 to 36, the Court concluded that the measure was justified under those provisions.[45] What is significant about the decision is that it is the only case where a restriction falling under Article 30 or Article 34 has been justified without the Court specifying the grounds for justification.

Advocate General Slynn in delivering his opinion referred to the argument advanced by the Commission that, as films were part of contemporary culture, it was legitimate to adopt restrictions on the free movement of goods which would override the restrictions contained in Article 30. The justification for this was to preserve or support cultural activities. Advocate General Slynn considered this to be a very broad principle, even assuming that cultural objectives could constitute one of the mandatory requirements. Having already decided on other grounds that the law at issue fell outside Article 30, Advocate General Slynn concluded:

> If, therefore, I had not come to the conclusion that this law fell outside Article 30 for the first reason given, I would accept that it is capable of doing so if the measure adopted can be shown to be justified as being necessary for the maintenance of the film industry and the supply of films to the consumer. That objective is a legitimate one.[46]

Does this mean that the protection of culture is too broad a concept to be a mandatory requirement? After all, the Advocate General rejected the Commission's approach as being too broad and formulated the principle in terms of the 'maintenance of the film industry and the supply of films to the consumer'. Even this principle gives rise to questions. Which film industry is being supported – national, European or the entire film industry? Had the Court chosen to deal with the issue of culture then some indication would have been forthcoming.

The question which has to be asked is why did the Court not rule on this matter. Oliver offers the following explanation for the dilemma facing the Court:

> The problem is most delicate. On the one hand, the protection of culture is obviously a worthy objective which should have its place in Community law and which is by no means covered by the exception in Article 36 relating to 'the protection of national treasures having artistic, historic or archaeological value.' On the other hand, to bring whole sectors of commercial activity virtually outside Article 30 on the grounds that they involve the production of 'cultural' goods would be unthinkable. Moreover, 'culture' is notoriously difficult to define.[47]

The Court has consistently managed to avoid having to decide the question of the inclusion of the protection of culture within the mandatory requirements.[48] It is to be regretted that the Commission did not take the opportunity provided by the 1982 Communication to offer its opinion on this question.

The second priority area of improving the living and working conditions of cultural workers constituted an amalgamation of various areas from the 1977 communication. So within this area came the freedom of movement and establishment of cultural workers, the harmonization of taxation in the cultural sector and the harmonization of laws on copyright and related rights.[49] In this latter area, the Commission expressed concern about the ability of legislation to keep pace with technological development. This problem arose indirectly in the case of *Commission v. France*.[50] In this case the Commission argued that a levy introduced by a French law of 1976 on the sale of reprographic machines, either domestically produced or imported, was contrary to Article 9 of the Treaty. The proceeds of the levy were used to subsidize literature in France through the purchase of journals and new books and the translation of foreign works. The French government argued that the levy served a dual purpose; to assist creativity in written form and to strengthen the entire protective scope of copyright law. The case was dismissed as unfounded, largely because the levy constituted a tax (and so Article 95 was relevant) rather than a levy on imports. The Court noted on the problem of technology: 'It is not disputed that the widespread use of reprography for the reproduction of printed works results in the loss not only by authors but also by publishers of the monetary gain which national copyright law guarantees them'.[51]

The French legislation undoubtedly was considered when the Commission recommended the introduction a component in the selling price of reprographic equipment in the 1977 Communication.[52] The Commission returned to this proposal in 1982 when it envisaged specific legislation which would protect cultural workers from the adverse effects of technological development on their existing intellectual property rights.[53] Further legislation was also envisaged to counteract the associated problem of piracy and to harmonize the differing copyright periods in the Member States.[54] The Commission also returned to the proposal made in its 1977 Communication relating to the resale rights of creative artists in the plastic arts sector.[55] Finally, it envisaged as an ultimate objective unlimited collective authors' rights to promote the greater dissemination of culture.[56]

In other areas of improving the living and working conditions of cultural workers, the Commission pointed to an amendment introduced by the Parliament to the 1982 Budget an article allowing for the promotion of the cultural sector. This stated: 'The purpose of this article is to contribute towards the financing of a variety of projects and pilot schemes aimed at offering the public a wider variety of forms of cultural expression, thereby reducing the level of unemployment among cultural workers'.[57] As part of the plan to reduce the level of unemployment the Commission envisaged a series of training and retraining programmes for cultural workers. In relation to advanced training the Commission envisaged making use of Article 50 of the Treaty on the exchange of young workers. Particular emphasis was given to the contribution which the promotion of culture could make to regional policy in the Community.[58] Once in employment it was considered important that the tax system should be amended to reflect the reality of the living and working conditions of cultural workers.[59]

Moving beyond the strict application of the Treaty to the cultural sector, the Commission's other priority areas were widening the audience and conserving the architectural heritage.[60] In the former area, technological development, especially in the audio-visual field, was seen as offering cultural workers more opportunities for work allowing them to enhance their earnings. However, the Commission considered that co-ordination between the Member States was necessary to ensure that maximum advantage would accrue from these developments. Other specific measures included cultural exchanges, a European Film Festival and a European Music Year.[61] In relation to the conservation of architectural heritage, among the measures which the Commission recommended included tax relief on the conservation of private architectural heritage and annual conservation operations. This aspect of the promotion of the culture of the Europe by the Community would also contribute to the development of the environmental policy of the Community.[62]

The Commission concluded that:

> There is no pretension to exert a direct influence on culture itself or to launch a European cultural policy; what stronger Community action in the cultural sector means in effect is linking its four constituents . . . more closely to the economic and social roles which the Treaty assigns to the Community, to the resources – mainly legislative – that it provides, and to various Community policies.[63]

Like the 1977 Communication, no cultural policy is envisaged, merely the application of the Treaty to the cultural sector. Several additional measures were also contemplated and in all the areas specific additional objectives were outlined; for example, cultural workers and regional policy and architectural heritage and the environment. However, in contrast to the previous Communication, the 1982 document elicited a response in the form of the first meeting of the Ministers of Culture of the Member States within the Council.

Although the first formal Council meeting did not take place in 1984, there had been informal meetings before then and the Commission communication was discussed before 1984. The first informal meeting was the result of an invitation of the Italian and French Ministers of Culture and was held in September 1982. The outcome was a joint press release which declared the intention of the Ministers of Culture to have further meetings.[64] There was also general agreement that more funds should be given to safeguard cultural heritage and ensure that Europe's film and audio-visual industries are competitive. Before the next informal meeting and the first formal meeting of the Council, there was further encouragement to the development of Community action in the cultural sector as a result of the 1983 European Council meeting in Stuttgart.[65] The Solemn Declaration issued as a result of the meeting committed the Community and the Member States to promote 'closer co-operation on cultural matters in order to affirm the awareness of a common cultural heritage as part of a European identity'.[66]

Further guidance on the scope of this cultural co-operation was provided by the listing of eight areas where Community action would be encouraged or facilitated.[67] Among the areas listed included an examination of the advisability of undertaking joint action to protect, promote and safeguard cultural heritage and an examination of the possibility of promoting joint activities in the dissemination of culture, in particular as regards audio-visual methods. In all of the areas, it was envisaged that the action of the Community would complement the activities of the Council of Europe.[68] As the President of the Commission noted at the time: 'it is encouraging that in the face of enormous difficulties which could have led to disintegration, the Heads of State and of Government have called for more integration and a relaunch of the European Community'.[69] At the next informal meeting of the Ministers of Culture of the Member States in November 1983, the Commission communication and the cultural section of the Solemn Declaration were discussed.[70]

In relation to the Commission communication, the Council identified priorities for future Commission action in the cultural sector. These were the social protection of cultural workers; action to adjust the intellectual property rights of cultural workers to reflect technological development; establishment of a list of the basic literary works of each Member State; the development of a grant system for young artists; and the establishment of record cards for all stolen works of art. In response to the Solemn Declaration, the Ministers made a number of suggestions to give effect to the co-operation envisaged by the Declaration. These suggestions were discussed at the first formal meeting of the Council and Ministers of Cultural Affairs meeting within the Council in June 1984. Broad agreement was reached on the following points:

(i) meetings and exchanges between individuals;
(ii) fostering the teaching of languages within the Community;
(iii) improved reciprocal knowledge of the other Member States, their inhabitants, their culture and their history;
(iv) cultural cooperation in non-member countries.[71]

Possible intensification of European cultural co-operation was not, however, forthcoming as was shown by the second meeting of the Ministers of Culture in November 1984 when a draft resolution on this was not adopted owing to the reservations of one Member State.[72]

In spite of this, agreement was reached on a work programme for the specific cultural projects set out in the draft resolution, for example, a European Music Year and a European youth orchestra. It was agreed that there should be greater recourse to the European Social Fund in respect of cultural workers.[73] The aim here was to alleviate the unemployment and underemployment in this sector by improving opportunities for vocational training and retraining. It was also agreed that there should be an annual event – the 'European City of Culture'.[74] To implement aspects of the Solemn Declaration it was further agreed that there should be a European sculpture competition.[75] Whereas these measures were in the form of resolutions of the Ministers responsible for Cultural Affairs meeting within the Council, in 1984 there were to be other resolutions with respect to cultural action passed by representatives of the governments of the Member States. All of these were concerned with the audio-visual sector.

One of the resolutions was concerned with measures to combat audio-visual pirating. After repeating the arguments concerning piracy, which had been noted by the Commission, the first paragraph of the resolution stated that the Member States: 'will endeavour to ratify, quickly, if they have not already yet done so, those international Conventions which they consider likely, by the reciprocal provisions which they contain, to facilitate the initiation of procedures against acts of audio-visual pirating'.[76] The relevant Conventions were the 1961 Rome Convention for the protection of performers, producers of phonograms and broadcasting organizations, the 1971 Geneva Convention for the protection of producers of phonograms against unauthorized duplication, and the 1974 Brussels Convention. In addition to accession to these conventions, it was recommended that national legislation in this area should be strengthened.

The fact that these measures were passed in the form of resolutions of the representatives of the governments of the Member States, indicates an unwillingness to consider the subject matter of the resolutions as falling within Community action in the cultural sector. This was despite the fact that the resolution of audio-visual piracy recognized the Community dimension of the problem.

However, intergovernmental action on cultural co-operation had been anticipated by the Solemn Declaration on European Union. As a result it could be argued that future co-operation would be on two or possibly three levels; through agreement at Community level, through agreement at the Council of Europe level and through agreement at the intergovernmental level between the Member States. Yet, by the next meeting within the Council of the Ministers responsible for Cultural Affairs in May 1985, the Member States had reaffirmed their intention to cooperate regularly and to develop cultural activities at Community level.[77]

Evidence of this increased co-operation emerged in the form of resolutions of the Council and the Ministers with responsibility for Cultural Affairs meeting within the Council on collaboration between libraries in the field of data processing,[78] on the access of young people to museums and cultural events[79] and on transnational cultural itineraries.[80] Although increasing use was being made of the Community framework, it could not be said that the action taken was substantial. Questions over the competence of the Community in this area, which seemed to lie behind the adoption of the resolution on audio-visual piracy, continued to impede progress in Community action in the cultural sector. As in the initial stages of action on education policy, there was a certain reluctance to allow the rapid development of Community action and Member States remained anxious to retain their sovereignty in this area. However, as in the case of education, further impetus to the development of Community action in the cultural sector emerged from the need to create a People's Europe and the drive to complete the Internal Market by 1993.

'*A FRESH BOOST*'

In the Foreword to the 1987 Commission document entitled 'A Fresh Boost for Culture in the European Community', the Commissioner responsible for Culture commented:

> Keen to build on the achievements of recent years, the Commission is convinced that increased cultural activity is now a political as well as a social and economic necessity, given the twin goals of completing the internal market by 1992 and progressing from a People's Europe to European Union.[81]

This document constitutes a new start for action by the Community in the cultural sector. Before discussing the impact of the goal of completion of the Internal Market by January 1993, the report of the *ad hoc* Committee on a People's Europe, the Adonnino Report, will be discussed.

The *ad hoc* Committee was established by the European Council meeting at Fontainbleau in June 1984.[82] It was given the mandate of pinpointing action which would enable the Community to respond to 'the expectations of the peoples of Europe by adopting measures to strengthen and promote its identity and its image both for its citizens and the rest of the world'. The first report was submitted to the European Council meeting in Brussels in March 1985 and concentrated on measures to promote the free movement of persons throughout the Community. A further report was requested for the next European Council and would concentrate on measures to add a new political, cultural and social dimension to the Community.[83] The second Adonnino Report had a specific section devoted to culture and communication, which recognized that through action in these areas 'which are essential to European identity and the Community's image in the minds of its people, that support for the advancement of Europe can and must be sought'.[84] Four particular areas were highlighted for special attention. The first of these areas was the audio-visual sector, where developments in technology were seen as necessitating greater encouragement at Community level of European audio-visual co-productions. This would improve the competitiveness of the European cultural sector. Further measures in this area included the promotion of a European Film and Television Year. The remaining areas included proposals for the establishment of a European Academy of Science, Technology and Art and a Euro-lottery and measures to ensure access to museums and cultural events by young people throughout the Community.

At the next meeting within the Council of the Ministers with responsibility for Cultural Affairs after the endorsement of the Adonnino Report by the European Council various resolutions were passed. For example, there was a resolution on the European Cinema and Television Year, as recommended by the Adonnino Report.[85] Further resolutions referred to the 1983 Solemn Declaration on European Union (the protection of Europe's architectural heritage)[86] and the 1982 Commission communication (conservation of works of arts and artefacts and on business sponsorship of cultural activities).[87] In the 1988 review of the progress towards the achievement of a People's Europe, the Commission noted:

> Anxious to enhance Europe's cultural potential in all its diversity, the Commission has embarked on a long-term operation to mobilize wider audiences, decentralize the arts and develop exchanges within the Community. The best examples are the setting up of the European Youth Orchestra and the development of the European City of Culture.[88]

The Commission also indicated that the experience which had been gained so far would be the basis of a plan to give a fresh boost to cultural activity to cultural activity in the Community during the period 1988 to 1992.

Additional assistance to the formation of this plan emerged from a conference held in Florence in March 1987 on culture and its relations with technology and the economy.[89] There was clear recognition that co-operation at the European level was necessary to enable Europe to meet the challenges of the future, especially the technological challenge. Two points emerged from the conference. First, the increasing economic significance of cultural activities. It was estimated that some 4 million people were employed in this sector generating between 3 and 6 per cent of the Gross Domestic Product of the Member States. Secondly, given the increasing economic significance of culture, it should be seen as a common denominator in all areas of economic activity. Investment in culture would, therefore, become increasingly significant in the future.[90] Building on the outcome of the Conference the Commission noted:

> A fresh boost for culture in the Community is a political necessity. There is growing concern within the Community as to the future of cultural cooperation in Europe. This concerns reflects an increasing awareness of what is at stake in the interrelationship between the economy, technology and culture.[91]

This fresh boost would be in the form of a definition of general guidelines and a priority programme for the period 1988 to 1992.

In one sense the general guidelines were an attempt by the Commission to clarify the scope of Community powers in the cultural sector. Existing provisions of the Treaty could be used to define the scope of the Community's powers. Thus there would be a continuation of past activities; the free movement of cultural goods, the freedom of movement and establishment of cultural workers and the emergence of a competitive cultural industry. Other Community policies would also have a Community dimension, for example, the conservation of the architectural heritage would be part of the environmental policy of the Community. Finally, action already begun by the Community would continue, for example, the European City of Culture scheme. The Commission concluded:

> These three lines of action do not, however, make up the entire cultural challenge facing the Community. The complexity and scale of this challenge and the minimal financial resources – whether public or private – available at regional, national and Community level suggest that those engaged in cultural activity need to work more closely together.[92]

The Commission would therefore act as a co-ordinator of the efforts in the cultural sector, thus ensuring a higher profile for Community activities in the cultural sector.

In terms of the framework programme for the period up to the end of 1992, five fields of activity were envisaged: the creation of a European cultural area; the promotion of the European audio-visual industry; access to cultural resources; training in the cultural sector; and dialogue with the rest of the world. In each of these areas various proposals for action were outlined. The Commission communication was discussed at an informal meeting of the Ministers of Culture in Copenhagen in December 1987. It was welcomed as 'an excellent basis for the work ahead'.[93] However, the areas for priority action were not to be those identified by the Commission. Instead there were to be three areas of further action; the audio-visual sector, books and the training of cultural workers. At the next formal meeting of the Council and of the Ministers responsible for Cultural Affairs meeting within the Council, four areas were selected; in addition to those identified at Copenhagen, priority would also be given to the issue of business sponsorship of cultural activities.[94] Each of these four areas will now be examined.

The Audio-visual sector

The promotion of the audio-visual sector was identified by both the Commission and the Council as a priority area. The

Commission pointed to the need to take concerted action at the European level and the efforts which it had made in the past in this area.[95] In addition to the existing directive on the adoption of a common technical standard for satellite broadcasting,[96] proposals had been made for a directive on broadcasting which would cover the free movement of television and radio broadcasts and the promotion of television productions. A further directive on broadcasting would provide for a percentage of programming time to be devoted to programmes of Community origin and impose a requirement on television companies to allocate a percentage of their budget to financing work for independent producers.

As part of the drive to complete the Internal Market, agreement had already been reached on the Media Programme. This programme would encourage the creation of a European film distribution system and assist in the introduction of new production technologies into the audio-visual industry. Other existing measures which fell within the scope of this area included the European Cinema and Television Year, which had been agreed on in 1986. The implementation of this 1986 resolution had led to two proposals which the Commission considered deserved especial attention. First, a proposal to establish a European Cinema and Audio-visual Arts Academy. The Academy would be based on US Academy of Motion Picture Arts and Sciences.[97] The second proposal was for the creation of an Audio-visual Charter laying down authors' rights. One outcome of both these proposals was the perceived need to ensure that the Community would be able to respond to the advent of the third television generation – high definition television. This was not considered a priority sector by the Council who limited themselves to commenting on the Media Programme. It also promised to consider 'other actions relating to the promotion of the audio-visual sector with all the attention which the importance of this sector warrants'.[98]

An indication of the importance of this sector was provided by the European Council in 1988 when they pointed out that:

> it is extremely important to strengthen efforts, including co-operation to develop Europe's audio-visual capacity, whether with regard to the free movement of programmes, the promotion of the European High Definition Television system, or, to a policy of encouraging creativity, production and broadcasting so as to provide an opportunity of demonstrating the richness and diversity of European Culture.[99]

An Annex to this declaration from the Rhodes European Council set out the French proposals for the development of a European audio-visual area and the promotion, experimentation and development of high definition television. This constituted a reversal for the Council who had not highlighted this area. The 1990 Commission communication established the broad parameters of audio-visual policy as being threefold; establishing the rules of the game, the technology of the programme industry and the creation of an audio-visual Europe.[100]

As part of the drive to establish the rules of the game for the European audio-visual market, Directive 89/552 co-ordinates the laws of the Member States on the pursuit of television broadcasting activities.[101] Based on Articles 57(2) and 66, the directive is designed to remove obstacles to the free movement of television services throughout the Community.[102] Article 1 defines the television services covered by the directive as including television broadcasting and television advertising. Member States according to Article 2 'shall ensure freedom of reception and shall not restrict retransmission on their territory of television broadcasts from other Member States'. The directive does contain a number of reasons for limiting the reception and retransmission, for example, Article 22 provides that Member States shall 'ensure that broadcasts do not contain any incitement to hatred on grounds of race, sex, religion and nationality'.

Under Chapter III of the directive various measures are advocated to promote the distribution and production of television programmes. For instance, under Article 4 Member States shall ensure that broadcasters reserve 'a majority proportion of their transmission time' for European works.[103] Further incentives to European works are provided by Article 5 which requires broadcasters to reserve 10 per cent of either their programming budget or transmission time for 'European works created by producers who are independent of broadcasters'. Chapter IV of the directive contains provisions designed to promote the free movement of television advertising and sponsorship.[104] The main provisions of this chapter are designed to restrict the content of television advertising; for example, advertising of tobacco products is prohibited and advertising of alcoholic products is subject to strict criteria. Article 18 of the directive restricts the amount of advertising to 15 per cent of daily transmission time. The Member States were required to implement the directive by October 1991 by which time the Council had passed further measures implementing the threefold audiovisual policy envisaged by the Commission.

The second aspect of the policy – the technology of the programme industry – is evident in Council Decision 89/337 on high definition television (HDTV).[105] The decision establishes a series of objectives which were to form the basis of a comprehensive strategy for the introduction of HDTV services in Europe. Objective 1, for example, stated that every effort should be made to ensure that 'the European industry develops in time all the technology, components and equipment required for the launching of HDTV services'. The target date set for the launch of HDTV services was 1992. An action plan for the introduction of HDTV services was to be drawn up by the Commission in consultation with the Member States, and would allow for the participation of other European countries. By 1992 it was necessary to pass a directive on the adoption of standards for satellite broadcasting of television signals, Directive 92/38.[106]

The purpose of the directive is to create a convergence of standards in relation to the future development of HDTV. The previous decisions in this area had led to the creation of different standards for different types of satellite broadcasting.[107] By establishing a common standard investment would be concentrated in one area with the result that the competitiveness of the European audio-visual industry would be promoted. The standard chosen was the HD-MAC and D2-MAC standard. The Member States are required under the directive to take all the necessary steps to ensure that as from 1994 all new television sets, domestic satellite receivers and video-recorders for sale or rent in the Community possess the relevant decoder.[108] Under Article 5, the Member States are also required to take all appropriate measures to ensure that all cable networks, either existing or new, have the necessary capacity to transmit the HD-MAC signals to their subscribers.

In June 1993 the Council passed a resolution on the development of technology and standards in the field of advanced television services.[109] The Resolution reinforces the measures discussed above through the approval of a framework agreement for an action plan for the introduction of advanced television services in Europe. The framework agreement seeks to promote the HD-MAC standard by providing Community funding of 160 million ECU. This funding will cover up to 50 per cent of the cost differential between the costs of producing and broadcasting in the customary format and the new format. The action plan will expire in four years. Finally, the Council also called for the revision of Directive 92/38 and required the Commission to present a communication and proposals on the future development of digital television.

The third and final aspect of the audio-visual policy can be seen in Decision 90/685 which gave Council endorsement to the continuation of the Media Programme also granted financial assistance to the scheme for the period 1991 to 1995.[110] The 200 million ECU allocated to the Media Programme would be used to implement the objectives listed in Article 2. These objectives relate to various aspects of promoting the adaptation of the European audio-visual industry to enable that industry to meet technological challenges. Annex I lists the six measures which can be taken to implement these objectives: distribution mechanisms; improvement of production conditions; stimulation of financial investment; improving the economic and commercial management abilities of professionals; development of potential in countries with small audiovisual production capacities and/or with a limited geographical and linguistic area; and participation in Audio-visual Eureka projects.

Annex II goes on to outline the involvement of the Community in Audio-visual Eureka, which is a transnational co-operation structure in the audio-visual area between twenty-six European countries and the Commission. Audio-visual Eureka is a structure promoting projects in production. Co-operation between Media and Audio-visual Eureka had been advocated at the European Council meeting in Strasbourg in December 1989.[111] The Community, according to Annex II, can participate in Audio-visual Eureka projects which are concerned with the measures outlined in Annex I.[112] The Commission is also required to open existing projects to nationals from non-member countries. The Commission has the responsibility for implementing the programme and in this task it will be assisted by an Advisory Committee. Specific operations have already been implemented under the programme marking a continuation of operations under the pilot programme.[113]

The Book Sector

The Commission Communication did not envisage that the book sector deserved especial attention, rather it was part of their programme to create a European Cultural Area. In this respect they did suggest a policy for publishing which would seek to reconcile the conflicting interests in this sector. Some indication of this conflict emerged in the 1985 Commission communication to the Council on the European dimension with regard to books.[114]

The aim of this communication was to create an environment in which books could be 'more easily written, published, sold and read in the Community and be made more accessible to the greatest possible number of readers'.[115] To achieve this aim the Commission envisaged progress in a number of areas. First, the creation of a framework for discussion and consultation so as to identify the particular problems which would have to be confronted. To this end the Commission established an Advisory Committee on Books.[116] The second area, which would become the main area of Commission concern over the next few years, was book pricing. In this area the various arrangements in each of the Member States with respect to pricing were examined and it was pointed out that should the arrangements have effects on trade between Member States then provisions of the Treaty may be relevant. This had already been established by the European Court of Justice in two cases. The first of these cases, *VBVB & VBBB v. Commission*, concerned the application of Article 85, the main competition provision of the Treaty.[117]

In this case, VBBB, a Dutch association of publishers, and VBVB, a Flemish association of publishers had notified the Commission in 1962 of an agreement laying down rules relating to the book trade between the Netherlands and Flanders which they had concluded in 1949 and which had been amended in 1958. The provisions of that agreement involved an exclusive dealing undertaking and a resale price mechanism. In 1978 the Commission sent their objections to the agreement to the parties and in 1981 they decided that the agreement was contrary to Article 85(1). The parties to the agreement applied for a declaration that the Commission decision was void for reasons of procedural irregularities and of substance. In relation to the latter, the parties argued that the decision breached Article 10 of the European Convention on Human Rights, guaranteeing freedom of expression, Article 10 bis of the Paris Convention for the Protection of Industrial Property and that Article 85(1) was not applicable.[118]

After concluding that there was an agreement between associations of undertakings within the meaning of Article 85, the Court moved on to examine the substantive arguments of the parties.[119] On the issue involving Article 10 of the European Convention on Human Rights, it concluded that it had not been breached.[120] Article 10 bis of the Paris Convention was then analysed by the Court. It was argued that a system of resale price maintenance was necessary to prevent the practice of loss leading and, as a result, unfair competition. In response, the Court noted: The fact that a system of resale price maintenance may have the incidental effect of preventing unfair competition of the kind described by the applicants is not, however, a sufficient reason for failing to apply Article 85(1) to a whole sector of the market such as the book trade.[121] There were other remedies for the abuses argued by the applicants and the fact that such abuses existed could not, therefore, justify the infringement of the Community rules on competition. The substantive arguments of the parties and the application were totally dismissed.

It is interesting to note that the Court assiduously avoided any mention of the cultural overtones of its decision. In its decision, the Commission had considered that cultural values could only be taken into account in a negative manner.[122] In response to a question from the Court, the Commission stated that 'Article 85(3) does not permit the Commission to conduct a cultural policy'.[123] This was discussed by the Advocate General who concluded that 'there can therefore never be any question of the absolute priority of cultural over economic considerations' in the application of Article 85(3).[124] Despite the opportunity provided by the case, the Court made no comments on the relationship between cultural policy and the rules on competition. This reluctance is also evident in the second case, *Leclerc v. Au Blé Vert*, concerning the application of Article 30, although Article 85 was also discussed.[125] This was a preliminary reference concerning the compatibility of a French law on book prices with various provisions of Community law.

The relevant law required all publishers or importers of books to fix the retail price for books which they publish or import. Retailers must then charge an effective price for sales to the public of between 95 and 100 per cent of that price. Failure to do so may result in civil or criminal proceedings against the offending party. Civil proceedings were brought against Leclerc, a chain of low-price retail outlets, for selling books at prices below those fixed by law. Leclerc argued that Article 85 had been infringed, whereas the French government considered the relevant provision to be Article 30.[126] The Court considered that the French law did not detract from the effectiveness of Article 85.[127] It continued:

> It follows that, as Community laws stands, Member States' obligations under Article 5 of the EEC Treaty in conjunction

> with Articles 3(f) and 85, are not specific enough to preclude them from enacting legislation to the type at issue on competition in the retail prices of books, provided that such legislation is consonant with other specific Treaty provision, in particular those concerning the free movement of goods.[128]

After analysing the law, the Court concluded that as it led to differences in treatment between domestic and imported books Article 30 had been breached. The French government's attempt to justify the measure by pleading the mandatory requirement of consumer protection, referring in particular to the need to protect role of books as a cultural media, was rejected.[129] Once again the Court avoided the opportunity of ruling on the cultural issues raised by the case.[130]

Commenting on these two cases, the Commission concluded: 'The Commission has no intention of intervening in the cultural policy choices made by Member States, always provided of course that these choices do not result in measures being taken which conflicts with Community law'.[131] It then went on to outline four possible arrangements for a Community framework system for book prices.[132] By 1988 no progress had been made on the adoption of any of these arrangements and the Commission promised to review the situation and possible remedies on a periodic basis.[133]

The remaining areas identified by the Commission were the promotion of translation, measures to assist libraries and the simplification of customs formalities for books. The Commission returned to these areas in 1988 when it outlined its policy for publishing. The policy also proposed priority action in other areas, notably, the need for Community rules on reproduction and the harmonization of procedures for the suppression of piracy. In their outline of the priority areas, the Council considered all aspects of this sector should be the subject of examination with a view to adopting appropriate proposals.[134] Reference was made to the earlier Resolution of 1985 on collaboration between libraries in the field of data processing and to the 1987 resolution on the promotion of translation of important works of European culture.[135] This resolution emerged from the section on cultural co-operation in the Solemn Declaration on European Union and the 1985 Commission communication on the European dimension with regard to books. The resolution encouraged the undertaking of pilot schemes to provide support for translation, with special attention to the translation from minority European languages.

The Council in 1988 urged the launching of such pilot schemes as soon as possible and in 1989 a further resolution of the Council and the Ministers responsible for Cultural Affairs meeting within the Council launched the pilot projects for a five-year period.[136] Total finance available to the schemes amounts to 1 million ECU and the guidelines favour the translation of works in minority Community languages.[137] This resolution was the result of a further Commission communication entitled 'Books and Reading: A Cultural Challenge for Europe'.[138] In addition to the pilot projects, the resolution also approved a series of actions by the Community to promote books and reading, ranging from a European Literary Prize to scholarships and travel awards for courses for literary translators to a campaign to increase public awareness of books and reading. At the same time as passing the resolution, the Ministers also held a discussion on the effect of the completion of the Internal Market on books and reading. The conclusions reached stressed that in the absence of an alternative system of book pricing acceptable to all the Member States, the existing national policies in this area would continue. The need to ensure the compatibility of these arrangements with the EC rules on competition was emphasized.[139]

Training in the Cultural Sector

The third priority area identified by the Council in 1988 was training in the cultural sector and in particular, the training of sound and vision specialists and restoration specialists.[140] This was a specific section of the Commission communication, although they did envisage action across a broader range of activities. In the areas highlighted by the Council, the Commission considered that the training of sound and vision specialists would contribute to the competitiveness of the audio-visual sector. In relation to the training of restoration specialists, the Commission pointed out that this had been one of the pillars of Community action on culture.[141] The way forward was to be the provision of financial support for scholarships and prizes.

The other areas of training identified by the Commission were for the benefit of cultural administrators, journalists and programme planners and translators and interpreters. As the Commission recognized: 'Training for the cultural sector must be available for all since it provides a guarantee that traditions will be preserved and artistic creativity encouraged, but it is also an essential investment if young people are to adapt to the new information and communication technologies'.[142] The Commission envisaged the creation of a specific mechanism to boost its general training efforts in the cultural sector and in 1990 it presented a Communication on Vocational Training in the Arts field.[143] The role of the Commission in this area was seen as that of a catalyst promoting co-operation in the context of the common vocational training policy.

Particular emphasis was given to existing Community programmes in the area of vocational training and education, for example, Comett and Erasmus. These programmes were designed to cover more than the arts field, so the programmes were not sufficiently tailored to the problems of the arts sector. In addition, the Commission highlighted the role which the structural funds could play with respect to the improvement of competitiveness of European cultural activities and the elimination of regional disparities.[144] Once again, this was seen as ancillary to the main purpose of such assistance. The Commission considered the best way forward was, therefore, the development of training programmes for specific areas rather than the general mechanism envisaged in the 1988 communication. The areas chosen for specific action were those identified by the Council, the audio-visual sector and conservation and restoration, plus the area of translation.

In relation to training in the audio-visual sector it was pointed out that the pilot phase of the Media Programme had training as one of its central activities.[145] The Commission recommended the intensification of this activity in its proposal for a second Media Programme.[146] In April 1991 the Commissioner responsible for Cultural Affairs opened the Media Business School in Madrid; the school will set up training projects in Member States which can prepare audio-visual professionals to cope with the demands imposed by the Single Market.[147] In the area of the training of cultural workers in conservation and restoration, the Commission indicated that the Council of Europe and other international organizations, had already devoted a considerable amount of energy in the promotion of such training. Community activity would, therefore, be limited to the programmes already in existence, such as Erasmus, and to ensuring co-ordination between the activities of the Member States and the relevant international organizations.[148] The final specific area, the training of translators, was considered important as a result of the connection with activities in one of the other priority areas – the book sector. As previously noted, the Council and the Ministers responsible for Cultural Affairs meeting within the Council had passed a resolution on the promotion of translation of important works of European culture and a pilot scheme had been introduced to provide financial assistance for translators of contemporary literary works. In addition, the resolution concerning the promotion of books and reading had called for the creation of a prize for the best translation of literary works.[149] Given the encouragement which these resolutions gave to the promotion of translation, a training scheme for translators was almost inevitable. Support for existing translation centres was stepped up and a plan of action called for the identification of existing problems in the area and potential solutions.[150]

The Commission communication was discussed at the November 1990 meeting of the Council and the Ministers responsible for Cultural Affairs meeting within the Council. In welcoming the communication, the Council, in addition to repeating their call for specific measures in the area already called for, urged greater co-operation between the Community and other international organizations, particularly the Council of Europe.[151] Existing programmes in the field of vocational training and education would be considered in the Commission's review of the situation and needs in the field of training for the arts. One positive result of these conclusions was the 1991 resolution on the training of arts administrators. As the Preamble of this resolution notes:

> the extension of the sphere of cultural activity, the closer relationship brought about with the economic aspects of development and the diverse levels at which it must be carried out and sustained (regional, inter-regional, transfrontier, as well as national and internationally), generate a need for improved training for all those involved in the promotion of the arts.[152]

The substance of the resolution called for greater encouragement under existing programmes in the area of vocational training and education to the exchange of information about arts training, the mobility of arts administrators and networks of training centres for arts administrators. The resolution concludes by calling on the Commission to co-operate 'more closely with the Council of Europe and Unesco so as to develop concrete measures to strengthen the European dimension' of training for arts administrators. Despite being a priority area no further action has been taken since 1991.

Business Sponsorship

The final area of priority designated by the Council and the Ministers responsible for Cultural Affairs meeting within the Council was that of business sponsorship.[153] reference was made in the resolution to the previous Resolution on this issue in 1986.[154] In this latter resolution, after noting that business sponsorship can enhance the cultural heritage the Ministers agreed to encourage:

(i) the promotion of greater business sponsorship of cultural activities within the Member States of the European Community, by calling attention to sponsorship as an activity which provides benefits to both parties, as well as helping to enhance cultural and economic activity;
(ii) consideration of the introduction within their own countries of measures to promote suitable sponsorship schemes;
(iii) the setting up of organizations to advise and help those businesses and arts which are interested in sponsorship;
(iv) the development of links between the sponsorship organizations concerned;
(v) the sharing of information on current sponsorship activities, thus permitting an assessment of the need for future initiatives.

It was envisaged that companies with strong European interests would be interested in transnational arts activities and the improvement of opportunities for cultural exchanges. The resolution concludes by noting that the Commission intended to contribute to the realization of measures in this area.

By the 1988 the Commission seemed to have made limited progress. It repeated the need 'to advance in the direction' identified by the 1986 resolution.[156] It did propose to focus Community activities not on companies with strong European interests but in the area of sponsorship by small business and industry. This would be accomplished by the adoption of Community legislation on taxation and special support to national 'Foundations for the Promotion of the Arts'. To assist these foundations, a European databank was to be established; this would be gradually extended to cover the other countries in the Council of Europe. The proposal for adoption of Community legislation on taxation did not progress, given that it involved changes to direct taxation, which is not an area of direct Community competence. Special support for national foundations was provided by the appointment by the Commission of an Association for Business Sponsorship of the

Arts. Due to the work of this body, in 1991 the European Committee for Business Arts and Culture, which links business sponsorship bodies from a number of Member States and some EFTA countries, came into being.[157]

Further Commission activity involved the calling of a conference held in Lisbon in April 1992 on the issue of 'Business Sponsorship of the Arts in Europe'.[158] In an era when public sponsorship of the arts is diminishing, it was considered essential to increase private sponsorship. The role of the Commission, and indeed the Community, in this area would be that of facilitator. A number of points of interest emerged from the Conference. Although changes had been made in some of the Member States to the taxation system to promote business sponsorship, this in itself was not considered sufficient. Further action was considered necessary and this action would be national and exhortatory in character. Only after the development of a national framework would sponsorship develop satisfactorily at a European level. In the interim the role of the Community would be to collect and collate relevant information – for example, on tax arrangements and intellectual property issues. The next step was left to the meeting of the Council and the Ministers with responsibility for Cultural Affairs meeting within the Council in 1992. No further action was taken in this area.

Other Areas

The Council and the Ministers with responsibility for Cultural Affairs meeting within the Council having highlighted four priority areas noted that these areas were 'without prejudice to actions which they consider desirable in other areas'.[159] Indeed, the Commission communication had argued for action across a much broader range of activities. Perhaps the most surprising omission from the list of priorities was action to complete the cultural aspects of the Internal Market. The Commission had advocated a range of measures which they considered necessary to promote the free movement of goods, services and people in the cultural sector in the run-up to 1992.[160] Chief among these measures was the presentation of proposals for the definition of criteria which the Member States would use to identify 'national treasures' to which Article 36 of the Treaty could be applied and the implementation of procedures to guarantee the protection of national treasures. These proposals were duly submitted.[161]

The proposals were discussed at the November 1990 meeting of the Council and the Ministers with responsibility for Cultural

Affairs. It was noted that with the abolition of controls on the free movement of goods at the end of 1992, trade in cultural goods would increase. The only protection would be afforded by Article 36 and the Member States agreed to a further examination of the impact of 1992 on the cultural aspect of this provision.[162] The end result of this further examination, and the Commission proposals, was the enactment of two measures related to the protection of national treasures. The first of these measures to be passed was Regulation 3911/92 on the export of cultural goods.[163] The primary purpose of the regulation is to ensure that exports of cultural goods are subject to uniform controls at the external borders of the Community.

The means chosen to achieve this purpose is the requirement that all exports of cultural goods outside the customs territory of the Community be subject to the presentation of an export licence.[164] The licence, which is valid throughout the Community, is issued by a competent authority in the Member State in which the cultural object is located. The licence may be refused according to Article 2(2) 'where the cultural goods in question are covered by legislation protecting national treasures of artistic, historical or archaeological value in the Member State concerned'. The Annex to the regulation lists the categories of cultural objects which are covered by the regulation. The objects covered range from certain archaeological objects more than 100 years old to pictures and paintings to books more than 100 years old. Financial thresholds for certain categories of cultural goods are also set out in the Annex; for example, the financial threshold for books more than 100 years old is 50,000 ECU. The regulation, according to Article 11, will enter into force three days after the publication of the directive on the return of cultural objects unlawfully removed from the territory of a Member State.

This Directive, Directive 93/7, was enacted in March 1993.[165] As the Preamble recognizes:

> Whereas, under the terms and within the limits of Article 36 of the Treaty, Member States will after 1992 retain the right to define their national treasures and to take the necessary measures to protect them; whereas they will, on the other hand, no longer be able to apply checks or formalities at the Community's internal frontiers to ensure the effectiveness of those measures.

The directive complements Regulation 3911/92 as it establishes a system to protect cultural objects within the Single Market. A cultural object is defined under Article 1(1) as falling within one of four categories. First, it may be an object which has been classified as possessing artistic, historic or archaeological value under national legislation. The next two categories are objects which forms an integral part of a public collection or the inventories of ecclesiastical institutions. For objects which do not fall within these latter categories, the Annex to the directive lists further categories.[166]

For goods unlawfully removed from the territory of a Member State, the directive establishes a system guaranteeing Member States the return of national treasures. The directive promotes co-operation between the competent authorities of the Member States. Under Article 5 of the directive, the Member State from which the goods have been removed may initiate proceedings before a court in the Member State in which the goods are now located. Such proceedings must be brought not more than five years after the Member State from which the goods have been unlawfully removed becomes aware of their location. Article 8 makes clear that the proceedings may not be brought after a period of thirty years has elapsed since the unlawful removal of the cultural object. In the event that the court orders the return of the cultural object, the acquirer of the object will be entitled to 'fair compensation' having proved the exercise of all reasonable care at the time of the acquisition of that object.[167]

One further area of concern noted in the 1988 Commission communication was the question of copyright. Despite not being mentioned as a priority area, the Commission had continued its work in this area, resulting in the presentation of a Green Paper,[168] and various follow-up papers, on copyright and neighbouring rights.[169] The Green Paper recognizes:

> The development of copyright laws in the Community and elsewhere reveals a continual re-examination of those laws to achieve an appropriate balance, in the light of conditions prevailing at the time, between important objectives that are partially in tension. Protection of the economic interests of the author and other creators, the promotion of ready access to information, and the pursuit of cultural goals have all had to be pursued and reconciled.[170]

The case law of the Court had effected a reconciliation between the existence of copyright and neighbouring rights and the provisions of the Treaty on the free movement of goods and competition.[171] Although recognizing this contribution, the Commission considered that technological advances threatened the effective exercise of copyright and neighbouring rights.

In an attempt to reconcile the conflicting interests in this area, the Commission proposed immediate action across six areas.[172] These area were; piracy; home copying of sound and audio-visual material; distribution rights, exhaustion and rental rights for particular classes of works; protection of computer programs; data bases; and the role of the Community in multilateral and bilateral relations affecting the above. Each chapter concludes with proposals for Community action in the relevant area. The Green Paper, as a consultative document, invited comments on each of these proposals before the Commission would propose specific measures in the six areas. In the 1990 follow-up paper, the Commission envisaged presenting a series of proposals. For example, there was to be a proposal for a directive on home copying of sound and audio-visual recordings.[173] In addition various studies were to be carried out, for example, on moral rights, reprography and resale rights.[174]

The endeavours of the Commission have resulted in certain actions being taken by the Council. Directive 91/250 institutes a system ensuring that all Member States should accord protection to computer programs under their copyright laws.[175] The directive details who is to be considered as the 'author' of the computer program (Article 2) and the rights that that person should have (Articles 4 to 7). The term of protection, according to Article 8, is the life of the author and fifty years. In recognition of the effect which differences in protection can have on the free movement of goods, the date for implementation of the directive was fixed for 1 January 1993, the date on which the Single Market entered into force. In May 1992, the Council passed a resolution on increased protection for copyright and neighbouring rights.[176] The resolution urges those Member States, who have not already done so, should accede to the Paris Act of the Berne Convention and the Rome Convention. The Member States were also urged to introduce legislation to ensure effective compliance with these conventions. To combat the problem of piracy, the Commission was urged to pay particular attention to the rights of copyright-holders and holders of neighbouring rights in the negotiation of agreements with third countries. Finally, Directive 92/100 introduces a rental and a lending right.[177] Once again, the object of the Directive is to harmonize the laws of the Member States in the areas of rentals and lending.[178] The directive also harmonizes the laws of the Member States on certain rights related to copyright: for example, fixation, reproduction and distribution.[179]

Various other Commission proposals are still awaiting decision by the Council. These include a directive on the legal protection of databases,[180] a directive on the copyright implications of satellite broadcasting and cable retransmission,[181] and a Directive on the harmonization of the term of copyright protection and certain related rights.[182] The latter is particularly important for in the case of *EMI Electrola* the effect of reducing copyright protection to that of the least generous Member States was seen by Advocate General Darmon as posing a major risk 'for artistic creativity in the Community, an essential aspect of this Europe of culture which everyone desires'.[183] The Court in this case noted that in the absence of harmonizing legislation it was for each Member State to determine the conditions and detailed rules for copyright protection. It continued:

> In so far as the disparity between national laws may give rise to restrictions on intra-Community trade in sound recordings, such restrictions may be justified under Article 36 of the Treaty if they are the result of differences between the rules governing the period of protection and thus is inseparably linked to the very existence of the exclusive rights.[184]

This was subject to the proviso that the restrictions were not a means of arbitrary discrimination or a disguised restriction on trade. The failure to pass the harmonizing directive on copyright means that the Single Market is not yet complete and that there remain restrictions on the free movement of cultural goods between the Member States.

CONCLUSIONS

Despite the absence of reference to Community action in the area of culture, the Community has developed a role in this area. As in education, it is the Commission, ably supported by the European Parliament, who deserves the credit for this development. The role of the Community in both areas shares some similarities but there are also important differences. What is similar is the structure of the co-operation between the Community and the Member States.

Meetings, conclusions and resolutions are the outcome of co-operation between the Council and the relevant Ministers of Education or Culture from the Member States. In its work on education this Council is assisted by the Education Committee established by the 1976 Action Programme on education. The equivalent committee for culture, the Committee on Cultural Affairs, was not established until 1988. A resolution of the Council and the Ministers responsible for Cultural Affairs meeting within the Council on the future organization of their work established this committee.[185] It has the task of preparing the meetings of this Council and of monitoring the implementation of actions decided on by it. As with the Education Committee, it is to be chaired by the representative of the Member State which holds the Presidency of the Council at the time of its meeting.

The role assigned to the Commission by this resolution is one of implementing the decisions reached by the Council, in close co-operation with the Committee, and, if agreed to by the Committee, it will also have a co-ordinating role. For their part, the Commission has established an Advisory Committee on Cultural Activities to act as a forum for discussion, as an advisor to the Commission on general strategy in this area and to provide co-ordination between various cultural sectors.[186] Thus the institutional structure of co-operation in cultural activities is similar to that of education. It is here, however, that differences begin to emerge, most notable on the scope of that co-operation. Whereas it is possible to trace the emergence of a gradually increasing competence of the Community in the field of education, no such pattern emerges with respect to culture. In the first period of Community action in this area, 1977 to 1982, only the Commission and the European Parliament were active. It was not until half way through the second period, 1982–7, that the first formal meeting of the Ministers responsible for Cultural Affairs met within the Community framework.

One consequence of this is that Community action in the field of culture is much more ancillary/supportive than the equivalent action in the field of education. Even in the third period, 1987–92, the impression gained is one of limited action. For example, the 1987 Commission communication on cultural co-operation in the run-up to the Single Market envisaged Community activity across a broad range of activities. Without wishing to diminish the importance of the areas highlighted by the Council, these were only four aspects from a particularly wide-ranging policy. Despite this, action did continue to be taken on other fronts, for example, in relation to the export of cultural goods and in the area of copyright and neighbouring rights. However, in this latter area, the action taken has been limited. Only three of six proposals have been adopted and the proposed decision on the accession of Member States to the Paris Act of the Berne Convention and the Rome Convention by 31 December 1992 became a resolution to be implemented by 1 January 1995.

It is interesting to speculate on why the Community's actions in the cultural sector have not developed in a manner similar to its activities in the education field. One reason which could be suggested is the attitude of the European Court of Justice. There is little doubt, as demonstrated above, that the Court played a significant role in the development and, more importantly, in the extension of Community competence in the field of education.[187] The attitude of the Court in the area of culture has not been so supportive. Cultural policy was not accepted by the Court as a reason for restricting the free movement of goods; no interpretation has been offered of the limited cultural exception to the free movement of goods in Article 36. The Court has held that cultural policy reasons can support restrictions on the freedom to provide services but it has not yet accepted any of the cultural policy reasons advanced by the Member States as objectively justified. Finally, the Court has not ruled on the impact of cultural policy on competition within the Community despite the opportunity to do so. Perhaps it is the very nature of the area which has prevented the Court from playing a role similar to the role which it has played in the area of education.

The nature of the area is the second reason which can be given for the differences between Community action in the cultural sector and action in the field of education. The Commission emphasized in 1977 that action in the cultural sector would be 'complementary and subsidiary to what is already being done internationally'.[188] The Council of Europe and other international organizations were already at work in this area. While the Council of Europe was also active in the field of education, Community activity could be clearly differentiated from it. For example, action was necessary by the Community to promote the assimilation of the worker and his/her children into the Member State to which the worker had moved. Community action in the cultural sector could not be so easily distinguished. In those cases where it could be distinguished from the Council of Europe's activities, it was necessary to involve other countries, for example, in the development of the audio-visual industry. Equally, it was necessary to co-operate with international organizations who were working in the area. For example, in the copyright area, the Berne and Rome Conventions are administered by the World Intellectual Property Organization. Moreover, the negotiations of the Uruguay Round conducted under the auspices of the GATT sought to include copyright, and other areas of intellectual property, within the rules of world trade.

Having discussed the gradual emergence and extension of Community competence in relation to cultural activities from its origin in 1977 to the creation of the Single Market, it only remains to discuss the likely future development of that competence as a result of the Treaty of Maastricht. Article 128 of that Treaty introduces a specific Community competence with respect to cultural activities. A number of questions arise. For example, will the competence of the Community be limited to those areas where it has already acted? Will new areas of competence be allocated to the Community? These questions will be answered in the next chapter which outlines the likely development of the competence of the Community in cultural affairs as a result of the implementation of the provisions of the Treaty of Maastricht.

Notes

6

From Maastricht to the Future

According to Article 3 of the Treaty of Rome as amended by the Treaty of Maastricht, the Community shall contribute to 'the flowering of the cultures of the Member States'. Furthermore, an amendment to Article 92(3) allows the Member States to grant aid to 'promote culture and heritage conservation where such is aid does not affect trading conditions and competition in the Community to an extent that is contrary to the common interest'. Article 3 is further developed in Article 128 which provides for the first time a specific Community competence in the field of culture. In any consideration of how the Community will contribute to the achievement of the goals specified in Article 128, an evaluation of past activities of the Community will be central. This will also assist in the interpretation of Article 128 and give some insight into the likely development of that provision. So before considering the provisions of the Maastricht Treaty, a brief review of the activities of the Community in the field of culture will be undertaken.

A REVIEW: 1977–93

As previously noted the history of the Community's activities in the field of culture can be divided into three phases; 1977 to 1982, 1982 to 1987; and 1987 to 1992. The first phase began with the presentation of the Commission communication advocating action in the cultural sector. This was defined as 'the socio-economic whole formed by persons and undertakings dedicated to the production and distribution of cultural goods and services'.[1] Despite the endorsement of the communication by both the European Parliament and the Economic and Social Committee limited progress was made in the implementation of the recommendations of the communication. One reason for this was the failure of the Council and the Ministers responsible for Cultural Affairs to meet during this period.

The Council and the Ministers responsible for Cultural Affairs did meet within the Council during the second period of Community action in the field of culture. Once again, this phase began with another Commission communication advocating stronger action in the field of culture.[2] In this communication the Commission established four priority areas for action; freedom of trade in cultural goods; improvement of the living and working conditions of cultural workers; enlarging the audience; and conservation of the architectural heritage. Within each of these areas various measures were proposed and the Commission went to great lengths to emphasize that Community action in the field of culture was to be complementary to that of the Member States and international organizations, such as the Council of Europe.[3] Perhaps as a consequence of this, the Ministers with responsibility for Cultural Affairs began to meet, first informally in 1982 and 1983 and then formally from 1984.

The activities of the Council in this period is marked by great uncertainty. On the one hand, there remained doubts as to the competence of the Community in the field of culture beyond the strict application of the Treaty to this sector. These doubts came to the fore in 1984 when the Council and the Ministers responsible for Cultural Affairs meeting within the Council did not endorse a resolution on the intensification of European cultural co-operation.[4] Further evidence is the passing of three resolutions on matters contained in the 1982 Commission communication in the form of resolutions of the representatives of the governments of the Member States. On the other hand, this Council was being urged to take action by the European Council as a result of the Solemn Declaration on European Union agreed at the 1983 Stuttgart meeting.[5] The Solemn Declaration urged 'closer cooperation in cultural matters in order to affirm the awareness of a common cultural heritage as an element in the European Identity'.[6] Further encouragement from the European Council would come from their endorsement in 1985 of the second report of the *ad hoc* Committee on a People's Europe, a committee which had been established by that Council.[7]

Institutional recognition of the role of the Community in the field of culture undoubtedly contributed to the gradual development of the competence of the Community. However, one particular institution, the European Court of Justice, seemed determined not to lend assistance to the development of that competence. In a series of judgments it had studiously avoided commenting on the role of cultural policy within the framework of the Treaty. The development of a Community competence in culture would not therefore benefit from the encouragement which the Court had provided, and would continue to provide, in another nascent area of Community competence, namely education. As in education, a major impetus to the further development of Community action in the field of culture would result from the movement of the Community to complete the Internal Market by 1993.

The third phase, 1987–92 began with another Commission communication on cultural activity, which considered the impact of the completion of the Internal Market on this sector.[8] On the basis of this document the Council and the Ministers responsible for Cultural Affairs meeting within the Council designated four areas as priority areas.[9] In the first of these areas, the promotion of the audio-visual sector, a series of measures were to be taken over the period which would promote the competitiveness of the European audio-visual industry.[10] Encouragement was given to the development of high definition television.[11] Television services, already subject to the Treaty rules on the freedom to provide services, would be subject to a directive establishing minimum rules for their free movement across national frontiers.[12] A programme would be agreed to promote the adaptation of the European audio-visual industry to technological challenges.[13] The emphasis of all these measures extended beyond the Member States of the European Community to include other European countries.[14]

In the second priority area, the book sector, various measures were agreed on by the Council and the Ministers responsible for Cultural Affairs meeting within the Council. These included measures such as a European Literature Prize and a European Translation Prize, a pilot scheme to provide financial assistance for the translation of contemporary literary works and grants to promote the training of translators.[15] In the third area, training in the cultural sector, it is possible to point to the institution of a training scheme for arts administrators as well as to training schemes instituted within the first two priority areas.[16] In the final area, although there has been great activity, it is not possible to point to particular legislative measures or even resolutions in the area of business sponsorship.[17]

In establishing the four priority areas, the Council made it clear that these areas were without prejudice to actions which were considered desirable in other areas. These actions have included measures to deal with the impact of the Internal Market on the free movement of cultural goods in the form of a regulation on the export of cultural goods[18] and a directive on the return of cultural objects unlawfully removed from the territory of a Member State.[19] Action has also been taken in the area of copyright.[20] In addition, the Community has continued a number of schemes established in the first and second phases of Community action in the field of culture. Action continues, for example, to protect the architectural heritage of the Community.[21] The scheme to have an annual European City of Culture event, instituted in 1985, is continuing and has been extended to allow for the participation of European cities outside the European Community.[22] Finally, cultural cooperation between the Member States and greater awareness of the shared cultural heritage of the Member States is encouraged through schemes such as Platform Europe and, its successor, Kaleidoscope.[23]

This brief overview of the activities of the Community in the field of culture serves to highlight the variegated nature of Community action in this area, from regulations establishing licences for the export of cultural goods to pilot schemes for the translation of important contemporary literary works. What this may demonstrate is that the problems in this area vary considerably and the Community and the Member States have chosen a wide range of instruments to deal with these problems. What the overview may also demonstrate is that the Member States are more committed to some aspects of the activities of the Community in the field of culture – for example, audio-visual services – than they are to other aspects of those activities – for example, the book sector. The question which arises is whether this difference of approach is reflected in the provisions of the Treaty of Maastricht on culture and in the guidelines for action in the next phase of Community activity in the field of culture.

THE MAASTRICHT PROVISIONS

As already noted, according to Article 3(p), the Community shall contribute to the 'flowering of the cultures of the Member States'. This is further developed in Article 128 which states:

1) The Community shall contribute to the flowering of the cultures of the Member States, while respecting their national and

regional diversity and at the same time bringing the common cultural heritage to the fore.

2) Action by the Community shall be aimed at encouraging cooperation between the Member States and, if necessary, supporting and supplementing their action in the following areas:
   - improvement of the knowledge and dissemination of the culture and history of the European peoples;
   - conservation and safeguarding of cultural heritage of European significance;
   - non-commercial cultural exchanges;
   - artistic and literary creation, including the audio-visual sector.
3) The Community and the Member States shall foster cooperation with third countries and the competent international organizations in the sphere of culture, in particular the Council of Europe.
4) The Community shall take cultural aspects into account in its action under other provisions of this Treaty.
5) In order to contribute to the achievement of the objectives referred to in this article, the Council:
   - acting in accordance with the procedure referred to in Article 189b and after consulting the Committee of the Regions, shall adopt incentive measures, excluding any harmonization of laws and regulations of the Member States. The Council shall act unanimously throughout the procedure referred to in Article 189b;
   - acting unanimously on a proposal from the Commission, shall adopt recommendations.

As in education, future Community action in the field of culture will have to respect the principle of subsidiarity, introduced by the Maastricht Treaty. Thus subsidiarity will be a general principle of Community action. Other references to the principle of subsidiarity are made in the Preamble to the Treaty which recognizes that the process of building an ever closer union among the peoples of Europe requires decisions to be 'taken as closely as possible to the citizen in accordance with the principle of subsidiarity'. A further reference is contained in the final paragraph of Article B of the Treaty which recognizes that in achieving the objectives of European Union, the principle of subsidiarity will be respected.

The exact meaning of the principle of subsidiarity has been the subject of much debate within the Community and a start has been made on the definition of the principle.[24] The application of the principle to the field of culture is a further question. The latest Commission communication on culture gives some indication as to the future scope of Community action in the field of culture. It points out that:

> The Community is on the threshold of a new era in which it will be able to grow beyond its purely economic dimension and enjoy unprecedented opportunity for cultural cooperation and support . . . thought should therefore be given to the future thrust of cultural action in this new environment.[25]

Action is envisaged on three fronts. First, a Community contribution to the flowering of culture in the frontier-free area. Secondly, bringing the common cultural heritage to the fore by providing support for three specific areas – cultural heritage, books and reading, and the audio-visual sector. Finally, increased co-operation with non-member countries and international organizations. Specific measures are advocated in each of these sectors.

In the first area, a contribution to the flowering of culture, the Commission envisaged two particular spheres of action. The first sphere would be encouraging co-operation between the Member States and to supplementing their action in four particular activities. The first of these activities is related to increasing the involvement of all those active in the field of culture.[26] To respect the separate traditions of the Member States, the involvement of all the bodies in the Member States in the cultural aspects of the Community would be increased. This would allow Community action in the field of culture to make a contribution to the elimination of regional disparities in the Community. Increased use would be made of cultural networks to promote co-operation through the exchange of information and experience, between facilities providing access to culture. This would also contribute to the third and fourth activities in this sphere of action which are improving the knowledge and dissemination of culture and making better use of cultural resources.[27]

The second activity is the encouragement of artistic and cultural creation. The Commission envisaged a three-pronged approach. The Community would improve access to existing programmes, such as Erasmus and Tempus, and the European Social Fund to promote culture-related training schemes. This would be complemented by an exchange programme involving cultural workers and by the promotion of pilot projects of Community interest.[28] Further action in the third and fourth activities, in addition to the cultural networks noted above, included measures to support the translation of important works and greater promotional activities on specific aspects of culture, such as books and reading. The issue of sponsorship is raised in the fourth area as a potential means of preserving existing cultural resources.

The second sphere of action in the contribution of the Community to the flowering of culture involved the consideration of cultural aspects in the implementation of existing Community policies and programmes.[29] Considering past Community activity in the field of culture, it is possible to point to a number of policies including the free movement of goods and persons, the environment and external relations. Other areas include the audio-visual sector, intellectual property rights and the rules on competition. These latter rules will become increasingly significant in the future as a result of the changes made by the Treaty of Maastricht to Article 92 of the Treaty allowing for aid to be granted 'to promote culture and heritage conservation'. As the body responsible for the supervision of the rules of the Treaty, the Commission will be able to monitor and control the assistance given by the Member States under this new provision.

The second front where the Commission envisaged future Community activity in the field of culture is bringing the common cultural heritage to the fore by providing support for three specific areas. These are the cultural heritage, books and reading and the audio-visual sector. The Commission justified its choice of a limited number of areas by arguing:

> The role of the Community in contributing to the flowering of our cultures must be subsidiary to that of the Member States. Given the vast area covered by culture careful prioritization is essential if the dissipation of effort is to be avoided. Community action must therefore be efficient, coherent and a valuable example and motive force.[30]

Given the constraints identified by the Commission the areas selected had to be areas where there was a pre-existing framework for Community action. Each of the areas had been to the fore of the Community's activities in the field of culture since 1988.

In relation to cultural heritage, the Community has already been active in measures to preserve the architectural heritage of the Community. It is envisaged that the concept of cultural heritage would be extended beyond this area to include cultural goods as part of the exploitation of existing resources and a highlighting of the diversity of the common cultural heritage of the Community.[31] In the area of books and reading, the Commission could point to the various schemes instituted since 1988. These included the promotion of translation and co-operation between libraries.[32] Finally, in the third area, the audio-visual sector, the Commission did not envisage a major change of approach. Efforts would, therefore, continue on the three fronts which had been established since 1988; establishing the rules of the game, the promotion of technology and the promotion of the programmes industry.[33] In this final area it was noted that co-operation in the audio-visual sector extended beyond the confines of the Member States of the Community to include other European countries. This extension was recognized in the final front of Community action in the field of culture – increased co-operation with non-member countries and international organizations.[34]

As part of a strategy to strengthen cultural co-operation with third countries, it was recognized that a breakthrough had been made by the inclusion of provisions on cultural co-operation in various agreements concluded by the Community with third countries.[35] Given the increasing number of agreements including provisions on cultural co-operation, the Commission considered that it would be necessary to ensure that such provisions fit within a more coherent framework and that the provisions are actually applied in the concerned countries.[36] As a further example of the internationalization of Community activity in the field of culture, it is possible to point to the European City of Culture scheme, instituted in 1985, which has already been extended to other European countries. In parallel with this event there is to be a European Cultural Month to be held each year in a European city outside the Community.[37] Finally, the Commission recognize that the Community should have close and harmonious relations with the various international organizations involved in this area, such as UNESCO and, in particular, the Council of Europe.

The Commission conclude their assessment of future Community action in the field of culture by emphasizing the need for a framework for action. It identifies a number of priority areas for this framework; essentially, these seek to build on the achievements of the past, and the three fronts identified by the Commission, while respecting the principle of subsidiarity. The Commission have continually emphasized that Community action in the field of culture has always respected the principle of subsidiarity:

> As and when cultural action develops, and in particular whenever specific programme proposals are made, care should be taken to ensure that the principle of subsidiarity is fully respected. This subsidiarity will produce action of Community interest geared primarily to the breaking down of barriers, to transparency and to genuine added value throughout the Community.[38]

The result may well be that, as the Commission have recognized, that there will be fewer Community measures but greater visibility. In contrast to education, where the Treaty of Maastricht seemed to confirm and promote the role of the Community in this sphere, the provisions on culture point to an apparent downgrading of Community activities in the field of culture.

Both the Council and the Parliament who will have power of co-decision in the field of culture have had the opportunity to examine the Commission communication. The result is that on consideration of these examinations it is possible to outline the future scope of Community activities in the field of culture. The Ministers of Culture meeting within the Council in November 1992 reached a series of conclusions on the Commission communication.[39] Although the conclusions do not define the precise scope of future activities, they do focus attention on a number of key areas and approaches to Community cultural action. As for the scope of Community cultural action, the Council concluded that the Community should develop the existing activities in the areas of cultural heritage, books and reading and the audio-visual sector. The Council continued:

> Future programmes may specifically include: encouraging the activities of European cultural networks of arts practitioners and cultural institutions such as museums, archives, libraries and monuments; encouraging business sponsorship of the arts; exchanges and training of personnel in the cultural field in support of the activities of Member States; increasing awareness of different cultures and safeguarding the Community's linguistic diversity, as well as promoting respect for shared values.[40]

This appears to be a full endorsement of the Commission's

proposals for the future direction of the activities of the Community in the field of culture. However, the Council continue by pointing to the limited financial resources available for Community activities.

This leads the Council to emphasize the complementary nature of Community activity in this area. Indeed such activity is placed below that which can be achieved at national or regional level, on the one hand, and at international level, on the other. Cultural co-operation with third countries will, therefore, become an increasingly important feature of Community action in the field of culture. For example, co-operation between the Community and EFTA countries was highlighted, especially as the agreement on the European Economic Area contains a declaration on the strengthening of cultural links between the two areas.[41] Special attention would be paid to the countries of Central and Eastern Europe.[42] The final area of future activity at the Community level, related to the cultural aspects of action under different Treaty provisions. The conclusions in this area urge the adoption of a standard practice of taking of culture into account in the preparation of new actions or policies under the Treaty. To improve the effectiveness and co-ordination of Community activity in the field of culture, the Ministers of Culture would regularly consider the cultural aspects of issues examined in other Councils.

The Council concluded that the Commission should present an annual outline of proposals to be considered. In addition to the work in progress, such as the Media Programme, the Council selected five areas of the Commission communication where proposals were to be made or discussion papers presented. These related to the cultural heritage; a survey of Community policies with a cultural impact; cultural co-operation with third countries and international organizations; strengthening dialogue in the cultural sector; and, development and exchange in the area of artistic and literary creation. The overall tenor of the Council conclusions is supportive of the approach of the Commission to the future scope of Community activity in the field of culture. Given the recognition by the Commission that future activity would be restricted, it seems that the impression of the downgrading of existing Community activity in the field of culture has been confirmed by the Council.

While being generally supportive of the thrust of the Commission's communication, the attitude of the European Parliament is more critical than the Council.[43] Although accepting the approach of, and proposals made by, the Commission, the Parliament advances various criticisms and additional proposals. In the first section, contributing to the flowering of culture, the Parliament endorses the approach of the Commission. However, it points out that the completion of the Internal Market has not been accompanied by an assessment of its impact on the cultural sector. In this area Parliament bemoans the elevation of competitiveness as the criterion of action to the exclusion of cultural goals.[44] To counter problems of financing in the field of culture, the Parliament considered that the cultural dimension of existing Community programmes in specific sectors should be enhanced.[45] In particular, more attention, according to the Parliament, ought to be devoted to exchange programmes and networks for those working in the cultural sector.[46] Greater Community support for cultural events is also recommended. The Parliament seems to question the sincerity of the Commission's, and the Community's, approach to all aspects of the cultural sector. The final paragraph of this section of the resolution records the hope that the Community 'will support the broadest range of cultural activities, including new ones, in a more even-handed manner than it does at present'.[47]

In the second area, bringing the common cultural heritage to the fore, although the Parliament sympathizes with the need to prioritize action, it considers that such prioritization could be a reason for withdrawing, or failing to provide, Community support to areas where that support would yield real benefits.[48] In the three areas selected by the Commission for priority action, cultural heritage, books and reading and the audio-visual sector, a number of additional proposals are made. For example, in the area of cultural heritage, it is recommended that the existing preoccupation with the awarding of prizes in the area of architectural heritage should give way to a more comprehensive strategy promoting restoration. In recognition of finite resources, the Parliament urge greater use of Structural Funds and ordinary budgetary resources. In the audio-visual sector, the Parliament considered that there is still a considerable amount of work to be done and it recommends further emphasis on the Media Programme as the way forward in this area.[49] In the final area, increased cooperation with third countries and international organizations, the Parliament fully endorses the approach of the Commission.[50]

The Parliament concludes its resolution by pointing out:

> having regard to the subsidiarity principle, that cultural action, both within and outside the Community, cannot be pursued to

> the full and yield its benefits, not least from the employment and economic point of view, unless the Member States and regional and local authorities take an open-minded, cooperative attitude in relation to the guidelines and programmes drawn up to reflect the increasingly authoritative influence that the Community is destined to exert as it grows into a European Union.[51]

Parliament has always been a great supporter of Community action in the field of culture and it appears that it has given a very expansive interpretation to the provisions on culture introduced by the Treaty of Maastricht. As a result it seems that the Parlaiment and the Council have different conceptions of the future scope of the Community's activities in the field of culture. One arguing for an enlargement of the existing policy and the other arguing for a refinement of that policy. Using the definition of subsidiarity which emerged from the European Council meeting in Edinburgh and considering the past history of Community activities in the field of culture, it seems probable that the conception advocated by the Council will be more accurate than that advocated by the Parliament. The impression that the Treaty of Maastricht actually restricts the competence of the Community to act in the field of culture rather than confirming and enlarging that competence is the correct impression.

A CONCLUSION

According to the Draft Treaty on European Union adopted by the Parliament:

1) The Union may take measures to:
   - promote cultural and linguistic understanding between citizens of the Union;
   - publicize the cultural life of the Union both at home and abroad;
   - establish youth exchange programmes.
2) The European University Institute and the European Foundation shall become establishments of the Union.
3) Laws shall lay down rules governing approximation of the laws of copyright and the free movement of cultural goods.[52]

The proposed article on culture predated Community activity in the field of culture so it is only natural that Community activity would extend beyond what the Parliament anticipated would be covered. What could not be anticipated is that the activities which would develop would be so limited.

An explanation as to why this has occurred has already been essayed. Two reasons were advanced. The first reason was the reluctance of the Court to lend support to the development and extension of the competence of the Community in the field of culture. Sufficient examples have been already given but one further example will serve to illustrate the attitude of the Court. The particular case is *Groener* v. *Minister of Education*.[53] The case was a preliminary reference on the interpretation of Article 48(3) and Article 3 of Regulation 1612/68 in the context of a dispute concerning the refusal to appoint the plaintiff to a permanent full-time position in a public educational institution as she had failed a test intended to assess her knowledge of the Irish language. National rules made appointment to this position conditional on proof of an adequate knowledge of the Irish language. Advocate General Darmon advanced the following opinion: 'It seems to me that every State has the right to try to ensure the diversity of its cultural heritage and, consequently, to establish the means to carry out such a policy .... Every State has the right to determine the importance which it wishes to attribute to its cultural heritage'.[54] The Advocate General went on to examine the particular provisions of Community law before concluding that the Irish rules were acceptable.

The Court in its judgment, after examining the various provisions of Community law, continued:

> The EEC Treaty does not prohibit the adoption of a policy for the protection and promotion of a language which is both the national language and the first official language. However, the implementation of such a policy must not encroach upon a fundamental freedom such as that of the free movement of workers.[55]

The Court found the rules to be acceptable provided that they were proportionate to the goal being pursued and would not be applied in a manner bringing about discrimination against nationals of other Member States. The ruling is typical of the approach of the Court in cases raising cultural issues. In case after case the Court had studiously avoided passing any comment on the role of cultural issues within the Treaty and instead concentrated on the issue of ensuring the maximum level of freedom, whether that be the freedom to trade or the freedom to move to another Member State.

To be fair to the Court, the approach which it has adopted in the cases involving culture may have been dictated by the second reason for the limited development of the competence of the Community in the field of culture. This is the nature of the area itself. In contrast to education which is a relatively well-defined field, culture is an area which cuts across a range of Community policies. It is much more general than education. In addition it has been the subject of international co-operation. Although education has also been the subject of international co-operation – notably through the efforts of the Council of Europe – within the Community it would be possible to define a specific area of Community competence in education. A specific area for culture is not so easy to define. Copyright and audio-visual development not only affect the creation of a Single Market within the Community but are problems which need to be addressed in either a multilateral or European framework. As a consequence of this the development of a specific Community competence in culture has been hamstrung by the need to consider the international or European dimension of particular problems. So, Community activity yields to international or European activity with the result that the specific competence of the Community is reserved for a narrow range of prestige or largely symbolic programmes.

In attempting to draw this examination of the future of the Community in the area of culture to a close, it is reasonable to conclude that future Community activity will remain peripheral to the activities of the Member States and international organizations, such as the Council of Europe. Despite sharing so many characteristics with the development of Community competence in the field of education, the Treaty of Maastricht marks a true turning point for both areas. In the future there will be a well-established and specific policy for education within the Community which will genuinely add value to the activities of the Member States in this area. This is confirmed by the Treaty of Maastricht. The same Treaty confirms that a similar future will not await Community activities in the field of culture. On the thirtieth anniversary of the signing of the Treaty of Rome the French government presented a paper on the future development of Community policies in the areas of education and culture. According to the French government:

> The need to improve European cooperation in the field of education and culture is accepted with so little hesitation that for years numerous initiatives have been taken to reinforce progress in this direction whether in meetings of the Ministers concerned at Council level, by the conclusions of the European Council, the work of the European Parliament on European Union, the conclusions of the Adonnino report or by the Commission's constant efforts to implement joint action. In both education and culture, we are forced to note that the efforts have not yet produced all the tangible results hoped for.[56]

Although Community action in the field of culture is sanctioned by the provisions of the Treaty of Maastricht, it will not produce all the tangible results hoped for.

Notes

Chapter 1 The Development of Community Competence

1 Kloss, G., 'Education Policy' in S. Bulmer, S. George, and A. Scott (eds), *The United Kingdom and the EC Membership Evaluated* (Pinter: London, 1992) p. 239.
2 EC Bulletin 1/70 First Part, Chapter 1 (see also point 16 of the communique).
3 See *European Educational Policy Statements* (1987, Council of the EC, Brussels) p. 11. See also Bulletin of the EC 12/71 pp. 28–30.
4 EC Bulletin Supplement 10/73 For a Community policy on Education, p. 5.
5 Ibid., pp. 6–8.
6 Ibid., p. 57.
7 Ibid., pp.58–9.
8 Ibid., p. 49.
9 The Treaties of Rome are the Treaty establishing the European Economic Community and the Treaty establishing the European Atomic Energy Community. On the question of the links between educational policy and cultural policy and educational policy and scientific policy see pp. 12–13.
10 Ibid., p. 51.
11 Ibid., p. 51 (see also p. 23).
12 Ibid., p. 23.
13 Ibid., p. 11.
14 Ibid., p. 24 on the various alternatives to harmonization.
15 Ibid., p. 52.
16 Ibid., p. 53 (see also pp. 30–5).
17 Ibid., pp. 35–40 for discussion of this area.
18 Ibid., p. 53.
19 Ibid., pp. 54–5 (see also pp. 40–4 for discussion of this area).
20 Ibid., p. 56.
21 EC Bulletin Supp. 4/74, p. 6.
22 Ibid., pp. 8–11.
23 This topic will be discussed in greater depth in Chapter 3.
24 Supra n. 21, pp. 11–12.
25 Ibid., p. 12.

26 Ibid., pp. 12–13.
27 Ibid., pp. 13–14.
28 Ibid., pp. 14–15.
29 Ibid., pp. 19–20.
30 Ibid., pp. 21–2.
31 OJ [1974] C98/2.
32 Ibid., point II of the resolution.
33 OJ [1976] C38/1.
34 OJ C308/1.
35 Ibid., point III of the resolution.
36 See resolution of the Council and of the Ministers of Education meeting within the Council of 15 January 1980, OJ [1980] C23/1.
37 Supra n. 3, pp. 49–71. For a more general account see EC Bulletin 6/80 pp. 76–7.
38 Ibid., pp. 64–6.
39 See, for example, COM (78) 499 Education Action Programme at Community Level: Equal Opportunities in education and training for girls.
40 The end result of all these activities was a resolution of the Council and Ministers of Education meeting within the Council on an action programme on equal opportunities for girls and boys in education – OJ [1985] C166/1.
41 Supra n. 3, p. 75.
42 See G. Neave, *The EEC and Education* (Trentham, Stoke, 1984) p. 15, for further discussion.
43 OJ [1982] C193/1.
44 OJ [1983] C166/1.
45 OJ [1983] C256/1.
46 Supra n. 3, pp. 93–6.
47 Ibid., p. 95.
48 OJ [1983] C193/2.
49 EC Bulletin Supp. 7/85, 'A People's Europe: Reports from the *ad hoc* Committee'.
50 Ibid., p. 13.
51 Ibid., p. 14.
52 Ibid., p. 23.
53 Ibid., pp. 23–6.
54 COM (85) 310.
55 Ibid., p. 26.
56 See for further discussion, Commission, 'The role of education and training in the completion of the internal market' *Social Europe* 3/88, p. 36.
57 *European Educational Policy Statements*, (Council of the EC, Brussels, 1987) pp. 143–4.
58 OJ [1988] C177/02.
59 Ibid., point II A of the resolution
60 Ibid., point II B of the resolution.
61 COM (88) 331 Communication from the Commission to the European Parliament: 'A People's Europe', p. 13.

62 These schemes had been envisaged by the Commission in its 1985 White Paper on the completion of the Internal Market, supra n. 54 , and will be discussed further below.
63 OJ [1989] C277/5.
64 See COM (89) 236, 'Education and Training in the EC Guidelines for the Medium Term 1989–92'.
65 Supra n. 63, first conclusion.
66 Noted above, see text accompanying n. 63.
67 This programme will be discussed in the next section.
68 This will be discussed further in Chapter 3.
69 OJ [1992] L209/25. The directive extends the scope of Directive 89/48 beyond higher education so as to facilitate the pursuit of all those professional activities which require the completion of a certain level of education and training.
70 Decision 88/348 OJ [1988] L158/42. See also Decision 91/387 OJ [1991] L214/69 amending the Petra scheme to allow for the participation of young persons.
71 OJ [1987] C211/5.
72 OJ [1989] C153/1 and C153/5.
73 OJ [1990] C27/1.
74 Decision 87/569 OJ [1987] L346/31, see also amending decision 91/387 OJ [1991] L214/69.
75 Decision 89/657 OJ [1989] L393/29. See also Decision 92/170 OJ [1992] L75/51.
76 Decision 90/267 OJ [1990] L156/1. See also Decision 92/170 OJ [1992] L75/51.
77 OJ [1987] C178/ 3.
78 This will be discussed further in the next section of this chapter.
79 See Article of the EEA Agreement. The EFTA countries may already participate in the Comett Programme (see Council Decisions 90/190–5 OJ [1990] L102 for details of the Agreements between the EEC and Norway, Finland, Iceland, Norway, Sweden and Switzerland on co-operation in the implementation of the Comett II Programme) and the Erasmus Programme (Council Decisions 91/611–17 OJ [1991] L332 for the details of similar agreements in relation to Erasmus). See also Part IV of the Agreement on the European Economic Area (Articles 78–88).
80 Supra n. 63, second conclusion of the Council and the Ministers of Education meeting within the Council.

Chapter 2 Specific Programmes

1 OJ [1974] C98/2.
2 OJ [1976] C38/1, p. 4.
3 European Educational Policy Statements. (Council of the EC, Brussels, 1987), p. 49, pp. 56–60. See also EC Bulletin 6/80, pp. 76–7.
4 For further discussion of these programmes, see Smith *Joint Programmes of Study: An Instrument of European Cooperation in Higher Education*. European Education Series No.7 (1979, Commission, Brussels.)
5 Supra n. 3, p.57–8.
6 Ibid., p. 59.

7 Ibid, pp. 89–90. See also EC Bulletin 6/83 p. 50.
8 Ibid., Conclusion 1.
9 Ibid., Conclusion 2.
10 Ibid., Conclusion 4.
11 Ibid., Conclusion 5.
12 EC Bulletin Supp. 7/85, 'A People's Europe': Reports from the *ad hoc* Committee', p. 25.
13 4th Recital to Decision 87/327 OJ [1987] L166/20.
14 Ibid., Article 2(i).
15 Ibid., Article 2(ii).
16 Articles 2(iii)–(v).
17 Ibid., 18th Recital to the Preamble.
18 Ibid., Article 4.
19 It is important to note that the nature of the Erasmus Committee differs fundamentally from the Education Committee. The latter appears to be a Committee of the Council whereas the former is to be chaired by a Commission representative.
20 Case 242/87 *Commission v. Council* [1988] ECR 1425.
21 COM (85) 756 Proposal for a Council Decision adopting Erasmus. The EC Action Scheme for the Mobility of University Students.
22 Supra n. 20, p. 1430–1.
23 Ibid., pp. 1432–3.
24 Ibid., p. 1434.
25 Ibid., p.1435. The intervening parties were the United Kingdom, Germany and France.
26 Ibid., p. 1438.
27 Ibid., pp 1439–40.
28 Ibid., p. 1445.
29 Ibid., p. 1447.
30 See, for example, Case 45/86 *Commission v. Council* [1987] ECR 1493.
31 Supra n. 20, p. 1453.
32 Ibid., para. 13.
33 These cases will be discussed at length in the section on vocational training in Chapter 3.
34 Supra n. 20, p. 1456.
35 Ibid., paragraph 28.
36 Ibid., p. 1457.
37 Ibid., p. 1458.
38 Decision 89/663 OJ [1989] L395/23.
39 Ibid., Article 1(3) which amends Article 4 of the original decision.
40 Ibid., Article 1(5) which amends Article 7 of the original decision.
41 Ibid., Annex to the decision.
42 OJ [1986] L222/17.
43 See G. Neave *The EEC and Education* (Trentham, Stoke, 1984) Chapter 9, 'The Micro Electronic Revolution' for discussion of early Community action in this area.

44 OJ [1983] C166/1.
45 Ibid., point III of the resolution.
46 OJ [1983] C256/1.
47 Supra n. 3, p. 115. See also EC Bulletin 6/84, p. 42.
48 See COM (85) 167, Communication setting out the broad lines of Community action for the period 1985–8 in the field of vocational training and the new information technology and COMs (85) 431 and 690 Proposal for a decision adopting an action programme of the Community in Education and Training for Technology 1986-92.
49 Supra n. 42, Article 1.
50 Ibid., Article 4.
51 Ibid., Annex to the decision.
52 See COM (88) 36 Comett Programme, Report on 1987 Activities. See also OJ [1988] C239/3.
53 OJ [1989] L13/28.
54 Ibid., Article 4.
55 Supra n. 42, Second Recital of the Preamble.
56 Joined Cases C-51/89, C-90/89 and C-94/89, *United Kingdom and others v. Council* [1991] ECR I-2757.
57 Ibid., p. I-2764.
58 Ibid., p. I-2765.
59 Ibid., pp I-2766–7.
60 Ibid., p. I-2769.
61 See discussion of this issue in the section on the concept of vocational training in Chapter 3.
62 Supra n. 56, p. I-2772.
63 Supra n. 20, p. 1454.
64 Supra n. 56, p. I-2791.
65 Ibid., pp. I-2776–8.
66 Ibid., pp. I-2774–5.
67 Ibid., pp. I-2781–2.
68 The Eurotecnet (OJ [1989] L393/29) and Force (OJ [1990] L156/1) programmes.
69 Supra n. 136, p. I-2785.
70 Ibid., p. I-2792.
71 Ibid., p. I-2795.
72 OJ [1974] C98/2.
73 OJ [1976] C38/1, paras 17–19.
74 *European Educational Policy Statements* (1987, Council of the EC, Brussels) p. 49, Part V of the Conclusions p. 61. See also EC Bulletin 6/80 pp. 76–7.
75 Ibid., pp 61–2.
76 Ibid., pp. 117–19.
77 EC Bulletin Supp. 7/85, 'A People's Europe: Reports of the *ad hoc* Committee', p. 23.
78 Supra n. 74, p.143.
79 See COM (88) 203 Communication from the Commission: The teaching of foreign languages and COM (88) 841, Proposal for a Council Decision establish-

ing the Lingua Programme to promote training in foreign languages in the European Community.

80 OJ [1989] L239/24.

81 Ibid., Article 10.

82 OJ [1990] C27/7.

83 OJ [1990] L131/21. (This decision was amended by Decision 92/240 OJ [1992] L122/43; the decision amends Article 1 of Decision 90/233 by stating that the Tempus Programme will run for four, rather than three, years.) See also Regulation 1360/90 which establishes a European Training Foundation (OJ [1990] L131/1); this is another aspect of the concern expressed European Council on the situation in Central and Eastern Europe.

84 Regulation 3906/89 OJ [1989] L375/11, last amended by Regulation 2334/92 OJ [1992] L227/1. See also Regulation 2157/91 OJ [1991] L201/2 – provision of technical assistance for economic reform and recovery in the USSR.

85 Supra n. 83, 7th recital of the Preamble.

86 This provision states one of the objectives of Tempus to be: 'to increase opportunities for the teaching and learning in the eligible countries of those languages used in the Community and *vice versa*.'

87 Supra n. 85, Article 8.

88 For details of this and the operation of the scheme see COM (93) 29, Evaluation of the Tempus Programme.

89 Supra n. 85, Article 4(a).

90 Ibid., Article 5.

91 Supra n. 88, and COM (92) 407, Proposal for a Council Decision adopting the second phase of the Trans-European Cooperation Scheme for Higher Education (amended by COM (93) 132).

92 OJ [1993] L112/34.

93 EC Bulletin 1/70, First Part, Chapter 1.

94 OJ [1979] C207/14 or COM (79) 215, see also COM (80) 358 and 649 for amendments to the proposal.

95 COM (89) 275 Proposal for a Council Decision on the Right of Residence of Students, on the Right of Residence for employees and self-employed persons who have ceased their occupational activity and on the right of residence.

96 Directives 90/364–6 OJ [1990] L180/26.

97 Ibid., OJ [1990] L180/30, 4th recital of the Preamble.

98 The rights of the children of migrant workers will be discussed in greater detail in Chapter 3.

99 Supra n. 97, 3rd and 6th recital of the Preamble.

100 Case C-295/90, *European Parliament v. Council* (Judgement of 7 July 1992 nyr in ECR.) See The Proceedings of the Court of Justice and the Court of First Instance of the EC No. 21/92.

101 Ibid., p. 4.

102 COM (93) 209, Proposal for a Council Directive on the Right of Residence of Students. See also OJ [1993] C166/16.

103 Ibid., 4th recital of the Preamble.

104 Supra n. 97.

105 Comment on Case C-295/90 (1993) 30, *CMLRev* 639, p. 650.
106 'Education and law: The Community context' (1989) 14 *ELRev* 363.
107 See COM (91) 349 Memorandum on Higher Education in the European Community. This will be discussed further in Chapter 4.
108 As an example of this see OJ [1992] C336/7, Conclusions of the Council and Ministers of Education meeting within the Council of 27 November 1992 on Community/United States cooperation in the field of education.
109 'Education' in Keatinge (ed.), *Ireland and EC Membership Evaluated* (Pinter, London, 1991), p. 260, at p. 262.

Chapter 3 The Extension of Community Competence

1 OJ Special Edition, [1968](II) p. 475.
2 OJ [1977] L337/12. This directive emerged from the 1976 Action Programme on Education discussed in Chapter 1. See also EC Bulletin Supp. 3/76, Action Programme in favour of migrant workers and their families. On the implementation of the directive see COM (84) 53, Report on the implementation of Directive 77/486 on the education of the children of migrant workers.
3 Ibid., Article 2 of the directive. This tuition is to be free and the host Member State is required to take measures for the training and further training of teachers who are to provide the tuition.
4 Ibid., Article 3 of the Directive.
5 Case 9/74 [1974] ECR 773.
6 Ibid, p. 781.
7 Such an approach was predictable given the decision of the ECJ in case 76/72 *Michel S* [1973] ECR 457. Although the case concerned the interpretation of Article 7 of Regulation 1612/68 in the context of a claim by the father of Michel S that the latter be registered as a handicapped person, the Court stated: 'The fact that the abovementioned Article 12 does not expressly refer to educational arrangements provided in favour of such children, is not to be understood as denoting the intention to exclude these arrangements from the scope of the Regulation, but is explained by the difficulty of mentioning all hypotheses exclusively, especially those of an exceptional nature, in view of which it is necessary to guarantee the equality of nationals of all the Member States, in order to ensure that the right of freedom of movement can be exercised to its full extent' (p. 463).
8 Supra n. 5, p. 779 (para. 9).
9 Ibid., p. 779 (para. 12).
10 Ibid., p.784–5 .
11 Ibid., p. 780.
12 Case 68/74 [1975] ECR 109.
13 Joined cases 389 and 390/87 [1989] ECR 723.
14 Ibid., p. 741 .
15 Ibid., p. 761.
16 Idem. My emphasis.

17 Supra n. 13, p. 759.
18 Ibid., p. 764.
19 Case 263/86 [1988] ECR 5365.
20 Ibid., p. 5380.
21 Ibid., p. 5382.
22 Ibid., p. 5381. The argument of the Italian government ran as follows: 'If the host State procures for the benefit of its own nationals the possibility of studying abroad on advantageous terms, that benefit must be extended equally to other Community nationals resident on its territory or at least those covered by Regulation 1612/68'. The purpose of such an interpretation was to promote the integration of the children of the migrant worker which would be frustrated if a contrary decision were reached.
23 Ibid., p. 5387.
24 Case C-308/89 [1990] ECR I-4185.
25 Ibid., I-4208.
26 This ruling was subsequently confirmed in case C-3/90, *Bernini* (nyr 26 February 1992). In this case Bernini, the child of an Italian migrant worker in the Netherlands, applied for a grant from the Netherlands Ministry of Education to fund a course of architectural studies in Italy. This was refused on the grounds that she could not be treated as a Netherlands national as she was resident in Italy. On a preliminary reference the ECJ declared, using Article 7(2) of Regulation 1612/68, that Bernini was entitled to a grant as a 'social advantage'.
27 [1982] 3 CMLR 91.
28 Ibid., p. 94.
29 Case 32/75 [1975] ECR 1085.
30 Case 65/81 [1982] ECR 33.
31 Supra n. 27, p. 96.
32 Ibid., p. 98.
33 Case 39/86 [1988] ECR 3161.
34 Case 197/86 [1988] ECR 3207.
35 Supra n.33, p. 3181.
36 The previous case law of the Court indicates that in order to be classified as a worker under the Treaty a person must engage in 'effective and genuine activities to the exclusion of activities on such a small scale as to be regarded as purely marginal and ancillary'. Case 53/81, *Levin* [1982] ECR 1035, p. 1050. Alternatively, the Court in case 66/85, *Lawrie-Blum* [1986] ECR 2121 classified a worker as a person who for a certain period of time performs services for and under the direction of another in return for remuneration.
37 Supra n. 33, p. 3183.
38 Ibid., pp, 3165–8.
39 Ibid., p. 3184.
40 Ibid., p. 3185.
41 Ibid., pp. 3187–8.
42 Ibid., p. 3196.
43 Ibid., p. 3197.
44 Ibid., p. 3198.

45 Ibid., p. 3200.

46 Ibid., p. 3185. He stated: 'It is, however, sought to qualify any right given on the basis that it only applies where the course undertaken is connected with the work previously done. I do not find this limitation in Article 7(3) either expressly or impliedly in relation to training in vocational schools. Such a limitation as is suggested in my view conflicts with the aim of the regulation which is directed to the mobility of labour on equal terms and which recognizes the "close links" which exist between freedom of movement for workers, employment and vocational training'.

47 Supra n. 27, p. 96.

48 Supra n. 33 pp. 3169–71.

49 Ibid., p. 3201.

50 The decision in *Lair* has been confirmed by the Court in the subsequent cases of *Raulin* (Case C-357/89) nyr 26 February 1992. The facts of the case were that Raulin, a French national, moved to the Netherlands in 1985. She did not register with the Office for the Control of Aliens and did not obtain a residence permit. In March 1986 she signed a contract obliging her to perform sixty hours of service as a waitress. In August 1986 she began a course in plastic arts and applied for a grant to finance her studies. This was refused on the grounds that she could not be treated as a Dutch national as she did not possess a residence permit. The plaintiff sought to rely on Regulation 1612/68 and Article 7 of the Treaty in her challenge to this decision. On reference to the ECJ the Court confirmed the ruling in *Lair* that to retain the status as a worker and so benefit from Article 7(2) of the Regulation the course must have some connection with the previous employment.

51 Steiner comments: 'It is regrettable that in its concern to appease the anxiety of member States it chose in *Lair* to limit the scope of Article 7(2) by denying a right to "social advantages" in the form of grants to migrant workers who have not become unemployed but who genuinely want to improve their prospects by retraining in a new field of activity. In an era of rapid technological and economic change such as will inevitably occur if the single market becomes a reality, flexibility in the work force is surely to be encouraged'. *Textbook on EEC Law* (3rd edn) (Blackstone, London, 1992).

52 Supra n. 34, p 3233.

53 Ibid., p. 3221.

54 Ibid., pp 3215-3220.

55 Ibid., p. 3235.

56 Ibid., p. 3235. The Advocate General did not consider the one year period to be 'an infallible yardstick.'

57 Ibid., pp 3231-3232.

58 Ibid., p. 3246. The Court stated after reviewing their case law on the definition of a worker:'Community law does not impose any additional conditions for a person to be classifiable as a worker and the Member States cannot unilaterally make the grant of the social advantages contemplated in Article 7(2) conditional upon the completion of a given period of occupational activity'.

59 Ibid., p. 3247.

60 Case 235/87 [1988] ECR 5589.
61 Ibid., pp. 5598–9.
62 Ibid., pp. 5599–600.
63 Ibid., pp. 6601–2.
64 Ibid., p. 6609.
65 Ibid., pp. 6611–12.
66 Ibid., p. 6611.
67 Case 293/83 [1985] ECR 593.
68 Case 152/82 [1983] ECR 2323.
69 Ibid., p. 2341.
70 Ibid., p. 2342.
71 Ibid., p. 2336.
72 A. Arnull, *The General Principles of EEC Law and the Individual* (Leicester University Press, Leicester, 1990) p. 33.
73 Hartley suggests that although 'the exact meaning of lawfully established is unclear: it certainly covers any Community immigrant with a right under Community law to reside in the Member State in question; it might also cover a Community immigrant with a right only under national law; it certainly does not, however, cover a student who comes expressly in order to study.' in N. Green, T. Hartley and J. Usher *Legal Foundations of the Single European Market* (OUP, Oxford, 1991) p. 177.
74 [1985] 1 CMLR 716.
75 Ibid., p. 724.
76 In *MacMahon* v. *Department of Education*, supra n. 27, p. 97, Dillon J. concluded that training in vocational schools 'covers any training in a school or college which is intended to prepare or qualify a person for a particular vocation or job, whether manual or technical or not'.
77 Most notably for the use of the guidelines from *Bulmer* v. *Bollinger* in relation to the question of whether or not to refer a question to the ECJ. See S. Weatherill & P. Beaumont, *EC Law* (Penguin, London, 1993), pp. 255–8 for discussion and criticism of these guidelines.
78 Supra n. 67.
79 Ibid., p. 595.
80 Ibid., p. 596.
81 Ibid., p. 599.
82 Ibid., p. 601.
83 Ibid., pp 601–4.
84 Ibid., p. 604.
85 Ibid., p. 611.
86 Ibid., p. 614.
87 See J. Steiner, 'Recipients of services – Some more equal than others' (1985) 10 *ELRev* 348.
88 See P. Watson (1987) 24 CMLRev 89.
89 For example in *MacMahon* [1982] 3 CMLR 91, Dillon J. noted: 'It is not necessary in this case to go so far as to say that it would cover all university courses, but it does cover training in a medical school, a law school, or a teacher

training college,' (pp. 97–8). In *ex parte Hinde*, Taylor J. cited this passage with approval but held that a university course leading to the award of an LLB was not vocational training.

90 Case 293/85 [1988] ECR 305. (Note: when the Commission lodged its main application, it also submitted an application for interim measures. These measures would ensure that students who were nationals of other Member States would have access to vocational training courses offered by Belgian Universities in the same conditions as Belgian nationals. The Court ordered these measures in the belief, *inter alia*, that it could not be ruled out that Article 7 of the Treaty covered vocational training offered by universities. Case 293/85R [1985] ECR 3521.)

91 Ibid., p. 313.

92 Ibid., p. 316.

93 Ibid., p. 334.

94 Ibid., p. 335.

95 Ibid., p. 336.

96 Ibid., pp. 337–8.

97 Ibid., p. 353.

98 Arnull points out that the ruling in this case raises serious questions about the Commission's power to bring cases under Article 169. He concludes that the attitude of the Court may have been different if the case had have stood alone. As it was the Court delivered judgment in the cases of Barra and Blaizot on the same day as the direct action: A. Arnull, 'Of strip cartoonists, vets and gunsmiths' (1988) 13 *ELRev* 260, 266.

99 Case 309/85 [1988] ECR 355.

100 Ibid., p. 367.

101 Ibid., p. 368.

102 Ibid., p. 369.

103 Ibid., p. 375.

104 Ibid., p. 367.

105 Ibid., p. 362.

106 Case 24/86 [1988] ECR 379.

107 Ibid., p. 396.

108 Ibid., p. 397.

109 Ibid., p. 404.

110 Ibid., p. 407.

111 See Case 43/75 *Defrenne* v. *SABENA* [1976] ECR 455 for the first occasion the Court restricted the temporal effect of its judgment. The case of *Blaizot* bears some similarity to *Defrenne*.

112 Supra n. 89.

113 Case 263/86 [1988] ECR 5365. See text accompanying notes 19–23 above.

114 Ibid., p. 5376.

115 Ibid., p. 5377.

116 Ibid., p. 5387.

117 Case 42/87 [1988] ECR 5445.

118 Ibid., pp. 5447–8.

119 Ibid., p. 5451.
120 Ibid., p. 5342.
121 Ibid., pp. 5455–6.
122 Ibid., p. 5370.
123 Ibid., p. 5372.
124 Joined cases 286/82 & 26/83 [1984] ECR 377, 403. My emphasis.
125 Ibid., p. 5378.
126 Ibid., p. 5379.
127 Ibid., p. 5388.
128 OJ [1974] C 98/1 . An alternative starting point would be the General Programme for the Abolition of Restrictions on Freedom of establishment (OJ Special Edition 2nd Series IX, p. 7) Title V dealt with mutual recognition of diplomas and other evidence of formal qualifications. The wording of this Title is repeated in the General Programme for the Abolition of Restrictions on Freedom to Provide Services – OJ Special Edition 2nd Series IX, p. 3.
129 Ibid., para. I.
130 Ibid., para. II.
131 Directives 77/452–5 OJ [1977] L176/1. See G. Morse (1977) 2 *ELRev* 363.
132 Directives 80/154–7 OJ [1980] L33/1. See G. Morse (1980) 5 *ELRev* 222.
133 Directives 78/686–9 OJ [1978] L233/1. See G. Morse (1978) 3 *ELRev* 494.
134 Directives 85/432–5 OJ [1985] L 253/34.
135 Directives 78/1026–9 OJ 1978 L362/1. See G. Morse (1979) 4 *ELRev* 111.
136 Directives 85/384–7 OJ [1985] L223/15.
137 OJ [1993] L165/1. The old Directives can be found in OJ [1975] L167/1. See G. Morse (1975–76) 1 *ELRev* 226 for a comment on the 1975 Directives.
138 See case C 61/89 *Bouchoucha* [1990] ECR I-3551 for an example of the application of this conclusion. See for discussion of this case, J. Lonbay, 'Picking over the bones: Rights of establishment reviewed' (1991) 16 *ELRev* 507.
139 Case 246/80 [1981] ECR 2311.
140 Directive 86/475 (OJ [1986] L267/16) now requires all Member States to provide specialized training in general medicine. This directive has been repealed; its provisions can now be found in directive 93/16 OJ [1993] L165/1.
141 Supra n. 139, p. 2331. For discussion see L. Gormley 'Registration of General Practitioners' (1982) 7 *ELRev* 37.
142 See also Case 115/78 *Knoors* [1979] ECR 399. On this point see S. Kon 'Aspects of discrimination in Community Law' (1981) 6 *ELRev* 75 and D.Pickup, 'Reverse discrimination and freedom of movement for workers' (1986) 23 *CMLRev* 135.
143 Case 11/77 [1977] ECR 1199.
144 Case 2/74 *Reyners* v. *Belgian State* [1974] ECR 631, pp. 654–5. See comment on this case R. Reichling (1974) 11 *CMLRev* 397 and H. Bronkhorst 'Freedom of establishment and freedom to provide services under the EEC Treaty' (1975) 12 *CMLRev* 245.
145 Supra n. 143, p. 1206. See A. Dashwood 'The Patrick case' (1977) 2 *ELRev* 293.

146 Case 71/76 [1977] ECR 765.
147 Ibid., p. 777.
148 Ibid., pp. 778-779. See comment on the case C. Crisham (1978) 15 *CMLRev* 366.
149 Case 222/86 [1987] ECR 4097.
150 Ibid., p. 4116.
151 See on a similar point case C-340/89, *Vlassopoulou* [1991] ECR I-2357. For discussion of this point see Lonbay supra n. 138.
152 See case 222/84 *Johnston* v. *RUC* [1986] ECR 1651, p. 1663.
153 Supra n. 149, p. 4117. See also R. Wallace 'Remedies for foul play' (1988) 13 *ELRev* 267.
154 EC Bulletin 6/84 pt. 1.1.9. para. 6. For details of the Reports see EC Bulletin Supp. 7/85 'A People's Europe: Reports of the *ad hoc* Committee'. See also COM (84) 466 'A People's Europe – Implementing the Conclusions of the Fontainbleau European Council'.
155 See COM (85) 355. Proposal for a Council Directive on a general system for the recognition of higher education diplomas. For discussion of this document see R. Wagenbaur 'Free movement in the professions: The new EC proposal on professional qualifications' (1986) 23 *CMLRev* 91.
156 Ibid., pp. 3–5.
157 OJ [1989] L19/16. See M. Ross 'Mutual recognition of Professional Qualifications' (1989) 14 ELRev 162.
158 Ibid., 5th recital of the Preamble. See also Directive 92/51 OJ [1992] L209/25 on a second general system for the recognition of professional education and training to supplement Directive 89/48. This directive extends the scope of Directive 89/48 beyond higher education to facilitate the pursuit of all those professional activities which in a Member State are dependent on the completion of a certain level of education and training. The system for recognition is similar to that provided by Directive 89/48.
159 OJ [1989] L19/24.
160 OJ [1977] L78/17. For an early commentary on this directive see P. Wilson 'EEC: Freedom to provide services for EEC lawyers' (1978) 19 Harv. Int'l LJ 379 or D. Walters 'Uncertain steps towards a European legal profession' (1978) 3 *ELRev* 265.
161 Case 271/82 [1983] ECR 2727.
162 Case 5/83 [1983] ECR 4233.
163 Case 96/85 [1986] ECR 1475.
164 Auer had previously been prosecuted before the expiry of the time limit for the implementation of the Directives. The Court concluded in that case: 'Article 52 of the Treaty must be interpreted as meaning that for the period prior to the date on which the Member States are required to have taken the measures necessary to comply with Council Directives 78/1026 and 78/1027, the nationals of a Member State cannot rely on that provision with a view to practising the profession of veterinary surgeon in that Member State on any conditions other than those laid down by national legislation'. See Case 136/78 Auer (No.1) [1979] ECR 437.

165 Supra n. 161, p. 2745.

166 Supra n. 162, p. 4246. The Court concluded: 'A Member State may not enforce a penal measure in respect of the improper practice of the profession of veterinary surgeon against a national of another Member State, who is entitled to practise as a veterinary surgeon in his own country, on the ground that he is not enrolled on the register of veterinary surgeons of the first Member State, where such enrolment is refused in breach of Community law'.

167 Supra n. 163, pp. 1485–6.

168 Case 107/83 [1984] ECR 2971.

169 Ibid., p. 2990.

170 Idem., the Court stated: 'In view of the special nature of the legal profession, however, the second Member State must have the right, in the interests of the due administration of justice, to require that lawyers enrolled at a Bar in its territory should practise in such a way as to maintain sufficient contact with their clients and the judicial authorities and abide by the rules of the profession. Nevertheless such requirements must not prevent the nationals of other Member States from exercising properly the right of establishment guaranteed them by the Treaty'. See L. Gormley, 'Freedom to practise at the Bar in more than one Member State' (1984) 9 *ELRev* 439.

171 Compare case 110/78 *Van Wesemael* [1979] ECR 35 and case 279/80 *Webb* [1981] ECR 3305 in relation to less regulated activities. This may change as a result of Directive 92/51 (supra n.158). See cases discussed below for the situation in relation to regulated professions. For discussion see G. Morse, 'Provision of services: The professional supervision exception' (1979) 4 *ELRev* 375.

172 OJ 1993 L 165/1.

173 Supra n. 159. See N. Skarlatos 'European lawyer's right to transnational legal practice in the European Community' [1991/1] LIEI 49.

174 See Case 427/85 *Commission* v. *Germany* [1988] ECR 1123 where the Court held that a provision of the German law implementing Directive 77/249 requiring a German lawyer to accompany a lawyer from another Member State even in cases under German law where there was no mandatory requirement of representation by a lawyer was an infringement of the Directive. Moreover, it was not justified in the public interest (p. 1159). See comment on this case, J. Lonbay 'Cross frontier provision of services by lawyers' (1988) 13 *ELRev* 347. See also case C-294/89 *Commission* v. *France* [1991] ECR I-3591 on a similar point.

175 See case 292/86 *Gallung* [1988] ECR 111. The Court stated: 'Directive 77/249 must be interpreted as meaning that its provisions may not be relied upon by a lawyer established in one Member State with a view to pursuing his activities by way of provision of services in the territory of another Member State where he had been barred from access to the legal profession in the latter Member State for reasons relating to dignity, good repute and integrity'.

176 N. Green, T. Hartley and J. Usher, *Legal Foundations of the Single European Market* (OUP, Oxford, 1991), pp. 191–2.

177 Ibid., pp. 192–3.

Chapter 4 From Maastricht to the Future

1 OJ [1974] C98/2.

2 OJ [1976] C38/1.

3 European Educational Policy Statements (1987, Council of the EC, Brussels) pp. 49–71.

4 Directive 77/486 OJ [1977] L337/12.

5 COM (93) 151, EC Education and Training Programmes 1986–92. Results and achievements: an overview p. 3.

6 Lonbay states: 'The spectacular blossoming of Articles 7 and 128 EEC and Articles 7 and 12 of Regulation 1612/68, by the nurturing hand of the European Court could not have been expected. The swift change from inter-governmental decisions, to 'mixed' decisions, to Community decisions proper was unexpected, and largely made possible by the European Court judgments. The *Gravier* judgment, for example, being widely credited for the ERASMUS programme, the *ERASMUS* judgment itself widely interpreting Community powers.'. J. Lonbay, 'Education and law: The Community context' (1989) 14 *ELRev* 363, p. 386.

7 See Community Charter of the Fundamental Social Rights of Workers (1990, Commission of the EC, Brussels).

8 Articles 130a–130e of the Treaty of Rome as amended by the Single European Act. See also Articles 117–22.

9 The areas are Freedom of Movement; Employment and Remuneration; Improvement of living and Working Conditions; Social Protection; Freedom of Association and Collective Bargaining; Vocational Training; Equal Treatment of Men and Women; Information, Consultation and Participation for Workers; Health Protection and Safety at the Workplace; Protection of Children and Adolescents; Elderly Persons; and, Disabled Persons.

10 Supra n. 7, p. 16.

11 COM (89) 568, Communication from the Commission on the Community Charter of basic social rights for Workers.

12 Ibid., Section 9.

13 OJ [1991] L214/69 amends Decision 87/569 OJ [1987] L346/31.

14 OJ [1989] L393/29. See also Decision 92/170 OJ [1992] L75/51 which merges the Eurotecnet and Force Committees.

15 Decision 90/267 OJ [1990] L156/1. See also Decision 92/170 OJ [1992] L75/51.

16 Decision 88/348 OJ [1988] L158/42. See also Council Decision 91/387 OJ [1991] L214/69 amending the Petra Programme to allow for youth exchanges.

17 See COM (91) 511 First Report on the Application of the European Community's Social Charter.

18 Preamble to the Protocol on Social Policy.

19 Article 2(1) of the Agreement on Social Policy attached to the Social Protocol.

20 The new Article 127 states:

(1) The Community shall implement a vocational training policy which shall support and supplement the action of the Member States, while fully

respecting the responsibility of the Member States for the content and organization of vocational training.

(2) Community action shall aim to:
- facilitate adaptation to industrial changes, in particular through vocational training and retraining;
- improve initial and continuing vocational training in order to facilitate vocational integration and reintegration into the labour market;
- facilitate access to vocational training and encourage mobility of instructors and trainees and particularly young people;
- stimulate cooperation in training between educational or training establishments and firms;
- develop exchanges of information and experience on issues common to the training systems of the Member States.

(3) The Community and the Member States shall foster cooperation with third countries and the competent international organizations in the sphere of vocational training.

(4) The Council, acting in accordance with the procedure referred to in Article 189c and after consulting the Economic and Social Committee, shall adopt measures to contribute to the achievement of the objectives referred to in this Article, excluding any harmonization of the laws and regulations of the Member States.

21 Supra n. 5, p. 6. (Table 2: Networks, Structures and Systems).
22 Ibid., p. 7. (Table 3: Mobility and Exchange).
23 Ibid., p. 8. (Table 4: Projects and Action).
24 Ibid., pp. 10–28.
25 The figure currently is between 6 and 7 per cent. See COM (93) 268 Report on the Erasmus Programme 1992.
26 OJ [1988] C177/2.
27 Supra n. 5, pp. 12–14.
28 Ibid., pp. 14–20.
29 Ibid., pp. 20–2.
30 Ibid., pp. 22–5.
31 Ibid., pp. 25–8.
32 Ibid., p. 20.
33 Ibid., p. 29.
34 COM (90) 334.
35 Ibid., pp. 4–5.
36 OJ [1989] C277/04. See also COM (89) 236, Education and Training in the European Community: Guidelines for the medium-term 1989–92.
37 Ibid., pp. 2–12. The particular policies where a contribution can be expected from higher education includes, the completion of the Internal Market, research and development, social policy, regional development, external relations and, cultural policy.
38 COM (91) 349, p. 13.
39 Ibid., pp.15–18.

40 Ibid., pp 18–19.
41 Ibid., pp. 20–4.
42 Ibid., p. 13.
43 Ibid., pp. 25–7.
44 Ibid., pp. 27–9.
45 Ibid., pp 33–4.
46 Ibid., pp. 29–31.
47 Ibid., pp. 31–3.
48 Ibid., p. 29.
49 Ibid., pp. 35–9.
50 OJ [1992] C336/4.
51 Ibid., p. 5.
52 See OJ [1992] C336/6, Conclusions of the Council and of the Ministers of Education meeting within the Council on criteria for actions on open and distance learning.
53 COM (92) 457.
54 Ibid., p. 31
55 Ibid., pp. 31–2.
56 See, for example, A. Toth, 'The principle of subsidiarity in the Maastricht Treaty' (1992) 29 *CMLRev* 1079; Lord MacKenzie Stuart, 'Subsidiarity – A busted flush?' in Curtin and O'Keefe (eds), *Constitutional Adjudication in European Community and National Law* (Butterworths, Dublin 1992), p. 19.; N. Emiliou 'Subsidiarity: An effective barrier against "the Enterprises of Ambition"?' (1992) 17 *ELRev* 303.; D. Lasok, 'Subsidiarity and the occupied field' (1992) 142 *NLJ* 1228.
57 See for example the case law of the Court on the Treaty-making powers of the Community, case 45/86 *Commission v. Council* [1987] ECR 1493.
58 See for example in relation to the powers of the Court itself: cases 267–9/81 *SPI & SAMI* [1983] ECR 801 and case 294/83 *Les Verts – Parti Ecologiste v. Parliament* [1986] ECR 1339.
59 Communication from the Commission to the Council and the European Parliament, 'The Principle of Subsidiarity', EC Bulletin 10-1992, Part 2, Ch. 2.
60 J. Coppel, 'Edinburgh subsidiarity' (1993) 44 *NILQ* 179, p. 186.
61 See R. Wallace and A. Wilke, *Subsidiarity: Approaches to Power Sharing in the European Community* (RIIA, London, 1990).
62 Conclusions of the Presidency (European Council in Edinburgh, 11–12 December 1992) Annex 1 to Part A, p.7. Reproduced in EC Bulletin 12-1992 Part 1, Ch. 1.
63 See, for example, T. Hartley, 'Constitutional and institutional aspects of the Maastricht Agreement' (1993) 42 *ICLQ* 213, pp. 214–18 for a discussion of the justiciability of the principle of subsidiarity.
64 COM (93) 183 Commission Working Paper: Guidelines for Community Action in the Field of Education and Training.
65 Ibid., p. 1.
66 Ibid., pp. 2–6.
67 Ibid., p. 9.
68 Ibid., pp. 10–11.

69 Ibid., p. 13.
70 Ibid., p. 13.
71 Supra n. 34, p. 9.
72 Supra n. 64, p. 15.
73 Ibid., pp. 14–15.
74 Ibid., p. 14.
75 Ibid., pp. 15–16.
76 Ibid., pp. 16–17.
77 Ibid., p. 16.
78 OJ [1983] C277/1. For a critical analysis of the draft Treaty see, R. Bieber et al., *An Ever Closer Union* (European Perspective Series, Brussels, 1985).
79 See European Integration in Education and Culture: The French Government Blue Paper EC Bulletin 3-1987, Part 3, Ch. 4.

Chapter 5 The Emergence and Development of Community Competence

1 OJ [1974] C62/5.
2 Point 4 of the communique, EC Bulletin 1-1970 Part One Ch. 1.
3 Point 3 of the declaration, EC Bulletin 10-1972 Part One Ch. 1.
4 EC Bulletin 12-1973, point 2501.
5 Reproduced in EC Bulletin Supp. 6/77.
6 Ibid., p. 5.
7 Ibid., p. 7.
8 Ibid., pp. 7–10.
9 Case 7/68 [1968] ECR 423.
10 Ibid., p. 428. See also Case 155/84, *Onnasch v. Hauptzollamt Berlin-Packhof* [1985] ECR 1149, where the Court considered the tariff classification of works of art.
11 Ibid., p. 430.
12 P. Oliver, *Free Movement of Goods in the EEC* (second edn) (ELC, London, 1988) p. 205.
13 Supra n. 5, p. 10.
14 Ibid., pp. 11–12.
15 Ibid., pp. 12–17.
16 Case 24/67 [1968] ECR 55, at p. 71.
17 Case 78/70 [1971] ECR 487.
18 Ibid., p. 500.
19 Case 15/74 [1974] ECR 1147.
20 Ibid., pp. 1162–3.
21 Cases 55 and 57/80 [1981] ECR 147.
22 Ibid., p. 161.
23 In addition to moral rights the Court stated that the other rights included 'the right to exploit commercially the marketing of the protected work, particularly in the form of licences granted in return for payments of royalties'. Ibid., p. 162.

24 Compare with Case 19/84, *Pharmon v. Hoechst* [1985] ECR 2281, where the Court held that the licence was of a compulsory character consent could not be said to be given to the licensee. The potential application of this case, which deals with patents, to copyright is an open question. See now Case 156/86, *Warner Bros v. Christiansen* [1988] ECR 2605 and Case 341/87, *EMI Electrola v. Patricia Im- und Export* [1989] ECR 79 where the Court was more lenient on the question of consent. For example, in *Christiansen* the Court stated: 'Where national legislation confers on authors a specific right to hire out video-cassettes, that right would be rendered worthless if its owner were not in a position to authorize the operations for doing so. It cannot, therefore, be accepted that the marketing by a film-maker of a video-cassette containing one of his works, in a Member State which does not have specific protection for the right to hire out, should have repercussions on the right conferred on that same film-maker by the legislation of another Member State to restrain, in that State, the hiring out of that video-cassette' (p. 2630).

25 Case 62/79 [1980] ECR 881 (See also on a similar point Case 52/79 *Procureur Du Roi v. Debauve* [1980] ECR 833.)

26 Ibid., p. 903.

27 Supra n. 5, p. 14.

28 Committee on Copyright and Design Law Cmnd 6732 Ch. 17.

29 Supra n. 5, p. 18.

30 Ibid., pp. 19–24.

31 Ibid., p. 19.

32 Ibid., p. 21.

33 Ibid., p. 26.

34 OJ [1979] C39 for the response of the European Parliament and OJ [1979] C128 for the response of the Economic and Social Committee.

35 Supra n. 5, p. 6.

36 EC Bulletin Supp. 6/82, Stronger Community Action in the Cultural Sector, p. 7 (reproduced from COM (82) 590).

37 Ibid., p. 8.

38 Idem.

39 Supra n. 19, p. 8.

40 OJ [1981] C227/2.

41 Supra n. 36, p. 16 (Annex I).

42 Case 120/78, *Rewe-Zentral v. Bundesmonopolverwaltung für Brantwein* [1979] ECR 649.

43 Ibid., p. 662.

44 Cases 60 and 61/84 [1985] ECR 2605.

45 Ibid., p. 2628.

46 Ibid., p. 2613.

47 Supra n. 12, p. 221.

48 See also case 229/83 *Leclerc v. Au Blé Vert* [1985] ECR 1.

49 Ibid., pp. 9–12.

50 Case 90/79 [1981] ECR 283.

51 Ibid., p. 299.

52 Supra n. 5, p. 13.
53 Supra n. 36, p. 16 (Annex II).
54 Ibid., p. 17.
55 Ibid., p. 22.
56 Ibid., p. 21.
57 Ibid., p. 18.
58 Ibid., p. 11.
59 Ibid., pp. 19–20.
60 Ibid., p. 12.
61 Ibid., p. 26.
62 Ibid., p. 14 and pp. 26–7.
63 Ibid., p. 32.
64 EC Bulletin 9-1982, point 2.1.112.
65 EC Bulletin 6-1983 Part 1, Ch. 5.
66 Ibid., Ch. 6.
67 Ibid., point 3.3.
68 In addition to taking the activities of the Council of Europe into consideration, the final area called for 'closer coordination of cultural activities in third countries within the framework of Political Cooperation' thereby promoting the international dimension of the Community's action in the cultural sector.
69 Supra n. 65, p. 23.
70 EC Bulletin 1-1983, point 2.1.93.
71 EC Bulletin 6-1984, point 2.1.63.
72 EC Bulletin 11-1984, point 2.1.75.
73 OJ [1985] C2/2.
74 OJ [1985] C153/2.
75 OJ [1985] C153/3.
76 OJ [1984] C204/1.
77 EC Bulletin 5-1985, point 2.1.59.
78 OJ [1985] C271/1.
79 OJ [1985] C348/2.
80 OJ [1986] C44/2.
81 EC Bulletin Supp. 4/87, p. 5.
82 EC Bulletin 6-1984, Part 1 Ch. 1, point 6.
83 EC Bulletin 3-1985, Part 1 Ch. 1, point 1.2.7.
84 EC Bulletin Supp. 7/85, p. 21.
85 OJ [1986] C320/4.
86 OJ [1986] C320/1. See also OJ [1984] C111, Commission publication of calls for proposals for pilot projects in the field of protection and conservation of the Community's architectural heritage. This call for proposals was repeated in subsequent years, although each year has a slightly different focus to the preservation and conservation projects: e.g., OJ [1987] C98, OJ [1988] C55.
87 OJ [1988] C320/2.
88 COM (88) 331. Communication from the Commission to the European Parliament: A People's Europe, p. 12.
89 EC Bulletin 3-1987, Part 1, Ch. 1.

90 The Commission in responding to the Conference noted that only 0.05 per cent of the EC Budget was devoted to cultural activities.
91 Supra n. 81, p. 6.
92 Ibid., p. 7.
93 EC Bulletin 12-1987, Part 1 Ch. 2.
94 OJ [1988] C197/2.
95 Supra n. 81, pp. 13–14.
96 Directive 86/259 OJ [1986] L311/28.
97 Supra n. 81, p. 16.
98 Supra n. 94, para. 3 of the Conclusions.
99 EC Bulletin 12-1988, Pt 1, Ch.1., point 1.1.9.
100 COM (90) 78 Audiovisual Policy, p. 3.
101 OJ 1989 L 298/23.
102 For the situation before this directive see Case 352/85, *Bond van Adverteerders* [1988] ECR 2085 and Case C-288/89, *Collective Antennevoorziening Gouda* [1991] ECR I-4007. The cases concerned restrictions on the retransmission of television broadcasts from other Member States in the Netherlands. In the latter case the Netherlands government argued that the restrictions were justified on grounds of cultural policy – i.e. to safeguard freedom of expression/pluralism in the media. This, according to the Court, may constitute a ground for restricting the freedom to provide services; however, the restrictions in this case had no necessary connection with the cultural policy being pursued (ibid., p.4043–4). The Advocate General reached a different conclusion (Ibid., p. 4026).
103 These are further defined in Article 6 of the Directive, supra n. 101. See also Case C-353/89 *Commission v. Netherlands* [1991] I-ECR 4069, which occurred before the date for the implementation of the directive had expired, where the Commission alleged that Articles of the Netherlands Law on Radio and Television requiring the use of the technical resources of a particular body for the production of radio and television programmes breached Article 59 of the Treaty. The Netherlands government argued that the restriction was necessary for cultural policy reasons – protection of freedom of expression. The Court held that the restriction went beyond what was necessary to achieve the requirements of protection of freedom of expression (ibid., I-4097).
104 Case C-353/89, *Commission v. Netherlands* [1991] ECR I-4069, p. 4102, for discussion of the law prevailing before the directive. In this case, the Commission maintained that Article 66 of the Netherlands law on radio and television, which limited advertising in the Netherlands, was contrary to Article 59 of the Treaty. It was argued that such restrictions were necessary to protect consumers and to pursue cultural policy objectives. The Court held these restrictions to be contrary to Article 59. See also cases cited supra n. 102.
105 OJ [1989] L142/1. See also Decision 89/630 (OJ [1989] L89/360) on the common action to be taken by the Member States with respect to the adoption of a single worldwide high definition television production standard.
106 OJ [1992] L137/17.
107 See, for example, OJ [1986] L311/28.

108 Supra n. 101, Article 4 of the directive.
109 EC Bulletin 6-1993, point 1.2.230.
110 OJ [1990] L380/37.
111 EC Bulletin 12-1989, Part 1, Ch. 1.
112 Supra n. 101, Article 4(1) states 'In implementing the programme, particular attention will be given to Community participation in Audiovisual Eureka projects which complement or extend the measures referred to Article 3 and satisfy the criteria for Community involvement set out in Annex II'.
113 See COM (90) 78 Audiovisual Policy and Production.
114 COM (85) 681.
115 Ibid., p. 2.
116 Ibid., p. 3.
117 Joined cases 43/82 and 63/82 [1984] ECR 19.
118 Ibid., pp. 33–4.
119 Ibid., p. 55. The Court stated that the agreement 'involved a restriction on competition within the common market by reason of both the exclusive dealing system and the collective resale price maintenance for which it makes provision'.
120 Ibid., p. 62. The Court concluded: 'To submit the production of and trade in books to rules whose sole purpose is to ensure freedom of trade between Member States in normal conditions of competition cannot be regarded as restricting freedom of publication which, it is not contested, remains entire [sic] at the level of both publishers and distributors'.
121 Ibid., p. 63.
122 See OJ [1982] L54/36, paragraph 60. The Advocate General noted that in response to questions asked by the Court, the Commission claimed: 'In appreciating an agreement in the light of Article 85(3) it neither can nor may attribute decisive significance to certain culturally desirable consequences of a given form of distribution without more ado' (ibid., p. 89).
123 Supra n. 117, p. 48.
124 Ibid., p. 89.
125 Case 229/83 [1985] ECR 1.
126 Ibid., pp. 19–20.
127 Ibid., p. 31. The Court noted: 'Whilst it is true that the rules on competition are concerned with the conduct of undertakings and not with national legislation, Member States are none the less obliged under the second paragraph of Article 5 of the Treaty not to detract, by means of national legislation, from the full and uniform application of Community law or from the effectiveness of its implementing measures; nor may they introduce or maintain in force measures, even of a legislative nature, which may render ineffective the competition rules applicable to undertakings'.
128 Ibid., p. 33.
129 Ibid., p. 35. The Court specifically stated: 'As far as that point is concerned, it must be pointed out that national legislation which requires traders to abide by specific retail prices and discourages the marketing of imported products can be justified solely on the grounds set out in Article 36 of the Treaty. Since it

derogates from a fundamental rule of the Treaty, Article 36 must be interpreted strictly and cannot be extended to cover objectives not expressly enumerated therein. Neither the safeguarding of consumers' interests not the protection of creativity and cultural diversity in the realm of publishing is mentioned in Article 36. It follows that the justification put forward by the French government cannot be accepted'.

130 See discussion above in relation to the mandatory requirements especially text accompanying notes 44–6.

131 Supra n. 114, p. 6.

132 Ibid., pp. 15–20. The four proposals were (a) Complete freedom to determine prices; (b) An obligation on the publisher to sell a book at the same price to all buyers in the Community; (c) Giving Member States the option of allowing publishers to set a retail price (which would then apply throughout the Community, according to a mechanism to be determined); (d) Obliging Member States to apply the system under (c) with some flexibility for the bookseller. The options represent the systems applicable in each of the Member States.

133 EC Bulletin Supp. 4/87, p. 13.

134 OJ [1988] C197/2.

135 OJ [1987] C309/3.

136 OJ [1989] C183/1.

137 For further details see OJ [1989] C225/2.

138 COM (89) 258.

139 OJ [1989] C183/3.

140 Supra n. 134, para. 3.

141 Supra n. 133, p. 24.

142 Ibid., p. 21.

143 COM (90) 472.

144 Ibid., p. 2.

145 COM (86) 255, Guidelines for an action programme to promote the European media software industry.

146 OJ [1990] C127/5.

147 EC Bulletin 4-1991, point 1.2.145.

148 Supra n. 114, p. 5.

149 For details of these resolutions see the discussion in the previous section – the Book Sector.

150 Supra n. 114 , pp. 6–9. See also the discussion of this issue in COM (89) 258, Books and reading: a cultural challenge for Europe.

151 EC Bulletin 11-1990, point 1.3.188.

152 OJ [1991] C188/1.

153 Supra n. 134, para. 3.

154 OJ [1986] C320/2.

155 Ibid., para. 5.

156 Supra n. 133, pp. 12–13.

157 See COM (92) 149, New Prospects for Community Cultural Action, Annex A, part IV.C.

158 Ibid., Annex B.

159 Supra n. 134, para. 2.
160 EC Bulletin Supp. 4/87, p. 10.
161 COM (89) 594, Commission communication to the Council on the protection of national treasures possessing artistic, historic or archaeological value; needs arising from the abolition of frontiers in 1992.
162 EC Bulletin 11-1990, point 1.3.187.
163 OJ[1992] L395/1.
164 Ibid., Article 2(1).
165 OJ [1993] L74/1.
166 The categories are roughly comparable to those in the Annex to Regulation 3911/92.
167 Ibid., Article 10.
168 COM (88) 172 Green Paper on copyright and the challenge of technology: copyright issues requiring immediate attention.
169 For example, COM (90) 584 Follow-up to the Green Paper: Working Programme of the Commission in the field of copyright and neighbouring rights.
170 Supra n. 168, p. 1.
171 See discussion of this point on pp. 124-7. See also Case 158/86, *Warner Bros. v. Christiansen* [1988] ECR 2605 and Case 341/87 *EMI Electrola v. Patricia Im- und Export* [1989] ECR 79.
172 The Green Paper devotes a chapter for discussion of each of these areas.
173 Supra n. 168, p. 13.
174 Ibid., pp. 34–6.
175 OJ [1991] L122/42.
176 OJ [1992] C138/1. See also Conclusions of the Ministers for Culture meeting within the Council on copyright and neighbouring rights OJ [1991] C188/4.
177 OJ [1992] L346/61.
178 See Articles 1 to 5 of the directive. Although before the directive, see also case 158/86 *Warner Bros v. Christiansen* (supra n. 171) a case concerning differences in the legislation of the Member States on rental rights.
179 Supra n. 175, Article 6 to 11 of the Directive.
180 OJ [1992] C156/4.
181 OJ [1993] C25/43.
182 OJ [1993] C27/7.
183 Supra n. 171, p. 91.
184 Ibid., p. 96.
185 OJ [1988] C197/1.
186 EC Bulletin 5-1988, point 2.190. See also EC Bulletin 11-1988, point 2.1.146 for the establishment within the Commission of a Committee of cultural consultants.
187 See in particular the discussion of the concept of vocational training in Chapter 3.
188 EC Bulletin Supp. 6/82 Stronger Community Action in the Cultural Sector, p. 7.

Chapter 6 From Maastricht to the Future

1 EC Bulletin Supp. 6/77, p. 5.
2 EC Bulletin Supp. 6/82.
3 Ibid., p. 7.
4 EC Bulletin 7-1984, point 2.1.175.
5 EC Bulletin 6-1983, Part 1, Ch. 6.
6 Ibid., point 1.4.3.
7 See EC Bulletin Supp. 7/85 for further details.
8 EC Bulletin Supp. 4/87 (COM (87) 603) A Fresh Boost for Culture in the European Community.
9 OJ [1988] C197/2.
10 For further details see the section on the audio-visual sector in Chapter 5.
11 For example, Directive 92/38 OJ [1992] L137/1.
12 Directive 89/552 OJ [1989] L298/23.
13 OJ [1990] L380/37.
14 Ibid., Annex II for an example of pan-European co-operation.
15 OJ [1989] C225/2 and OJ 1993 C 160/1. For further details see the section on the Book Sector in Chapter 1 of this Part.
16 OJ [1991] C188/1.
17 For further discussion, see the section on business sponsorship in Chapter 5.
18 OJ [1992] L395/1.
19 OJ [1993] L74/1.
20 For details see the section on other areas in Chapter 5.
21 See for example, OJ [1990] C304 and OJ [1991] C284.
22 OJ [1985] C153/2 and OJ [1990] C162/1.
23 OJ [1990] C167/2 (Platform Europe) and OJ [1991] C205/19 (Kaleidoscope).
24 See discussion of this area in Chapter 4.
25 COM (92), New Prospects for Community Cultural Action, p. 1.
26 Ibid., p. 4.
27 Ibid., pp. 6–7.
28 Ibid., p. 5.
29 Ibid., pp. 7-8.
30 Ibid., p. 8.
31 Ibid., p. 10.
32 Ibid., pp. 11-12.
33 Ibid., pp. 13.
34 Ibid., pp. 14–17.
35 For example, Lomé IV concluded in 1990 contains a chapter on cultural co-operation.
36 Supra n. 25, p. 16.
37 OJ 1990 C 162/1.
38 Supra n. 25, p. 3.
39 OJ [1992] C366/1.
40 Ibid., para. 4.
41 The declaration 'declares the intention to strengthen and broaden cooperation in

the area of cultural affairs, in order to contribute to a better understanding between peoples of a multicultural Europe and to safeguard and further develop the national and regional heritage that enriches European culture by its diversity'. A further declaration records the parties intention to cooperate against illegal traffic in cultural goods.

42 The Parliament had previously passed a resolution on cultural relations between the Community and Central and Eastern Europe. (OJ [1991] C267) The resolution recommends that cultural relations be developed in nine areas: information; language and translation; training; the audio-visual sector; art; publishing; libraries; the architectural and cultural heritage; and town twinning.

43 OJ [1993] C42/173.

44 Ibid., para. 30(k).

45 Ibid., para. 29(m).

46 Ibid., para. 29(q).

47 Ibid., para. 29(t).

48 Ibid., para. 30(b).

49 Ibid., para. 30(n).

50 Ibid., para. 31.

51 Ibid., para. 34.

52 OJ [1984] C77/33. See for a critical analysis of the Draft Treaty, R. Bieber *et al.* (eds), *An Ever Closer Union* (European Perspectives Series, Brussels 1985).

53 Case C-379/87 [1989] ECR 3967.

54 Ibid., p. 3982.

55 Ibid., p. 3993.

56 EC Bulletin 3-1987, Part 3, Ch. 4.

Table of European Communities Legislation

Treaty of Rome

Article 3: 97; 161; 164
Article 3b: 112; 113; 165; 166
Article 7: 44; 68; 69; 71; 78; 81
Article 7(2): 45
Article 30: 121; 130; 132; 146; 147
Article 34: 121
Article 36: 121; 123; 124; 129; 130; 132; 156
Article 48: 7
Article 50: 133
Article 52: 85
Article 54: 81
Article 57: 3; 22; 81; 82; 85; 142
Article 59: 71; 80; 127
Article 66: 142
Article 85: 145; 146
Article 86: 125
Article 92: 161; 167
Article 100: 127
Article 118: 3
Article 128: 3; 25; 29; 32; 33; 34; 35; 39; 44; 45; 49; 68; 159; 164
Article 222: 124
Article 235: 25; 28; 34; 35; 39; 44

Regulations

Regulation 1612/68: 43; 51; 81
Article 7(2): 59–66
Article 7(3): 59–66
Article 12: 7; 51; 52–9; 66; 79
Regulation 1360/90 OJ [1990] L131/1: 40n
Regulation 2157/91 OJ [1991] L201/2: 40n
Regulation 2334/92 OJ [1992] L227/1: 40n
Regulation 3911/92 OJ [1992] L395/1: 153

Directives

Directive 64/221 OJ Special Edition [1964], 117: 46
Directive 68/360 OJ Special Edition [1968] (II), 475: 21n
Directive 77/249 OJ [1977] L78/17: 90; 93
Directive 77/452 OJ [1977] L176/1: 82n
Directive 77/486 OJ [1977] L337/12: 52
Directive 78/686 OJ [1978] L233/1: 82n
Directive 78/1026 OJ [1978] L362/1: 82n
Directive 80/154 OJ [1980] L33/1: 82n
Directive 85/384 OJ [1985] L223/15: 82n
Directive 85/432 OJ [1985] L253/34: 82n
Directive 86/259 OJ [1986] L311/28: 141n
Directive 86/475 OJ [1986] L267/16: 84n
Directive 89/48 OJ [1989] L19/16: 87–90
Directive 89/552 OJ [1989] L298/23: 142
Directive 90/364 OJ [1990] L180/26: 43n
Directive 90/365 OJ [1990] L180/28: 43n
Directive 90/366 OJ [1990] L180/30: 43; 46; 47
Directive 91/250 OJ [1991] L122/42: 155
Directive 92/38 OJ [1992] L137/17: 143; 144; 163n
Directive 92/51 OJ [1992] L209/25: 18; 18n
Directive 92/100 OJ [1992] L346/61: 155; 156
Directive 93/7 OJ [1993] L74/1: 153; 154
Directive 93/16 OJ [1993] L165/1: 83; 84n; 93

Decisions

Decision 86/365 OJ [1986] L222/17: 30
Decision 87/327 OJ [1987] L166/20: 24; 28
Decision 87/569 OJ [1987] L346/31: 19n
Decision 88/348 OJ [1988] L158/42: 18n
Decision 89/27 OJ [1989] L13/28: 100n
Decision 89/337 OJ [1989] L142/1: 143
Decision 89/489 OJ [1989] L239/24: 38
Decision 89/657 OJ [1989[L393/29: 19n; 100
Decision 89/663 OJ [1989] L395/23: 28n
Decision 90/190 OJ [1990] L102/1: 19n
Decision 90/233 OJ [1990] L131/21: 40
Decision 90/267 OJ [1990] L156/1: 19n; 100
Decision 90/685 OJ [1990] L380/37: 144
Decision 91/387 OJ [1991] L214/69: 18n; 19n; 100
Decision 91/611 OJ [1991] L332/1: 19n
Decision 92/170 OJ [1992] L75/51: 19n
Decision 92/240 OJ [1992] L122/43: 40n
Decision 93/246 OJ [1993] L112/34: 41

Table of Cases from the European Court of Justice

A: Numerical

Case 24/67, *Parke Davis* v. *Centrafarm* [1968] ECR 55: 124; 125
Case 7/68, *Commission* v. *Italy* [1968] ECR 423: 123
Case 78/70, *DGG* v. *Metro* [1971] ECR 487: 125
Case 2/74, *Reyners* [1974] ECR 631: 84
Case 9/74, *Casagrande* [1974] ECR 773: 52; 53; 70
Case 15/74, *Centrafarm* v. *Sterling Drug* [1974] ECR 1147: 125
Case 68/74, *Alaimo* [1975] ECR 109: 54; 55
Case 32/75, *Cristini* [1975] ECR 1085: 59
Case 43/75, *Defrenne* v. *SABENA* [1976] ECR 455: 77n
Case 71/76, *Thieffry* [1977] ECR 765: 85
Case 11/77, *Patrick* [1977] ECR 1199: 84; 85
Case 110/78, *Van Wesemael* [1979] ECR 35: 93n
Case 115/78, *Knoors* [1979] ECR 399: 84n
Case 120/78, *Rewe-Zentral* v. *Bundesmonopolverwaltung für Brantwein* [1979] ECR 649: 130
Case 136/78, *Auer* (No. 1) [1979] ECR 437: 91n
Case 52/79, *Procurueur du Roi* v. *Debauve* [1980] ECR 833: 126n
Case 62/79, *Coditel* v. *Ciné Vog* [1980] ECR 881: 126; 127
Case 90/79, *Commission* v. *France* [1981] ECR 283: 132
Cases 55 & 57/80, *Music-Vetreib* v. *GEMA* [1981] ECR 147: 126
Case 246/80, *Broekmeulen* [1981] ECR 2311: 83; 84
Case 279/80, *Webb* [1981] ECR 3305: 93n
Case 53/81, *Levin* [1982] ECR 1035: 60n
Case 65/81, *Reina* [1982] ECR 33: 59
Cases 267–9/81, *SPI & SAMI* [1983] ECR 801: 112n
Cases 43 & 63/82, *VBVB & VBBB* v. *Commission* [1984] ECR 19: 145; 146
Case 152/82, *Forcheri* [1983] ECR 2323: 67; 70; 77
Case 271/82, *Auer* (No.2) [1983] ECR 2727: 91

Case 5/83, *Reinks* [1983] ECR 4233: 91
Cases 286/82, & 26/83 *Luisi and Carbone* [1984] ECR 5445: 79
Case 107/83, *Klopp* [1984] ECR 2971: 92
Case 229/83, *Leclerc* v. *Au Blé Vert* [1985] ECR 1: 146; 147
Case 293/83, *Gravier* [1985] ECR 593: 27; 63; 70; 71; 72; 75
Case 294/83, *Les Verts – Parti Ecologiste* [1986] ECR 1339: 112n
Case 19/84, *Pharmon* v *Hoechst* [1985] ECR 2281: 126n
Cases 60 & 61/84, *Cinéthèque* [1985] ECR 2605: 131; 132
Case 155/84, *Onnasch* v. *Hauptzollamt Berlin-Packhof* [1985] ECR 1449: 123n
Case 222/84, *Johnston* v. *RUC* [1986] ECR 1651: 86n
Case 66/85, *Lawrie-Blum* [1986] ECR 2121: 60n
Case 96/85, *Commission* v. *France* [1986] ECR 1475: 91; 92
Case 293/85R, *Commission* v. *Belgium* [1985] ECR 3521: 72n
Case 293/85, *Commission* v. *Belgium* [1988] ECR 305: 72; 73
Case 309/85, *Barra* [1988] ECR 355: 74; 75
Case 352/85, *Bond van Adverteerders* [1988] ECR 2085: 142n
Case 427/85, *Commission* v. *Germany* [1988] ECR 1123: 93n
Case 24/86, *Blaizot* [1988] ECR 379: 27; 75; 76
Case 39/86, *Lair* [1988] ECR 3161: 60; 61; 65
Case 45/86, *Commision* v. *Council* [1987] ECR 1493: 27n; 112n
Case 158/86, *Warner Bros.* v. *Christiansen* [1988] ECR 2605: 155n
Case 197/86, *Brown* [1988] ECR 3207: 62; 63; 65
Case 222/86, *Heylens* [1987] ECR 4097: 86; 90
Case 236/86, *Humbel* [1988] ECR 5365: 27; 56; 57; 72; 77; 79; 80
Case 292/86, *Gallung* [1988] ECR 111: 93n
Case 235/87, *Matteucci* [1988] ECR 5589: 64; 65
Case 242/87, *Commission* v. *Council* [1988] ECR 1425: 25n
Case 341/87, *EMI Electrola* v. *Patricia Im- und Export* [1989] ECR 9: 155n; 156
Case 379/87, *Groener* v. *Minister of Education* [1989] ECR 3967: 173
Cases 389 & 390/87, *Echternach and Moritz* [1989] ECR 723: 55; 56; 58
Cases C-51/89, C-90/89 & C-94/89, *United Kingdom & Others* v. *Council* [1991] ECR I-2757: 32n
Case C-61/89, *Bouchoucha* [1990] ECR I-3551: 83n
Case C-288/89, *Collective Antennevoorziening Gouda* [1991] ECR I-4007: 142n
Case C-308/89, *Di Leo* [1990] ECR I-4185: 57; 58
Case C-340/89, *Vlassopoulou* [1991] ECR I-2357: 86n
Case C- 353/89, *Commission* v. *Netherlands* [1991] I-ECR 4069: 142n
Case C-357/89, *Raulin* (nyr 26 February 1992): 62n
Case C-3/90, *Bernini* (nyr 26 February 1992): 59n
Case C-295/90, *European Parliament* v. *Council* (nyr 7 July 1992): 46; 47

B: Alphabetical

Alaimo [1975] ECR 109, Case 68/74: 54; 55
Auer (No. 1) [1979] ECR 437, Case 136/78: 91n
Auer (No.2) [1983] ECR 2727, Case 271/82: 91
Barra [1988] ECR 355, Case 309/85: 74; 75

Bernini (nyr 26 February 1992), Case C-3/90: 59n
Blaizot [1988] ECR 379, Case 24/86: 27; 75; 76
Bond van Adverteerders [1988] ECR 2085, Case 352/85: 142n
Bouchoucha [1990] ECR I-3551, Case C-61/89: 83n
Broekmeulen [1981] ECR 2311, Case 246/80: 83; 84
Brown [1988] ECR 3207, case 197/86: 62; 63; 65
Casagrande [1974] ECR 773, Case 9/74: 52; 53; 70
Centrafarm v. *Sterling Drug* [1974] ECR 1147, Case 15/74: 125
Cinéthèque [1985] ECR 2605, Cases 60&61/84: 131; 132
Coditel v. *Ciné Vog* [1980] ECR 881, Case 62/79: 126; 127
Collective Antennevoorziening Gouda [1991] ECR I-4007, Case C-288/89: 142n
Commission v. *Belgium* [1985] ECR 3521, Case 293/85R: 72n
Commission v. *Belgium* [1988] ECR 305, Case 293/85: 72; 73
Commission v. *Council* [1987] ECR 1493, Case 45/86: 27n; 112n
Commission v. *Council* [1988] ECR 1425, Case 242/87: 25n
Commission v. *France* [1981] ECR 283, Case 90/79: 132
Commission v. *France* [1986] ECR 1475, Case 96/85: 91; 92
Commission v. *Germany* [1988] ECR 1123, Case 427/85: 93n
Commission v. *Italy* [1968] ECR 423, Case 7/68: 123
Commission v. *Netherlands* [1991] I-ECR 4069, Case C- 353/89: 142n
Cristini [1975] ECR 1085, Case 32/75: 59
Defrenne v. *SABENA* [1976] ECR 455, Case 43/75: 77n
DGG v. *Metro* [1971] ECR 487, Case 78/70: 125
Di Leo [1990] ECR I-4185, Case C-308/89: 57; 58
EMI Electrola v. *Patricia Im-und Export* [1989] ECR 79, Case 341/87: 155n; 156
Echternach and Moritz [1989] ECR 723, Cases 389 & 390/87: 55; 56; 58
European Parliament v. *Council* (nyr 7 July 1992), Case C-295/90: 46; 47
Forcheri [1983] ECR 2323, Case 152/82: 67; 70; 77
Gallung [1988] ECR 111, Case 292/86: 93n
Gravier [1985] ECR 593, Case 293/83: 27; 63; 70; 71; 72; 75
Groener v. *Minister of Education* [1989] ECR 3967, Case 379/87: 173
Heylens [1987] ECR 4097, Case 222/86: 86; 90
Humbel [1988] ECR 5365, Case 236/86: 27; 56; 57
Johnston v. *RUC* [1986] ECR 1651, Case 222/84: 56n
Klopp [1984] ECR 2971, Case 107/83: 92
Knoors [1979] ECR 399, Case 115/78: 84n
Lair [1988] ECR 3161, Case 39/86: 60; 61; 65
Lawrie-Blum [1986] ECR 2121, Case 66/85: 60n
Leclerc v. *Au Blé Vert* [1985] ECR 1, Case 229/83: 146; 147
Les Verts [1986] ECR 1339, Case 294/83: 112n
Levin [1982] ECR 1035, Case 53/81: 60n
Luisi and Carbone [1984] ECR 5445, Cases 286/82 & 26/83: 79
Matteucci [1988] ECR 5589, Case 235/87: 64; 65
Music-Vetreib v. *GEMA* [1981] ECR 147, Cases 55&57/80: 126
Onnasch v. *Hauptzollamt Berlin-Packhof* [1985] ECR 1449, Case 155/84: 123n
Parke Davis v. *Centrafarm* [1968] ECR 55, Case 24/67: 124; 125

Patrick [1977] ECR 1199, case 11/77: 84; 85
Pharmon v. *Hoechst* [1985] ECR 2281, Case 19/84: 126n
Procureur du Roi v. *Debauve* [1980] ECR 833, Case 52/79: 126n
Raulin (nyr 26 February 1992), Case C-357/89: 62n
Reina [1982] ECR 33, Case 65/81: 59
Reinks [1983] ECR 4233, Case 5/83: 91
Rewe-Zentral v. *Bundesmonopolverwaltung fur Brantwein* [1979] ECR 649, Case 120/78: 130
Reyners [1974] ECR 631, Case 2/74: 84
SPI & SAMI [1983] ECR 801, Cases 267 & 269/81: 112n
Thieffry [1977] ECR 765, Case 71/76: 85
United Kingdom & Others v. *Council* [1991] ECR I-2757, Cases C-51/89, C90/89 & C-94/89: 32n
Van Wesemael [1979] ECR 35, Case 110/78: 93n
VBVB & VBBB v. *Commission* [1984] ECR 19, Cases 43&63/82: 145; 146
Vlassopoulou [1991] ECR I-2357, Case C-340/89: 86n
Warner Bros. v. *Christainsen* [1988] ECR 2605, Case 156/86: 155n
Webb [1981] ECR 3305, Case 279/80: 93n

UK Cases

MacMahon v. *Department of Education* [1982] 3 CMLR 1085: 59; 60; 62; 69n
R v. *Inner London Education Authority ex parte Hinde* [1985] 1 CMLR 716: 69; 70; 72n

Bibliography

EC Publications

COM (78) 499, Education Action Programme at Community Level: Equal Opportunities in education and training for girls

COM (82) 590, Stronger Community Action in the Cultural Sector

COM (84) 466, A People's Europe: Implementing the Conclusions of the Fontainbleau European Council

COM (85) 134, Report on Education and vocational training within the EC

COM (85) 167, Communication setting out the broad lines of Community action for the period 1985–88 in the field of vocational training and the new information technology

COM (85) 310, White Paper on the Completion of the Internal Market

COM (85) 355, Proposal for a Council Directive on a general system for the recognition of higher education diplomas

COM (85) 431, Proposal for a decision adopting an action programme of the Community in Education and Training for Technology 1986–92

COM (85) 681, The European Dimension with regard to Books

COM (85) 756, Proposal for a Council Decision adopting ERASMUS

COM (86) 255, Guidelines for an action programme to promote the Euroepan media software industry

COM (87) 603, A Fresh boost for Culture in the European Community

COM (88) 36, Comett Programme – Report on 1987 Activities

COM (88) 172, Green Paper on Copyright and the challenge of technology; Copyright issues requiring immediate attention

COM (88) 192, Erasmus Programme Annual Report 1987

COM (88) 203, The Teaching of Foreign Languages

COM (88) 280, Education in the EC: Medium-term Prospects 1988–92

COM (88) 331, Communication from the Commission to the European Parliament: A People's Europe

COM (88) 841, Proposal for a Council Decision establishing the Lingua Programme to promote training in foreign languages in the European Community

COM (89) 236, Education and Training in the EC: Guidelines for the Medium-Term 1989-92

COM (89) 258, Books and Reading: a cultural challenge for Europe

COM (89) 275, Proposal for a Council Decision on the right of Residence of Students, on the Right of Residence for employees and self-employed persons who have ceased their occupational activity and on the right of residence

COM (89) 372, Proposal for a Council Directive in a second general system for the recognition of professional education and training which complements Directive 89/48

COM (89) 59, The protection of national treasures possessing artistic, historic or archaelogical value; needs arising from the abolition of frontiers in 1992

COM (89) 568, Community Charter of Basic Social Rights for Workers

COM (90) 78, Audio-visual Policy

COM (90) 334, The Rationalisation and Coordination of Vocational Training Programmes

COM (90) 472, Vocational Training in the Arts Field

COM (90) 584, Follow-up to the Green Paper: Working Programme of the Commission in the field of copyright and neighbouring rights

COM (91) 349, Memorandum on Higher Education in the European Community

COM (91) 511, First Report on the Application of the EC's Social Charter

COM (92) 149, New Prospects for Community Cultural Action

COM (92) 407, Proposal for a Council Decision adopting the second phase of the Trans-European Cooperation Scheme for Higher Education

COM (92) 457, European Higher Education-Industry Cooperation: Advanced training for Competitive Advantage

COM (93) 29, Evaluation of the Tempus Programme

COM (93) 151, EC Education and Training Programmes 1986–92

COM (93) 183, Guidelines for Community Action in the Field of Education and Training

COM (93) 194, Report on the Lingua Programme 1992

COM (93) 209, Proposal for a Council Directive on the Right of Residence of Students

COM (93) 268, Report on the Erasmus Programme 1992

EC Bulletin Supp. 10/73, 'For a Community Policy on Education'

EC Bulletin Supp. 4/74, 'Commission Communication on Education in the European Community'

EC Bulletin Supp. 3/76, 'Action Programme in favour of Migrant Workers and their families'

EC Bulletin Supp. 12/76, 'From Education to Working Life'

EC Bulletin Supp. 6/77, 'Community Action in the Cultural Sector'

EC Bulletin Supp. 6/82, 'Stronger Community Action in the Cultural Sector'

EC Bulletin Supp. 7/85, 'A People's Europe: Reports from the *ad hoc* Committee'

EC Bulletin Supp. 4/87, 'A fresh boost for Culture in the European Community'

European Educational Policy Statements (1987, Council of the EC, Brussels)

Community Charter of the Fundamental Social Rights of Workers (1990, Commission of the EC, Brussels)

Social Europe, 'The role of Education and Training in the Completion of the Internal Market', 3/88 p. 36

Baron, B. and Smith, A. (eds), 'Study abroad in the EC', *Higher Education in the EC* (1987)

Cox, E., 'Academic Recognition of diplomas in the EC: Present state and Prospects', *European Education Series No. 10* (1979)

Dalichow, F. and Teichler, U., 'Recognition of study abroad in the EC', *Higher Education in the EC* (1986)

Smith A., 'Joint programmes of study: An instrument of european co-operation in higher education', *European Education Series No. 7* (1979)

Other Publicatons

Arnull A., *The General Principles of EEC Law and the Individual* (Leicester University Press, Leicester, 1990)

Arnull A., 'Of strip cartoonists, vets and gunsmiths' (1988) 13 *ELRev* 260

Bieber R. *et al.*, *An Ever Closer Union* (1985, *European Perspective Series*, Brussels)

Bronkhorst, H., 'Freedom of establishment and freedom to provide services under the EEC Treaty' (1975) 12 *CMLRev* 245

Coppel, J., 'Edinburgh subsidiarity'(1993) 44 *NILQ* 186

Crisham, C., 'A comment on thieffry' (1978) 15 *CMLRev* 366

Dashwood, A., 'The Patrick case' (1977) 2 *ELRev* 293

Emiliou, N., 'Subsidiarity: An effective barrier against "the Enterprise of Ambition"?' (1992) 17 *ELRev* 303

Evans, A., 'European citizenship' (1982) 45 *MLR* 497

Flynn, J., 'Vocational training in Community Law and practice' (1988) 8, *Yearbook of European Law* 60

Gormley, L., 'Registration of General Practitioners' (1982) 7 *ELRev* 37

Gormley, L., 'Freedom to practise at the Bar in more than one Member State' (1984) 9 *ELRev* 439

Gould, M., 'Equality of access to education' (1989) 52 *MLR* 540

Green, Hartley, T. and Usher, J., *Legal Foundations of the Single European Market* (OUP, Oxford,1991)

Hartley, T., 'Constitutional and institutional aspects of the Maastricht agreement' (1993) 42 *ICLQ* 213

Kloss, G., 'Education policy' in Bulmer *et al.* (eds), *The United Kingdom and EC Membership Evaluated* (Pinters, London, 1992)

Kon, S., 'Aspects of reverse discrimination in Community Law' (1981) 6 *ELRev* 75

Laslett, J., 'Mutual recognition of diplomas, certificates and other evidence of formal qualifications in the European Community' [1990/1] *LIEI*

Lasok, D., 'The professions in the EC: The Treaty framework' (1991) 29 *Colombia Journal of Transnational Law* 41

Lasok, B., 'Subsidiarity and the occupied field' (1992) 142 *NLJ* 1228

Leneen, A., 'Recent case law of the Court of Justice of the European Communities on the freedom of establishment and the freedom to provide services' (1980) 17 *CMLRev* 259

Lonbay, J., 'Cross frontier provision of services by lawyers' (1988) 13 *ELRev* 347

Lonbay, J., 'Education and law: The Community context' (1989) 14 *ELRev* 363

Lonbay, J., 'Picking over the bones: Rights of establishment reviewed' (1991) 16 *ELRev* 507

Lord MacKenzie-Stuart, 'Subsidiarity – A busted Flush?' in Curtin and O'Keefe (eds), *Constitutional Adjudication in European Community and National Law* (Butterworth, Dublin, 1992)

Mancini, G. F., 'The free movement of workers in the case-law of the European Court of Justice' in Curtin and O'Keefe (eds) *Constitutional Adjudication in European Community and National Law [Butterworth, Dublin, 1992]*

Mohr, B., 'Education and culture' in Scheitzer and Karsten, Federal Republic of Germany and EC Membership Evaluated [Pinter, London, 1991]

Morse, G., 'Freedom of establishment. Freedom to provide services. Legislation since 1973' [1975–6] 1 ELRev 225

Morse, G., 'Provision of services: The professional supervision exception' (1979) 4 *ELRev* 375

Morse, G., 'Facilitating directives: Reverse discrimination' (1979), 4 *ELRev* 377

Morse, G., 'Establishment: Restrictions based on qualifications' (1979), 4 *ELRev* 379

Neave, G., The EEC and Education (Trentham, Stoke, 1984)

O'Leary, S., 'A Comment on European Parliament v. Council' (1993) 30 *CMLRev* 639

O'Toole, F., 'Culture and Media Policy' in Keatinge (ed.), *Ireland and EC Membership Evaluated* (Pinter, London, 1991)

Oliver, P., *Free Movement of Goods in the EEC* (2nd ed) (ELC, London, 1988)

Pickup, D., 'Reverse Discrimination and Freedom of Movement for Workers' (1986) 23 *CMLRev* 135

Reichling, R., 'A Comment on Reyners' (1974) 11 *CMLRev* 397

Ross, M., 'Mutual recognition of professional qualifications' (1989) 14 *ELRev* 162

Roth, W., 'The European Community's law on services: Harmonisation' (1988) 25 *CMLRev* 35

Scott, D., 'Education' in Keatinge (ed.), Ireland and EC Membership Evaluated (Pinters, London, 1991)

Skarlatos, N., 'European lawyers' right to transnational legal practise in the European Community' [1991/1] *LIEI* 49

Steiner, J., 'Recipients of services: Some more equal than others' (1985) 10 *ELRev* 348

Steiner, J., Textbook on EC Law (3rd edn) (Blackstone, London, 1992)

Toth, A., 'The principle of subsidiarity in the Maastricht Treaty' (1992) 29 *CMLRev* 1079

Wagenbaur, R., 'Free movement in the professions: The new EC proposal on professional qualifications' (1986) 23 *CMLRev* 91

Wallace, R., 'Remedies for foul play' (1988) 13 *ELRev* 347

Wallace, R. and Wilke, A., *Subsidiarity: Approaches to Power Sharing in the European Community* (RIIA, London, 1990)

Walters, D., 'Uncertain steps towards a European legal profession' (1978) 3 *ELRev* 265

Watson, P., 'Freedom of establishment and freedom to provide services: Some recent developments' (1983) 20 *CMLRev* 767

Watson, P., 'A Comment on Klopp' (1985) 22 *CMLRev* 736

Watson, P., 'A Comment on Gravier' (1987) 24 *CMLRev* 89

Watson, P., 'Wandering students: Their rights under Community Law' in Curtin and O'Keefe (eds.), *Constitutional Adjudication in European Community and National Law* (Butterworth, Dublin, 1992)

Weatherill, S. and Beaumont, P., *EC Law* (Penguin, London, 1993)

Wilson, P., 'EEC: Freedom to provide services for EEC Lawyers' (1978) 19 Harv. Int'l LJ 379

Index

Action Programme 1976: assessment of, 12, 48; background to, 9–10, 97, 98; scope of, 10; significance of, 11, 157

Adonnino Report: Commission report on, 18, 139; culture in, 138, 162; education in, 15, 24, 48; first report of, 15, 138; mandate of, 14, 138

Architectural Heritage, 128, 133, 138, 138n, 140, 168

Audio-Visual Sector: Eureka programme in, 144; general, 133, 138, 140, 141, 163; high definition television, 141, 143, 144; Media programme in, 141, 144, 149, 170; piracy in, 136; satellite broadcasting, 141; television broadcasting, 142, 142n, 143

Books: communication on, 144, 145, 147, 168; effect of Treaty rules on, 145, 145n, 146, 146n; pricing of, 146n; translation of, 147, 148, 150, 163

Business Sponsorship, 138, 163; conference on, 152; resolution on 151

Central and Eastern Europe (*see also* Tempus), 19, 170

City of Culture, 136, 139, 164, 168

Comett: amendment of, 32; future of, 106, 107, 110, 115, 116; general, 17, 101, 149; history of, 30, 31; legal basis of, 32–6; measures of, 31, 32, 102; objectives of, 31, 101; Tempus and, 40

Committee on Cultural Affairs, 157

Common Agricultural Policy, 1

Copyright (*see also* Harmonization), 122, 164; computer programs and, 155; impact of Treaty on, 126, 126n, 127, 154

Council of Europe, 129, 149, 158, 174

Cultural Cooperation: areas of, 140; boost to, 139, 163; future of, 166, 167, 169, 174, 179; scope of, 135, 152, 157, 158, 161, 162

Cultural Sector (*see also* Vocational Training), 122, 123; goods in, 127, 129, 130, 140; policy in, 128, 129, 134; workers in, 124, 129, 132, 133; workers in, exchanges of, 128

Discrimination: education and, 68, 70, 71, 78; mutual recognition and, 84, 85

EEA, 19, 19n, 170

Education Committee, 9, 10, 98; 1980 proposals of, 12

Equal Opportunity, 10, 12, 12n

Erasmus: amendment of, 28, 29; future of, 106, 107, 110, 115, 116; general, 17, 149; history of, 21, 22, 101; measures of, 24, 25, 102; legal basis of, 25–8; Lingua and, 39; objectives of, 24, 101; significance of, 29, 30; Tempus and, 40

European Court of Justice: role of, in culture, 158, 162, 163, 173, 174; role of, in education, 94, 95, 98, 98n
European Dimension: education, in, 7, 16, 17, 48, 103, 110; education, in, future of, 116
European Identity, 122
European Parliament: culture, 122, 156, 161, 170–2; education, 117
Eurotecnet, 100
Exchanges (*see also* Comett, Erasmus, Lingua and Tempus): future of, 109; general, 6, 19; review of, 102, 103

Film Festival, 134
Force, 100

GATT, 159

Hague Summit: culture, on, 122; education, on, 2, 8, 43
Harmonization: copyright, of, 122, 124, 154, 155, 156; goods, of, 131; taxation, of, 122, 124, 132
High Definition Television *see* Audio-Visual Sector
Higher Education: admission to, 6; Commission Memorandum on, 107, 108; Commission Memorandum on Council Resolution, 108, 109; future of, 115, 116; finance of, 103, 104; mobility in, 23

Intellectual Property Rights: impact of Treaty on, 124, 125
Internal Market: culture, 137, 138, 164; education, 15, 16, 104; education, resolution on, 17, 19; social dimension of, 99; students and, 43

Janne Report, 4–6, 18, 121; Commission response to, 6

Language Training, 7; Adonnino Report on, 15, 37
Lingua: Erasmus and, 39; future of, 106, 107, 110, 115, 116; general, 19, 101; history of, 36, 37; measures of, 38, 39, 101, 102; objectives of, 38, 101; Tempus and, 40

Maastricht Treaty (*see also* Subsidiarity): culture, on, 121, 159, 161, 164, 165; education, on, 97, 110, 114, 115, 118; education, on, background to, 105, 106; Social Protocol, 100, 101; subsidiarity under, 112, 113, 165; vocational training, in, 101, 101n
Migrant Workers: children, of, 7, 51, 52, 98; children of, education of, 52–9; children of, grants to, 54, 55, 57; social advantages to, 59–66; social advantages to, grants as, 59, 60, 62, 62n, 64; social advantages to, residence requirement for, 60, 61, 62, 63, 63n, 73n
Mutual Recognition: general, 18, 82; general directive on, history of, 87; general directive on, key concepts in, 88, 89, 89n; general directive on, purpose of, 87, 88; general directive on, rule of recognition in, 89, 90, 91; general principles of, 84–7; specific directives on, 82–4

National Policies: education, 11, 12
National Treasures, 121, 123, 124, 130, 152
New Information Technology, 13, 31n, 98

People's Europe *see* Adonnino Report
Petra, 19
Professional Conduct, 91–4; legal services, rules of, 92, 93, 93n
Public Lending Right, 127, 155

Quantitative Restrictions, 121, 123, 129; books on, 146, 147; cultural exception, 130, 131, 132; cultural exception, legislation on, 153, 154, 164

Resale Rights, 127, 128, 155
Right of Residence: persons of independent means, 43; retired persons, 43; students, conditions of, 45–7; students, legal challenge to, 44, 45

Services: education as, 79, 80
Social Charter, 99, 99n, 106; vocational training in, 100
Social Protocol, 100, 101
Solemn Declaration, 134, 135, 136, 138, 162
State Aid, 161, 167
Students *see* Right of Residence
Subsidiarity: definition of, 112, 113; effect on, culture, of, 166; effect on, education, of, 114, 115, 118; Maastricht Treaty on, 112

Tempus: amendments to, 40n; future of, 106, 107, 110, 115, 116; general, 19, 101; history of, 39, 40; measures of, 4, 101, 102; objectives of, 40, 40n, 101; other programmes and, 40; resources for, 40, 41; review of, 41, 42

Unemployment, 12; cultural sector, 136; education, 13, 14, 98

Vocational training: access to, 78, 101; cultural sector, in, 136, 148, 163; cultural sector, in, resolution on, 150; definition of, initial, 68–74; definition of, refinement of, 74–9; free movement of persons and, 71; migrant workers and, 61, 62, 63; secondary education as, 77, 78; Social Charter, aspects of, 100; university education as, 69, 70n, 73, 75, 76

Worker: definition of, 60n, 61, 63

Youth Exchanges, 18, 19, 172; Youth for Europe, 100
Youth Orchestra, 136